THE REFLECTIVE LIFE

The Reflective Life

Living Wisely with our Limits

VALERIE TIBERIUS

OXFORD
UNIVERSITY PRESS

OXFORD

UNIVERSITY PRESS

Great Clarendon Street, Oxford OX2 6DP

Oxford University Press is a department of the University of Oxford.
It furthers the University's objective of excellence in research, scholarship,
and education by publishing worldwide in

Oxford New York

Auckland Cape Town Dar es Salaam Hong Kong Karachi
Kuala Lumpur Madrid Melbourne Mexico City Nairobi
New Delhi Shanghai Taipei Toronto

With offices in

Argentina Austria Brazil Chile Czech Republic France Greece
Guatemala Hungary Italy Japan Poland Portugal Singapore
South Korea Switzerland Thailand Turkey Ukraine Vietnam

Oxford is a registered trade mark of Oxford University Press
in the UK and in certain other countries

Published in the United States
by Oxford University Press Inc., New York

© Valerie Tiberius 2008

The moral rights of the author have been asserted
Database right Oxford University Press (maker)

First published 2008

British Library Cataloguing in Publication Data

Data available

Library of Congress Cataloging in Publication Data

Tiberius, Valerie.
The reflective life: living wisely with our limits / Valerie Tiberius.
p. cm.
Includes bibliographical references and index.
ISBN-13: 978-0-19-920286-7 (alk. paper) 1. Conduct of life. I. Title.
BJ1581.2.T525 2008
170'.44—dc22
2008000202

Typeset by Laserwords Private Limited, Chennai, India
Printed in Great Britain
on acid-free paper by
Biddles Ltd, King's Lynn, Norfolk

ISBN 978–0–19–920286–7

1 3 5 7 9 10 8 6 4 2

For Walker

Preface

This is a book about how to live life wisely. You might think, given the title, that my answer would be to think and reflect more. But this is not my answer. I think that when we really take account of what we are like—when we recognize our psychological limits—we will see that too much thinking, rationalizing, and reflecting is bad for us. Instead, I think we need to think and reflect *better*. In a nutshell, this means that we need to develop the habits of thought that constitute wisdom: we need to care about things that will sustain us and give us good experiences; we need to have perspective on our successes and failures; and we need to be moderately self-aware and cautiously optimistic about human nature. Perhaps most importantly, we need to know when to think seriously about our values, character, choices, and so on, and when not to. A crucial part of wisdom is knowing when to stop reflecting and to get lost in experience.

Despite these cautions about too much reflection, I have titled the book in a way that emphasizes the reflective aspect of life. Why? I think that philosophical questions about how to live engage us insofar as we are reflective creatures. So, a philosophical answer to the question "How should I live?" has to speak to the reflective part of us. The answer has to be one that satisfies us when we are in a curious and thoughtful frame of mind. I argue in this book that if we cultivate the habits of wisdom, our lives will be successful from our own reflective point of view.

This is also a book about the more abstract topic of how to philosophize about how to live. A recent trend in moral philosophy has been toward what some are calling empirically informed ethics. This trend began with those interested in moral cognition, and it has spread to meta-ethics, philosophy of action, and moral psychology generally. The empirically informed methodology has not yet caught on in normative ethics (the branch of ethics that aims to answer questions like "How should I live?" and "What is the right thing to do?"). There are good reasons for this. The main one is the worry that we cannot conclude anything about what *ought* to be the case from the facts about what *is*. While I certainly agree that this leap should be avoided, I also think that empirical psychology can inform our philosophical theories in interesting ways. Showing how this is so is a subsidiary aim of this book.

Acknowledgements

I feel extremely fortunate to have received many kinds of help while writing this book. My home institution, the University of Minnesota, awarded me a sabbatical in 2006 and the McKnight Land Grant Professorship in 2002–4, which freed up time and gave me the resources to present my work in many distant places. My thanks are due to the Graduate School and the McKnight family for this generous award. I am also grateful to the Dean of the College of Liberal Arts, Steven Rosenstone, whose continued support was crucial to finishing the book. These resources allowed me to hire two research assistants, whose help has been tremendous. Mike Steger helped early in the process when I was beginning to look into the psychology literature. Matt Frank's help in the later stages—which ranged from formatting the bibliography to providing detailed comments on the manuscript—was truly indispensable. I would also like to thank my department and colleagues, my fellow ethicists Sarah Holtman and Michelle Mason in particular, for supporting me and putting up with my absence while working on the book. For more help with the final stages, I am grateful to the Rockefeller Foundation for allowing me to spend a month at the Bellagio Study and Conference Center in northern Italy, an inspiringly beautiful place to work. Having such a wonderful interdisciplinary group of scholars to talk to for a month was also helpful in unanticipated ways.

Many people have read and generously commented on parts of the book at various stages. I am grateful to Julia Annas, Elizabeth Ashford, Thomas Augst, Ruth Chang, Tim Chappell, Bridget Clarke, Roger Crisp, Julia Driver, Carl Elliott, Martin Gunderson, Thomas E. Hill Jr., Sarah Holtman, Christopher Hookway, Rosalind Hursthouse, Mark LeBar, Michelle Mason, Andrew McGonigal, Lisa McLeod, Elijah Millgram, Michelle Moody-Adams, Tim Mulgan, Jesse Prinz, Vance Ricks, Patricia Ross, David Schmidtz, Martin Seligman, George Sher, Henry Shue, Thomas Spitzley, Karen Stohr, L. W. Sumner, Corliss Swain, Christine Swanton, R. Jay Wallace, C. Kenneth Waters, Gary Watson, Jennifer Whiting, and Eric Wiland. Particular thanks are due to John Doris, who, in addition to providing constructive comments on the longest chapter of the book, invited me to join the moral psychology research group that has fueled my interest in empirically informed ethics.

I have also benefited greatly from presenting and discussing parts of the book at the following conferences and departments: the Department of Philosophy at the University of Arizona, the British Society for Ethical Theory, the Central Division meeting of the American Philosophical Association, the Central States Philosophical Association meeting, the Young Scholar at Cornell program, Daniel Andler's seminar at the École Normale Supérieur, the Joint Session of the Mind Association and the Aristotelian Society, the Ockham Society at Oxford University, the Rocky Mountain Virtue Ethics Summit, Radbound University Nijmegen's Conference on Selfhood, Normativity, and Control, the Scots Philosophical Club, the Department of Philosophy at the University of Sheffield, Daniel Haybron's seminar at St Louis University, the Syracuse Philosophy Annual Workshop and Network (SPAWN) at Syracuse University, John Doris's seminar at Washington University, and the Department of Philosophy at the University of Wisconsin Colleges.

I owe special debts of gratitude to Dan Haybron and Jimmy Lenman, who each read the manuscript more than once and provided me with detailed, helpful comments and encouragement when needed. Though there are still many flaws, the book is much better than it would have been without them. I am very fortunate to have parents, step-parents, and sisters who enjoy spending our limited time together discussing philosophical ideas, and who have given me excellent advice about the process of writing. Finally, my greatest thanks are to my partner John David Walker, who put up with my book-related moodiness, read anything I asked him to, provided criticism when I was ready for it and cheerleading the rest of the time. If this book is half as good as he believes it is, I would be very pleased.

Parts of this book have been published elsewhere. A version of Chapter 3 appeared as "Wisdom and Perspective", *The Journal of Philosophy*, 102/4 (April 2005): 163–82. A version of Chapter 4 was published as "Perspective: A Prudential Virtue", *American Philosophical Quarterly*, 39/4 (Oct. 2002): 305–24. I am grateful for the permission to include this material.

Contents

PART I

THE REFLECTIVE LIFE
AND REFLECTIVE VALUES

1

Introduction

1.1. LIVING WELL AND YOUR POINT OF VIEW

How should you live? Should you devote yourself to perfecting a single talent or try to live a balanced life? Should you lighten up and have more fun, or buckle down and try to achieve greatness? Should you be a saint, if you can? Should you be a parent, a career woman, a socialite, a good friend? How should you decide among the paths open to you? Should you consult experts, listen to your parents, do lots of research? Should you be self-critical or self-accepting? These are questions about how to live that are addressed to the first-person point of view, to you, the one who is living your life.

We might think that the way to answer these questions is to argue for a theory of the human good, well-being, or happiness. Should you try for greatness? That depends on the content of the good life, or the nature of human flourishing. If the best life for you is the life of perfecting your talents, then try for greatness. If the best life is a life of pleasure, you should find reliable sources of pleasure and forgo perfection. To know how to live, we need to know what we're aiming at, and this is what a good theory will define: the target. The problem with this approach is that it is difficult to get consensus about the target, especially if it is described in enough detail to be helpful to us. Philosophers and, more recently, psychologists have presented us with a diverse array of options, none of which is the obvious answer to everyone.

A different approach is to ask how to live our lives given that we don't know just what the target is, and without assuming that we would agree about the matter. This is the approach I take in this book: I defend a first-personal, process-based account of how to live, as opposed to an impersonal, goal-based theory of the good life. To put it another way, we begin with the question "How should I live?" instead of questions like "What is a happy life?" or "What is a good life for a human being?" My account of how to live well is addressed to the first-person point of view; it invokes the perspective of the deliberator. It is an account that aims to answer the questions we have when we are trying to figure out how to live our lives and we have limited knowledge about how things will work out, what we're like, and which theory of the human good is the right one.

An obvious question about such a first-personal account is this: What is the relevant first person point of view? How do we characterize the point of view of the person who wants to know how to live? We can distinguish two broad possibilities that derive from the familiar division between reason and passion. First, we might think that the relevant point of view is a reflective or rational point of view. On this hypothesis, you live your life well by living in accordance with the plans you arrive at through reasoning and deliberation, or by using reason to keep your desires and passions in check. Alternatively, we might think that the relevant point of view is an emotional, appetitive, unreflective point of view. On this hypothesis, you live your life well by doing what you want or by letting your feelings be your guide; a good life for you is one in which you feel good, get what you desire, or enjoy your experiences.

There is a long philosophical tradition that follows the first path, putting reason in the driver's seat and identifying the person (and hence the person's point of view) with the rational or reflective part. Plato used the metaphor of the chariot and the charioteer to illustrate the point: we live well, according to Plato, when the rational part of our soul (the charioteer) is in charge of the appetites and emotions (the chariot). You do best when your rational self has the reins. There are some attractions to this picture: the rational self seems to be unified in a way that appetites and passions are not, which makes it a better candidate for representing your point of view. Further, the rational self seems designed to hold the reins and direct things. At the very least, when our passions pull us in different directions, the rational self seems to be there to figure out which way to go.

But it turns out that the rational or reflective self isn't all that good a charioteer after all. Recent investigations in empirical psychology show us that the self-conscious, rational processor is more fallible than we imagined.[1] The rational self makes inaccurate predictions about what we'll find satisfying, is plagued by biases, and has a tendency to distraction. When we try to be

[1] For an introduction to some of this research see Wilson 2002 and Gilbert 2006. I discuss the research in Ch. 5.

reflective about our choices, we end up confused about our reasons, and we choose things we don't ultimately like. The rational self is hardly the reasonable, responsible, and prudent leader we took it to be. Given these problems, letting reason rule may not result in a life we find satisfying even upon later reflection. Furthermore, the non-reflective self is not so easy to control as we may have thought. It sometimes feels as if our attention and energy get hijacked by emotions or desires that are immune to our powers of reason. Worse, it turns out that non-rational, subconscious mental processes explain a great deal of our behavior in ways that are almost entirely out of our control. As psychologist John Haidt describes it, Plato's metaphor of the chariot and the charioteer ought to be replaced by the metaphor of the elephant and the rider: the non-reflective self is like a great big, determined elephant, and the reflective self is the little rider sitting on top, with rather limited control (2005: 2–4). Our reflective selves are neither as smart nor as powerful as is required by the ideal of rational control.

Perhaps, then, we should abandon the reflective self and identify with the elephant. But this won't work either, for two reasons. First, our non-reflective, emotional selves are not the best leaders either. The most obvious problem here is that we can have passions that lead us in opposite directions, leading to a lot of frustration. Even without conflict, momentary passions can lead us in directions that frustrate our long-term interests.

Second, it is as *reflective* creatures that we want to know how we ought to live our lives. People who ask questions like "What is the best life for me?" or "How should I live?" are already engaged in some reflection about their lives, and so these questions need an answer that will satisfy us insofar as we are being reflective. When we ask these kinds of questions, we presuppose that we have some kind of control over our lives, and that there are reasons for doing things one way rather than another. In other words, these questions are normative questions that require normative, action-guiding, or reason-giving answers.[2] To abandon the reflective self in our account of how to live would be to ignore the real source of our questions about how to live and, hence, to risk not really answering the questions we have.

A benefit of the traditional picture according to which we are identified with our rational capacities, and living well is living rationally, is that it seems to provide an obvious and satisfying answer to our normative concerns. On

---

[2] Here I mean "normative" in the philosophical sense in which it is contrasted with "descriptive" and carries a claim to justification. "Normative" in this sense does not have to do with statistical norms or conformity to cultural expectations.

one way of looking at it, the rational self is thought to be acting under the authority of rational principles that provide a satisfying stopping point for our questions about how to live. Insofar as we find rational principles to guide our choices, the thought goes, we will necessarily have found reason-giving answers. Once we've found a rational principle to tell us what to choose, we don't have to ask why that choice would be a good one. The rational self is the right guide for us because discovering and choosing in accordance with rational principles is its job. Unfortunately, though, I don't think we can look at it this way. Above I suggested one kind of reason to be skeptical of views like this that overestimate our capacity to choose rationally. Now we can see a further reason for skepticism: the promise that there *are* rational principles that these capacities track is controversial. This book does not presuppose that there are rational principles with inescapable action-guiding authority. Instead, my approach, in the tradition of Hume, is to look to our experience as the only source of answers to our normative questions. An account of how to live, on my view, must be genuinely normative in a way that gives satisfying answers to the questions we have in a reflective frame of mind; but it must also be compatible with a naturalistic picture of the world, one that contains neither imperatives from God nor principles or values that exist independently of our commitments to them.[3]

If we can't abandon the reflective self, but can't trust our reflective capacities either, how should we proceed? One obvious thought is that we should try to improve our reflection. There are different ways to improve our reflective processes and different ways of thinking about what role these improved processes should have in our thinking about how to live a good life. One idea is that we should first describe an ideal or perfect form of rationality, free from all our normal faults and constraints. This strategy identifies the best life for a person with the life that she *would* live if she were ideally reflective; that is, if her reflection did not suffer from any of the problems that afflict real reflection. In thinking about the good for a person, this strategy has seemed attractive.[4] While this might be a helpful way to

---

[3] This claim is intended to be cautious. It is not my intention to suggest that Kantian approaches in general are incompatible with naturalism. While it seems to me that some Kantian positions make extravagant assumptions about rational principles, the views of Kantians such as David Velleman and Thomas Hill certainly do not.

[4] This is one thing that animates full information theories. See, e.g., Griffin 1986. To be sure, these theories do not recommend that we actually become fully informed as a means to improving

think about "a person's good" from the outside, it is not promising as a way to think about how to live from the first-person point of view. Given that we are not, nor ever will be, ideally or perfectly rational, it is not obviously helpful to be told that we should choose whatever we would choose if we were.[5] Further, given the particular limitations of our reflective capacities, it is just not clear that trying to emulate a perfectly rational being will benefit us: an elephant rider who believes she is holding the reins of a horse might do much worse in controlling her elephant than one who recognizes what she's got.

A different strategy is to think about how to train the rational and reflective capacities we actually have so that they can function together with our emotions, moods, and desires to get us somewhere we'd like to be. This strategy is the one I favor. It involves being more humble about the powers of reflection and acknowledging the importance of our non-reflective experience. Learning how to live with the fallibility of reflection does not (cannot) mean accepting the results of our actual reflection without criticism. But we can make sense of improving our reflection without thinking about the reflection of a perfectly rational being who is not very much like us. To do this, we need to think about standards for improvement that take seriously the ways in which explicit reflection tends to go wrong and the ways in which non-reflective experience can lead us in the right direction. I propose to do this by thinking of the improvement of reflection in terms of developing certain virtues, qualities of mind, or habits of thought, that are useful for us, given our needs and limitations.

There are, surely, many qualities that foster appropriate reflection and living well. My focus will be on those that come to our attention when we acknowledge the fallibility of reflection and rational control. The four virtues I discuss focus on different limitations or problems with reflection as a guide, and they are each a part of reflective wisdom.[6] A person

our reflective capacities; they are not intended to give guidance to deliberators. This highlights the fact that full information theories are theories of the good, not theories of how to live. What I say here, therefore, is not intended as an argument against full information theories of normative concepts.

[5] The best idealizing accounts of the good are actually more complicated than this; they make use of an advice model according to which the good for me is what the ideal me would recommend for the actual me (e.g., Railton 1986). Again, while such theories may provide a compelling analysis of the good, the move to an advice model doesn't help when our questions are about how to live, given our distance from the ideal.

[6] In my preferred terms, both reflective wisdom (which has to do with living your own life well) and moral wisdom (which has to do with understanding what is at stake from the moral point

with the virtue of perspective brings her actions and feelings in line with her values; perspective helps us cope with reflection's limited motivational power. Another part of wisdom, attentional flexibility, contends with the fact that appropriate reflection does not mean reflecting all the time; the wise person has a reflective conception of a good life for her, but she also knows when it is best to experience life without reflecting. The virtues of self-awareness and optimism are shaped by competing forces: the demand for good information to make rational choices, the tendency toward various biases in reflection, and the benefits of certain kinds of distortion of the facts. These virtues acknowledge that appropriate reflection does not mean relentlessly seeking the truth. The habits of thought that a reflective person has must be responsive to the fallibility of our rational powers, and alive to the presence of the elephant under our seats.

There are, then, three important features of a first-personal, process-based account of how to live well. First, it must aim at reflective success; that is, it must give us guidance that will be satisfying from a person's actual reflective point of view.[7] Second, it must include norms of improvement for our reflection that are not derived from an unachievable ideal. And, third, it must recognize the importance of our passions and experiences both as a source of information and as a motivational force. In this book I develop an account of how to live that meets these three criteria, the Reflective Wisdom Account. According to this account, to live well, we should develop the qualities that allow us both to be appropriately reflective and to have experiences that are not interrupted by reflection, and we should live our lives in accordance with the ends, goals, or values that stand up to appropriate reflection. I call these beneficial qualities reflective virtues, and I take them to be components of wisdom. To live well, then, is to live wisely, and the wise person knows how to live with her limits.

In the remainder of this introduction I elaborate on the thoughts covered rather quickly in this section. I will also try to situate the Reflective Wisdom Account in the larger philosophical literature and to anticipate a few concerns one might have at the outset. Finally, at the end I will provide a road map for what is to come.

---

of view) are part of practical wisdom. Only the first kind of wisdom is covered in this book. For convenience, I sometimes use the term "wisdom" to refer simply to "reflective wisdom".

[7] "Reflective success" is Korsgaard's phrase, though she uses the notion to argue against a Humean account. See, in particular, Korsgaard 1996: 93–7.

1.2. PROCESS AND GOAL: WHY START WITH THE FIRST-PERSON POINT OF VIEW?

The fact that the subjective point of view plays such an important role in the Reflective Wisdom Account will draw comparisons to subjective theories of well-being. According to such theories, whether or not something contributes to a person's well-being depends on that person's attitudes toward it. Among these theories there are two front-runners: the Informed Desire Account and the Authentic Happiness Account. The former tells us that the good for you is the fulfillment of the desires you would have if you were fully informed.[8] The latter, according to its main proponent L. W. Sumner (1996), tells us that the good for a person is her authentic happiness, which in turn is defined as her informed and autonomous endorsement of the conditions of her life.

Subjective theories of well-being make the good for a person relative to individual subjects, and in this sense they take the first-person point of view seriously. But these theories are intended to answer a different kind of question from the one I am addressing here. These accounts are well suited to answering third-person questions about the quality of life that a person is achieving, but not for answering first-person questions about how one ought to live. Subjective theories of well-being or welfare are about the target rather than the process or practice. Given that these accounts do not recommend embodying the ideals they invoke—they do not say that we will be better off fully informed, for example—and given that we cannot know what an ideal version of us would recommend, specific recommendations about how to live do not follow directly.

One response to this difference between accounts of well-being, on the one hand, and accounts of how to live, on the other, would be to say that there are two different questions here and two different kinds of theories needed to answer them.[9] This is not incorrect, but I think the matter is more complicated than this answer makes it seem. Surely questions about the substance of the good life and questions about the process of how to live

---

[8] Defenders of Informed Desire Accounts include Railton (1986), Rawls (1971), Griffin (1986), and Brandt (1979). Griffin (1986: 32–3) denies that his theory is appropriately characterized as subjective; he claims that his theory has elements of both subjective and objective views.

[9] I thank Nicholas Wolterstorff and Julia Annas for helpful discussion about this distinction.

your life are closely related. Subjective accounts, and, I would add, Objective List Theories as well, can shed some light on the question of how to live by defining the target or aim of life.[10] If so, what reason do we have to start here rather than there? There is a rich literature on well-being and the prudential good that focuses on defining the target. Why not advance that literature rather than change the topic? Very briefly, my first answer is that the guidance we get from a theory like mine is better than the guidance we can infer from a theory of well-being. And good guidance about a profoundly important practical question is worth pursuing. Second, the focus on the process motivates an exploration of the nature of wisdom, which is interesting in its own right. Third, an investigation of the process may shed light on the nature of the target. To explain these advantages further, it will help to say more about the approach I am taking.

As I have explained, the primary focus of this book is the process of how to live, rather than the target or goal; it is primarily an account of the practice of conducting life wisely rather than a substantive account of the goods that a wise person would choose. That said, the process of living wisely surely must aim at something, and it will be helpful to clarify what that is. The thing to do is to begin with a description of the aim that is presupposed by anyone who asks questions about how to live. Such a description can't be substantive; it can't spell out the content of the good life; but what we can say is enough to be helpful when taken together with various facts about what we are like.

Importantly, the question "How should I live?" is a normative question. It is a request for guidance and for reasons to live one way or another. The aim that is presupposed by anyone who asks normative questions about how to live is that of living a life you can reflectively endorse, a good life from your own point of view. By this I do not mean "a life that seems good to you". A person's own point of view is a subjective point of view in the sense that it belongs to the subject, but it is not the point of view from which anything goes. Rather, a good life from your own point of view is a life you can affirm upon reflection; it is a life that you approve of on the basis of the standards you take to be important. Once we see what it means to live a good life from your own point of view, we can also see what a natural goal it is, and how very odd it would be for a person not to care about it. A person who

---

[10] Objective List Theories define the good life in terms of a list of goods. For example, see Kraut 1997. The label was coined by Parfit 1984: 493–502.

doesn't care about her own reflective judgment on the way her life is going is a person who has, in an important sense, abandoned the project of directing her own life.[11]

The idea that questions about the nature of a good life for you are normative questions that arise from reflection about how to live is central to the account defended in this book. One might worry that not everyone asks these questions, and that the kind of reflectiveness I am presupposing is the peculiar interest of professional philosophers. But I think that this pronouncement either is arrogant or misunderstands the kind of reflection I mean. The kind of reflection I have in mind, as we shall see, is not beyond anyone who has an interest in thinking about how to live.[12] A reflective person, on my view, is concerned to live a life that she can affirm, and because of this concern she sometimes thinks about what matters to her and why. If we do not insist that "thinking about what matters" is an analytic or highly intellectual kind of thinking (as I believe we should not), then it seems a bit of academic hubris to say that only academics think about these things.[13] There is perhaps a distinctive way in which academics and intellectuals engage in reflection about their lives, but nothing in my account of reflection requires this particular way of thinking. (In fact, one might think that academics are at least equally susceptible to certain barriers to good reflection on how to live, such as the capacity for rationalization, a tendency toward self-deception and self-aggrandizement, and a lack of sensitivity to others.)

A related worry about the starting point of this book is that there are people whose direction in life is largely determined by their social roles, their religion, or their community, who live perfectly well without having these normative concerns about how to live. There may be some truth to this. Indeed, the importance of perspective, flexibility, self-awareness, and optimism is highlighted by features of life in contemporary Western culture that give rise to the need for skills different from the ones emphasized in the traditional virtues. Life in contemporary industrial democratic societies

[11] Of course there may be people, such as the severely depressed, who ought to abandon control over their own lives, at least temporarily. Theories of how to live, however, are directed at agents who do have an interest in, and the capacity for, directing their own lives.
[12] Certainly there are people for whom these questions about how to live well are not pressing. For a person whose basic needs are not met, living a reflective life is an extraordinary luxury. This does not mean, however, that such people are incapable of reflection, or that they would not be interested in living well in this sense if they were at liberty to do so.
[13] In thinking about this issue, I have been influenced by Tom Augst's *The Clerk's Tale* (2003); and Arthur Kleinman's *What Really Matters* (2006). Both books, in very different ways, demonstrate a capacity for, and an interest in, reflection on the part of people who are not academics.

is characterized by competing demands and sources of stress, pressing and often overwhelming moral problems, and the imperative to be yourself in the context of a society that does not always foster the development of autonomy or approve of what people autonomously decide. This point about the relevance of culture to what counts as wisdom highlights a limitation that any account grounded in experience must acknowledge: namely, that it cannot claim to be truly universal. Rather, an empirically grounded account must start with people who have certain commitments and concerns as a matter of contingent fact.

Ultimately, the scope of my account depends on how universal are the various facts about human psychology on which I rely. This is a large question, beyond the scope of this book, and probably not one to which we yet know the full answer. That said, there are a few more things to say in defense of the starting point I have chosen. First, it should be pointed out that a self-directed life is not the same as a selfish life. As we will see in more detail in the next chapter, some of the most important commitments we have are our commitments to others. This means that a concern to live a life that succeeds by your own lights does not rule out a sense of your own good that is deeply identified with the good of your family or community; a person could have both. Second, the kind of life that would make reflection on what matters unnecessary is increasingly unavailable to people. Contemporary trends in technology, economics, and politics are breaking down traditional networks of social roles very quickly and introducing a lot of options that give rise to reflection.

The theory defended in this book is addressed to those of us who do reflect on how to live our lives and who are concerned to find satisfying answers. These are the people I am referring to when I talk about how it makes sense for "us" to live, and what habits "we" ought to adopt. I think this is a limitation, but, for the reason outlined above, not a troubling one. With this qualification in mind, we can continue to explore the nature of the first-person, reflective point of view.

According to the Reflective Wisdom Account, then, a well-lived life is a life we endorse or approve of upon reflection. In other words, paraphrasing David Hume, to live well is to live a life that can bear your reflective survey.[14] Now

---

[14] Hume (1978 [1739–40]) seems to assume that bearing one's own survey is an important goal in human life when he embarks on a brief exhortation to virtue at the end of the *Treatise*. Other philosophers who share this assumption include Bittner (1989: 123), Hill (1991: 173–88), Rawls (1971: 422), and C. Taylor (1976).

for our standards or our "reflective survey" to sustain genuine evaluation and justification, it must be possible to go wrong. If we take a person's standards to be whatever standards she happens to have, then the resulting notion of the good life will not answer our normative concern, which brings with it the assumption that we can be wrong about various things, including what standards we ought to use to assess how well our lives are going. This implies that the point of view from which we evaluate our lives must be one from which we can recognize the possibility of error and improvement. If this were not the case, living well would simply amount to thinking you are living well; but the deep concern we have to live a good life is not a concern merely to think we are living good lives.

Given the nature of our concern to live well, the relevant point of view has to be one that we can take up to a greater or lesser degree, where doing a better job of taking up the point of view is something we see as an improvement. In other words, the relevant point of view must be something we aspire to, an ideal. Moreover, if we are to have an account that is action guiding in the right way, this ideal must be something we can actually aspire to, not an ideal that is far out of reach. What kind of point of view is ideal enough to make sense of the *normative* notion of 'the good life' and is also something to which ordinary people can aspire? I suggest that it is the point of view of a person with reflective wisdom. Reflective wisdom is the right kind of ideal because, as we will see, it grounds criticism of our actual standards and values, and it is an ideal easily recognizable as an improvement to our current point of view.

An obvious question for any account that makes use of idealization in this way is this: How wise must we be to count as living well? The first thing to point out is that, on my view, wisdom and appropriate reflection are not unachievable ideals. Given how I will characterize appropriate reflection, it is a state that is within our grasp; it does not include full information, perfect rationality, or full moral virtue. Second, thinking of the idealization in terms of the development of virtue allows me to refuse to settle on a principled stopping point for improvement outside the context of deliberation about how to live. From the first-person point of view, the question "How wise must we be?" is a practical question to be addressed along with other practical questions about how to live. The aspects of wisdom I discuss—perspective, flexibility, self-awareness, and optimism—give us guidance about such matters as how informed we should be, or how much we should reflect before making a choice. But, as we will see, these virtues take account of what we are really like; they do not describe an impossible ideal.

Now that we have a better idea of what the relevant first-person point of view is and how the ideal to which it aspires is shaped by the concern to live a good life, we can return to the question about the value of focusing on the process rather than the target. First, beginning with the first-person question about how to live results in an account that addresses people on their own terms and, therefore, has a foothold in people's practical reasoning. This is the sense in which I suggested above that the guidance that comes from the Reflective Wisdom Account will be better than the guidance that comes from theories that aim to articulate the nature of the target: the best guidance is guidance we can follow. This foothold is one that eludes all varieties of third-personal theories of the prudential good, because different substantive claims about the nature of the good life will be accepted by some and rejected by others.[15]

One might object here that while the guidance we get from a first-personal account of how to live is guidance we *can* follow, it is not the guidance we need or want. Someone pressing this line of objection might say that what many people want is to live *good lives*, not to live good lives from their own point of view. Even if we make efforts to develop the virtues that would improve our reflective capacities, these capacities could be misguided enough that the Reflective Wisdom Account will lead us to live objectively bad lives. Essentially, the worry here is that aiming to live a life that you can endorse upon reflection (the rather formal target of my account) will not result in living a good life. But I think this worry is misguided, because it assumes that there is a way to live a good life without beginning from your own point of view. Even if your goal is to live an objectively good life in some sense, what else can you do besides reflect on what a good life consists in and attempt to live in accordance with those values? In short, the only reasonable way to pursue a good life, whatever its content turns out to be, is to try to lead a life that's good from your point of view. It is possible that living well from your own point of view you will do worse than you would if your life were governed by someone else. But we should certainly hope this is not the case, as it amounts to giving up on living our own lives. Ultimately, I

---

[15] Given this, we might wonder why contemporary accounts of well-being and prudential value have not taken this direct, first-personal approach; why, that is, they focus on the question of what a good life consists in, rather than the question of what it is to live a life well. I suspect that the explanation lies partly in the fact that many of the main proponents of these theories are consequentialists, whose interest is in what ought to be promoted or produced from the point of view of all concerned. This is a legitimate interest, but it is not the only important question about our lives.

think the only way to vindicate this hope is to show that the result of starting from a person's own point of view is compelling as an account of a good human life. Making good on this promise takes the whole of the book: we have to wait and see where we get by starting from a person's own point of view.

The second reason to begin with the first-personal question of how to live is that doing so motivates the development of an account of practical wisdom, which is important in its own right. Surprisingly, philosophers have not had very much to say about the nature of practical wisdom in recent years. When they have discussed it, they have emphasized two common and related themes: the uncodifiability of wise judgment and the analogy between wisdom and perception.[16] Wise judgment is thought to be analogous to a perceptual capacity, so that a wise person sees the right thing to do without applying a code of rules or general principles. While I accept the idea that having practical wisdom is not a matter of having the right code or decision procedure that one mechanically applies, I also think that the analogy to perception leaves the nature of wisdom mysterious and opaque. By breaking down wisdom into a set of skills, I hope to illuminate its nature without having to rely on rules or decision procedures.

There is, furthermore, an advantage to situating a characterization of reflective wisdom in the context of a naturalistic account of how to live. Given the constraints I have imposed on the construction of the Reflective Wisdom Account, the accompanying picture of wisdom will be one that takes seriously the facts about our psychology and the limitations of our rational capacities. This is, to my mind, a substantial benefit that should be appreciated by anyone who is committed to fitting ethics into the natural world. This last point introduces one more consideration in favor of starting where the Reflective Wisdom Account starts: for naturalists of a certain stripe, a psychologically realistic account of reflective practice may be a fruitful starting point for ethical theorizing in general, or at least an important constraint on the development of defensible ethical theories. For those who think that ethical theory must provide action-guiding reasons, and that such reasons must ultimately derive from a person's psychology, a theory of good reflective practice that is tied to our psychology and aspires to an ideal is a natural resource.

---

[16] See, e.g., McDowell 1979; Nussbaum 1986. An exception to this generalization, and to the lack of philosophical attention to the nature of wisdom, is John Kekes (1995) who has developed a detailed and illuminating account of what he calls moral wisdom.

1.3. ARISTOTLE AND VIRTUE

Aristotelian accounts of the good life, and eudaimonist accounts generally, do focus on the first-person question of how we ought to live our lives (Annas 1993). In this respect and in others, the strategy of argument described above resembles the Aristotelian strategy for defining human flourishing. Yet my account of the reflective life is not really Aristotelian, at least not on one standard interpretation of the Aristotelian project.[17] According to this interpretation, the Aristotelian project is naturalistic in a particular sense: it begins with thoughts about the human being as a natural organism (like other natural organisms such as lions and bees) and proceeds to think about what is good for a human being, given this nature.[18] The Reflective Wisdom Account, on the other hand, begins with thoughts about the concerns embedded in the normative questions of reflective creatures. This difference makes a difference to which virtues are discussed, and to the justificatory structure of the theory. Furthermore, the account of how to live discussed here is contingent in a way that Aristotle's is not usually taken to be. My account is addressed to people with a specific concern to live well, it relies on claims about the values that people tend to, but might not have, and it is influenced by facts about culture that are historically and geographically specific. Aristotle's account of flourishing is not meant to be contingent in any of these ways.[19] That said, there are some important similarities that should be identified.

Naturalistic Aristotelians are very sensitive to what people are like insofar as they rely on a conception of our nature to justify the virtues. A similar attention to the facts about us will be evidenced here. My attempts to explore what people are like in this book will be informed by empirical psychology

---

[17] I should emphasize that my intention here is merely to elucidate the nature of my own project, not to engage in scholarly debate or interpretation of Aristotle.

[18] Foot (2001) strongly suggests this interpretation. For a different interpretation of Aristotle see Nussbaum 1995. For a helpful general discussion of Aristotelian naturalism and its alternatives, see Stohr 2006. Other interpretations of the Aristotelian project may be closer to my view, though I do not know of any such project that brings empirical psychological research to bear on the question about the nature of practical wisdom.

[19] There is a sense in which the conception of a good life for eudaimonists is contingent on the concerns of reflective agents. As Annas (1993: 39) explains, the ancients thought that we have "an instinctive tendency to think of our lives as wholes ... .This is why we do not typically find arguments to show that it is rational to think of one's life as a whole, to see one's activity as given shape by a single final end. This is taken to be what we do anyway; at least we all do it instinctively, and the more reflective do it in a reflective way."

and, in particular, by positive psychology, a new field that has arisen within psychology, which emphasizes the study of mental health, well-functioning, and related strengths of character. Given the sensitivity of what counts as a virtue to facts about human beings and our commitments, it seems reasonable to refer to this literature in our discussion of wisdom.

Second, at least on one standard interpretation, the Aristotelian strategy does not divide moral values from non-moral values and attempt to ground the one in the other. The ancients did not draw a hard distinction between these two "types" of value; nor did they assume that one or the other was primary (Nussbaum 1986: 5). So too in my investigation, the intent is to take people as they are with a variety of commitments, some that would fall into a traditional conception of morality, some that would be categorized as prudential, and others that defy neat categorization (such as commitments to friends and friendship). What I hope to establish through this investigation also echoes the Aristotelian tradition according to which morality and prudence (as normally conceived today) are much closer than might appear to us post Hobbes. The intention here is not to prove that it is always prudentially rational to be moral; rather, the intention is to show that when we begin our inquiry from the right place, the question about whether acting morally is prudentially rational is much less pressing.

Third, both the Aristotelian account and the Reflective Wisdom Account emphasize virtues, which sets them apart from subjective accounts of well-being and the prudential good. Virtues, in my view, are sets of dispositions to think, act, and feel in certain ways, that work together as a regulative ideal for reflection and conduct. To say that a virtue is a regulative ideal is to say that it plays a particular role in a project of character development. A virtue must be a state at which it makes sense to aim, and there must be reasons for cultivating it that people can grasp. The reasons we have to cultivate the virtues essential to the reflective life derive from our interest in living well. It makes sense to cultivate these virtues because we will live better from our own point of view with them than without them.

Unlike the Aristotelian account, the account of virtue I favor is not highly unified. Which particular dispositions count as virtues depends upon the role that is played by the quality in question. Some virtues will include dispositions to overt behavior, others will include dispositions to have certain emotional responses. Further, virtues are identified, not with respect to human nature, but by reference to the idea of a reflectively successful life and the identified limits of our reflective capacities. That there is this variation does not mean that the virtues have nothing in common. A reflective virtue, on my view, comprises (i) a set of cultivatable habits of thought, strategies, or skills (ii) organized around a practical need (iii) that is likely to contribute to living well in a way that can be appreciated from the first-person point of view. I take the components of reflective wisdom to have two kinds of benefit. First, they are instrumental to achieving components of a good life. For example, I shall argue that optimistic realism is a means to the end of pursuing certain ideals in a satisfying way. Second, reflective wisdom is, in some respects, constitutive of the kind of good life that answers to the concerns of a reflective person.

Philosophical discussions of the virtues have been under attack recently by those who think that broad and stable traits of character have been shown by social psychologists not to be widely instantiated in creatures like us (Doris 2002; Harman 1998–9, 2000). Virtue ethicists have responded in various ways (Annas 2005; Kamtekar 2004; Sreenivasan 2002). The best response for my purposes is that the kinds of virtues at work in the Reflective Wisdom Account are not the kinds of virtues that have recently been under attack. The virtues I discuss, as we shall see, are more like habits and problem-solving strategies than like the robust character traits familiar to Aristotelian virtue ethics. When we think of virtues this way, we can rely on some of the work done by positive psychologists (who share this view of virtues) that makes a good case for the possibility of cultivating reliable habits and developing skills. Furthermore, when it comes to what we can do to live well, the recommendations of the Reflective Wisdom Account do not preclude attending to the role of situational factors in determining how we see things, what considerations we are likely to be moved by, and what we value. These factors may be very important in the project of character development.[20]

1.4. A ROAD MAP

For our lives to go well from our own point of view, we must have commitments to serve as standards of evaluation. For these standards to count as normative, it must be possible for us to be wrong about them and for us to reflect on whether they are good standards to have. These

---

[20] For an account that emphasizes the importance of social factors to the development of character see Merritt, forthcoming.

two observations lead to a characterization of a value commitment that emphasizes stability and justification. I define stability as the feature of our commitments that allows us to take these commitments seriously and yet have critical distance when we need it.[21] Chapter 2 begins with a discussion of value commitments and a characterization of what I call "reflective values". It proceeds to address the question of what value commitments most people have that would withstand appropriate reflection. Some value commitments are implied by the basic concern to live a life that sustains reflection. I argue that the value of life-satisfaction and self-direction are of this kind. To discover other reflective values, I propose that we filter the evidence about what people do in fact value through the norms that constitute good reflection. I survey some of the empirical literature on human values and argue that reflective values are plural, and that, for most people, they include close relationships with other people and certain moral ends. These generalizations about human values provide a foundation for claims defended in subsequent chapters.

Of course, having stable value commitments that constitute our point of view is not sufficient for a good life. We also need to act in accordance with our value commitments, and to reevaluate them when things don't seem to be working. Sometimes, then, we need to reflect on what matters to us and how the various things that matter fit together to form a conception of a good life. At other times we must be completely absorbed by our values in a way that is incompatible with this sort of reflection. Knowing when to reflect and when not to, and being able to shift our attention among the various evaluative perspectives that engage us, is a crucial component of wisdom. This aspect of reflective wisdom, attentional flexibility, is the topic of Chapter 3. We also need the ability to stand back from our current focus in order to remind ourselves of what really matters to us, and then to bring our feelings, thoughts, and actions in line with these reflective values. In other words, we must have the virtue of perspective, a part of wisdom which is the topic of Chapter 4.

Reflection must be limited in other ways too. A relentless search for the reasons why we care about something can end up undermining our commitment to it, and an uncompromisingly accurate picture of what other people are like can be harmful to our relationships with them. My

---

[21] "Stability" can have an unfortunate connotation of stubborn endurance. As we shall see in the next chapter, stability as I intend it is quite different from stubbornness.

characterizations of the virtues of self-awareness (Chapter 5) and optimism (Chapter 6) take account of these facts.

This investigation of the reflective habits of a wise person will provide an empirically grounded description of the person who lives well. Whether the Reflective Wisdom Account presents a compelling vision depends, in part, on how the reflective life matches up with other normative notions. In Chapter 7 I consider the relationship between the reflective life and morality, in order to show that the good life from a person's point of view gives an appropriate place to moral concerns.

Chapter 8 takes up a challenge to the very idea that the Reflective Wisdom Account constitutes a normative, action-guiding theory of how to live. This challenge stems from meta-ethical concerns about the relationship between facts and norms. Now, on the one hand, the Reflective Wisdom Account need not make any meta-ethical assumptions about the nature of values and norms. We can think of it as describing a path that it makes sense to take whatever the nature of the good, given that we must start with the rational and informational limitations we have.

On the other hand, the Reflective Wisdom Account does fit naturally with a certain meta-ethical position: namely, a Humean conception of normativity according to which the norms that govern how we ought to live are contingent on our commitments.[22] On this natural reading, according to the Reflective Wisdom Account, claims about our reflective values are based on contingent facts about the kinds of commitments and concerns people actually have. Further, claims about how we ought to develop our character are dependent on these contingent claims about values, and on facts about our psychology and the pressures of modern life. I do not intend to argue for this Humean view against the alternatives. I do think that it is the obvious view for naturalists to have, and I want to consider it because I think that the Reflective Wisdom Account helps make the Humean picture more attractive and clears the way for a fruitful avenue for ethical theorizing. In particular, the main concern about naturalistic explanations of normativity such as the Humean one is that our own commitments cannot provide us with any real normative force, because they are ultimately arbitrary. As I will argue in Chapter 8, however, the commitments that

---

[22] The label "Humean" means different things to different people. As I intend it, the essential Humean commitment is to the rejection of claims about evaluative authority that are independent of contingent human nature. In another familiar sense, a "Humean" is an instrumentalist about practical reason. The view I defend here is not Humean in this sense.

the Reflective Wisdom Account relies on are not arbitrary in any troubling sense.

For naturalists in the Humean tradition, ethics must fit into the natural world. As Simon Blackburn puts it, the Humean naturalist ambition is

To ask no more of the world than we already know is there—the ordinary features of things on the basis of which we make decisions about them, like or dislike them, fear them and avoid them, desire them and seek them out. It asks no more than this: a natural world, and patterns of reaction to it. (Blackburn 1984: 182)

One contribution I hope this book will make is to demonstrate by example one respectable way in which Humean naturalists can proceed in normative ethics. Philosophers committed to naturalism of this kind have largely turned away from normative philosophy and have focused their attention on meta-ethical analysis of the questions being asked and the status of the possible answers to them.[23] If I am right, then there is another role for Humean ethicists: by drawing out the implications of our commitments in light of our ideals and aspirations about how to live, we can derive normative conclusions about the reasons we have to choose to live one way rather than another. If my defense is persuasive, we should conclude that naturalists of this sort can defend first-order, normative theories. Such normative theories will (naturally) be dependent on people turning out to be a certain way or being committed to certain norms and ideals. But this is not a problem if our assumptions about what people are like are well informed and justified. Pursuing this methodology requires philosophers to leave their armchairs, of course, but it should not surprise us that a commitment to fitting ethics into the natural world requires us to investigate what that world is like.

Leaving the armchair has recently become a fashionable thing for philosophers to do.[24] While the movement toward empirically informed ethics is gaining strength and attracting interest, very few philosophers interested in well-being and the good life have entered the fray. Some of the reluctance may be due to a general philosophical concern about empirically informed ethics: namely, that there is a distinction between what is and what ought to be that is ignored or downplayed in this new empiricist movement. But I

---

[23] Simon Blackburn (1998) and Allan Gibbard (1990 and 2003) have done very important and influential work in this area. I do not mean to suggest that there is anything wrong with this approach; my point is just that Humeans are not limited to it.

[24] For an excellent introduction to the new field of experimental philosophy, see Knobe 2006. For other examples of how moral philosophy might be informed by empirical research see Nichols 2004 and Doris 2002.

think that illegitimate moves from empirical psychology to normative theory can be avoided without claiming that the science is irrelevant. A subsidiary aim in this book, then, is to provide a preliminary model for how such work in empirical moral psychology might be taken account of by philosophers working on normative questions about how we should live.

The question "How should I live?" is addressed to people for whom this is a normative question, people who have a concern for justification and standards. How to answer this question in the context of a naturalistic world view is the subject of this book. The scope of the answer developed here is not universal, and its recommendations are not rationally inescapable. If there are people who do not have these concerns, who do not care about what reasons they have to live one way rather than another, I have no argument to compel them to care. I do hope that the description of the reflective life I provide is attractive in its own right, and that it will therefore be natural to identify with the concerns that motivate this characterization. The concerns I identify as the concerns we have about our lives might be at times something to aspire to rather than something that already guides us. If this is the case, the Reflective Wisdom Account is relevant to our practical lives insofar as we aim to live in accordance with our aspirations.

2

Reflective Values

In order to live well from our own point of view, we need to have a point of view, and, given the nature of the concern to live well, this point of view must involve the reflective self. As reflective creatures, we give our approval when it is warranted: that is, when our lives are measuring up to some standards that we think are good ones to follow. The standards we apply to our lives give us reasons for thinking that what we've done is worthwhile (not necessarily from the point of view of the universe, but at least for us), and they must be ones we take to be appropriate, justified, or good to have. Another way of putting this demand is that our commitments need to be normative for us;[1] we think our values could be better or worse according to some norms of appropriateness, and we aim to have the better ones. When I talk about our "value commitments" I mean commitments that we take to be normative in this way. For convenience, I often refer simply to our "values" or our "commitments".[2] Value commitments that *are* appropriate according to these norms, I call our "reflective values".

The notion of a reflective value is a kind of regulative ideal in the sense that it represents the ways in which our values might be improved. To take a value commitment to be normative is to hold it to the standards (of appropriateness or justification) that define a reflective value. Insofar as we take our value commitments to guide us appropriately, we take these commitments to be (or at least to closely approximate) reflective values. So, we could say that value commitments exist along a continuum, at one end of which is a commitment that would be unlikely to survive the slightest reflection, and at the other end of which we have the notion of a reflective value. Wherever our value

[1] This is Christine Korsgaard's (1996: 93) way of putting it. Michael Smith's (1994) definition of normativity also includes both motivation and justification.

[2] I take "value" to be the more natural word when the description of its object is very general (e.g. "friendship" or "life-satisfaction"), and "commitment" to be more natural when we are talking about the particular value commitments of individual people ("my friendship with Lisa" or "the satisfaction of writing a book"). I intend no principled difference between the two terms.

commitments fall on this continuum, they play two important roles for us. They serve as action-guiding goals, and they also function as standards of evaluation or justification for other value commitments and for general reflection on how our lives are going.[3] The importance of the notion of a reflective value is that it is in virtue of this regulative ideal that we take ourselves to be appropriately or rightly guided by our values.

In this chapter I first outline a philosophical account of value commitments and reflective values that highlights the importance of stability, justification, and experience. This account is intended only to explicate the features that a value commitment must have in order to serve as a standard of evaluation in reflection. There may be other features that value commitments have, and there may be different ways of filling in the details.[4] My aim is to describe what's needed in the least controversial terms, so that people with a variety of views can follow me to the next step.

In the second half of the chapter, I argue for the claim that our reflective values are plural and include life-satisfaction, self-direction, social relationships, and moral ends. Here I use two kinds of arguments. The first (the subject of section 2.2.1) is familiar in philosophy: I argue that certain values are simply presupposed by the Reflective Wisdom Account. The second kind of argument (the subject of section 2.2.2) uses empirical findings in psychology as a basis for claims about reflective values. Because the psychological literature about values is still developing, and because the studies that have been done are not tailored to philosophical questions, this argument will be somewhat programmatic. The aim here is to model a way of using psychological research to argue for value claims without making a fallacious leap from *is* to *ought*.

2.1. VALUE COMMITMENTS AND JUSTIFICATION

Our value commitments are the ends we take to be normative for us; we endorse or avow them as things that it makes sense to care about, pursue, or promote. I mean to be very inclusive about what counts: value commitments can include activities, relationships, goals, aims, ideals, principles, and so on,

---

[3] Hence the kind of justification I am proposing is coherentist. See Stanovich 2004 for a sympathetic discussion of what he calls the Neurathian process of rational integration as a response to psychological findings about the large role of unconscious mental processing in our lives.

[4] See Tiberius 2000*b* for the details of my own account.

whether moral, aesthetic, or prudential. In this section I provide an account of value commitments and reflective values by thinking about what it is to be a reflective person. The claims I make here about how our commitments function in our deliberation and planning are not purely psychological claims; instead, they are claims about what we are like insofar as we are guided by the concern to live well described in the previous chapter.

There are several distinctive features of the commitments we take to be normative. The first thing to notice is that in paradigm cases of value commitments we are motivated to pursue or promote that to which we are committed. I take this to be a conceptual point about the particular sense of "value commitment" that I have in mind. To value something is to care about it in a particular way, and to care about something is, at least in part, to have some positive affective orientation toward it.[5]

But there is more to a value commitment than motivation. If value commitments were simple motivational or affective states, they could not play the various roles that they do. If our value commitments are going to serve as the basis for deliberation and planning and for assessments of how well our lives are going, they must include more than good feelings. Not every pro-attitude plays an important role in planning and in the assessment of our lives. Some of our motives are ones we wish we did not have and would be better off without; for example, the addict's desire for heroin or the fleeting urge to jump from a tall building do not seem like desires that provide reasons.[6] What we are motivated to pursue does not automatically give us reasons, then, even from our own point of view. In Christine Korsgaard's terms, we do not take every motivational state to be normative for us. True value commitments have two other features that allow them to play this role: stability and justification. In the remainder of this section I elaborate on these two features in turn, and then discuss how they function together.

The second feature of a value commitment is stability. We need some endurance in our value commitments to compensate for the fact that

[5] The view that value commitments have an affective component is very widely shared. See, e.g., Blackburn 1998; D'Arms and Jacobson 2003; Gibbard 1990; Nichols 2004; Prinz 2007.

[6] For further discussion and support of the point that our desires do not give us normative reasons by themselves, see Scanlon 1998: ch. 1. One might think that desires do give us reasons, but that these reasons are defeasible. However, it is consistent with common sense to think that some desires, such as Gary Watson's (1975) case of the frustrated mother's desire to throw her baby out of the window, provide us with no reason to act at all. Therefore, it seems that the position that all desires provide defeasible reasons should be resorted to only in case no other explanation of normativity can be defended. I thank David Schmidtz for pressing me on this point.

although we do feel strongly about them, our motivations can wax and wane. Sometimes we lose the motivation to pursue our commitments because we are distracted, sad, frustrated, or just in a bad mood. We counteract the influence of frustration, distraction, and other such factors by intending to continue to be motivated in the way we had been motivated without these influences. Further, stable commitments provide parameters within which deliberation typically takes place. Without stable attitudes toward some of our commitments, deliberation would be much more difficult, because in every deliberative context everything would be open for consideration; there would be no fixed points to give structure to our reasoning. The lack of stability and structure would also make it difficult to succeed in long-term planning for values that require it.[7] For example, commitments to learning the guitar, becoming an excellent basketball player, or reducing global poverty all require a sustained effort even for you to believe that you've done your best to live up to them.

Diachronic consistency, then, is an important feature of the paradigm case of a value commitment. Given its purpose, I suggest that we understand stability in terms of a defeasible disposition not to reconsider our values. How much stability a particular value commitment has will depend partly on how generally it is described. A commitment to friends and family is likely to last a lifetime, though the implications and specific objects of this commitment will no doubt change. What level of generality we require will depend on the purpose of our discussion. When we deliberate about specific choices in our own lives, it might make sense to characterize our commitments quite specifically. In this chapter, and later in the book, however, we will need to describe value commitments at a fairly high level of generality, so that we can draw out the implications of these commitments for people in general.

To pursue the ends we value in a satisfying way, we need to be willing not to reconsider these values incessantly. However, a *rigid* disposition not to reconsider our commitments under any circumstances would not be a good thing either. What we need, I suggest, is stability that is sustained by a conviction that one is justified in valuing some end; this is a reasonable form of stability because it allows a person to reconsider her commitments when she has new beliefs about the end in question, or when there is some other compelling case for deeper reflection. Appropriate stability, then, is a

---

[7] The point here is analogous to the point Michael Bratman (1987) makes about intentions and their role in planning.

disposition not to reconsider our commitments that is sustained by confidence in the value of the ends to which we are committed, or, in other words, by the conviction that we are justified in being committed to those ends.

This leads us to the third important difference between value commitments and mere pro-attitudes, which is that our value commitments have a certain kind of authority for us. (In other words, as suggested at the beginning of this chapter, they are normative for us.) We think it makes sense to plan around these commitments; we endorse them as important to our lives. For my purposes, I will say that a commitment has authority for us when we take ourselves to be justified in pursuing it or feeling as we do about it, which in turn means that we have something to say in answer to the question "Why go for that?" A justification in this context is a set of considerations or a story that fosters confidence, prevents undermining doubt, and contributes to stability. For a Humean theory like this one, this "something to say" will draw on other commitments or on the very attitudes that express the commitment itself. The fact that the other commitments we have support, or at least do not conflict with, a particular value will contribute to the justification for that value, as will the strength and depth of our attitudes toward the value itself.

The claim that we take our value commitments to be justified may strike some as hyper-rationalistic and false to experience. To address this concern, it will be helpful to compare my characterization of value commitments with Harry Frankfurt's recent work on volitional necessity and the will.[8] Frankfurt's picture is rich and compelling, and there is, in fact, much in his work that I want to accept. But Frankfurt rejects any important role for reasons in the commitments that are essential to a person's will, and, therefore, we might think his arguments will be a challenge to the idea that justification is crucial to value commitments. According to Frankfurt,

The fact that people ordinarily do not hesitate in their commitments to the continuation of their lives, and to the well-being of their children, does not derive from any actual consideration by them of reasons; nor does it depend even upon an assumption that good reasons could be found. Those commitments are innate in us. They are not based upon deliberation. They are not responses to any commands of rationality. (Frankfurt 2004: 29)

---

[8] Frankfurt is not trying to characterize value commitments *per se*. However, the comparison is useful because Frankfurt is also trying to capture a kind of authoritative motivation. Therefore, I think the objections Frankfurt raises to overly intellectualized accounts of autonomy and the will apply equally well here.

Frankfurt's discussion of these commitments makes this view attractive. We can see the point best in the case of love for another person, especially a child or spouse:

> It goes without saying that love is a contingent matter; unlike the dictates of the pure will, those of love are not supported by rational necessity. The fact that love and its commands are logically arbitrary does not mean, however, that they can be abandoned or invalidated at will. We are certainly not free to decide "at our own liking" what to love or what love requires of us. (Frankfurt 1994: 136)

I think we can acknowledge the phenomena that Frankfurt identifies here without giving up on the claim that a sense of justification is essential to value commitments insofar as they are different from other kinds of motivations. To see this, we need to recognize that taking your commitments to be justified in the sense I intend is different from providing reasons for them. Taking yourself to be justified, in my view, means that you think a story could be told, not that you are actually prepared to tell it. More importantly, this story need not be one that is philosophically illuminating; nor does it need to be a story that appeals to universal reasons. Instead, the story might have a lot to do with how you feel when you are guided by these commitments.[9]

Some, siding with Frankfurt, may find even this weaker notion of justification to be too much. Here it will be helpful to distinguish two different points that Frankfurt makes about reasons, only one of which is in conflict with my conception of a value commitment. First, one of Frankfurt's observations is that reasoning and reflection are not the means by which each of us discovers what has value for us. As he aptly puts it, "If we are to resolve our difficulties and hesitations in settling upon a way to live, what we need most fundamentally is not reasons or proofs. It is clarity and confidence" (Frankfurt 2004: 28). I agree with Frankfurt that the strong commitments we have to our friends, families, and projects are not caused by reflection. But this is compatible with the claim that we take our attitudes to be justified. I think that much of the attraction of Frankfurt's picture stems from this point about the origins of love and commitment. What seems quite right is that "[s]ome of our deepest desires, which express our natures most fully and most authentically, do not accommodate themselves to our thinking. Rather,

---

[9] It is worth noting that we may not be very good at ascertaining our own feelings, particularly if we rely on introspection to reveal them. This is a point that will be taken up in Ch. 5. My point here is just that assuming there is a story to tell is a part of the package that allows our values to play a certain practical role in our lives. I am not assuming that the stories we would tell are accurate.

our thinking accommodates itself to them" (Frankfurt 2002*b*: 224). So it is. But, again, this does not mean that we have nothing to say about why these commitments are worth having. Further, it doesn't contradict the idea that we assume we do have something to say.

Once we distinguish the point that justification plays a role in *causing* our commitments from the point that we *have* a sense of justification for our value commitments, we can see that the argument against the latter is less compelling. To see why, consider an objection that Frankfurt himself takes up to the idea that volitional necessities comprise an essential part of a person's will. Taking seriously what he says about love, we might wonder how love is to be distinguished from other irresistible motivations that do not seem to give us obligations, or to be related to what our final ends should be. As Frankfurt puts it, "We are vulnerable not only to being captivated by love, but also to being enslaved by jealousy or by a compulsion to take drugs. These passions too may be beyond our voluntary control, and it may be impossible for us to elude their rule" (1994: 136). In response to this problem, Frankfurt first points out that in many cases irresistible passions such as jealousy or desire for drugs will present themselves to the person as alien. But, as he admits, this is not always the case. We can imagine, for example, someone plagued by a desire to change her physical appearance who wishes this were not so, but for whom this desire is part of who she is, entirely *un*-alien. The real difference between love and other irresistible passions, according to Frankfurt, is that love necessarily carries with it a second-order volitional response:

However imposing or intense the motivational *power* that the passions mobilize may be, the passions have no inherent motivational *authority* .... Love is different. Love is not an elementary psychic datum, which in itself implies no particular evaluative or practical attitude on the part of the lover toward its motivational tendency. To be sure, a person may regret loving what he loves. He may have attempted to avoid loving it; and he may try to extinguish his love .... But since love is itself a configuration of the will, it cannot be true of a person who does genuinely love something that his love is entirely involuntary. (Frankfurt 1994: 137)

The necessity of love is voluntary in a sense; it is, as Velleman (2002a: 94) says, a "willing inability of the will". But now we need an understanding of this voluntariness that distinguishes love from other irresistible passions. Insofar as I understand Frankfurt's (1993: 111–12) view here, it seems to be that the constraints that love imposes on our will are endorsed by us. Again, as Velleman (2002a: 93) explains Frankfurt's position, "An inability becomes voluntary ... when it is due to a motive with which the subject identifies by means of a reflective endorsement."

This move, it seems to me, invites justification back into the picture, because reflective endorsement is approval that seems reasonable or grounded to us. Moreover, if we focus on the value commitments that shape the decisions we make about how to live our lives, the need for justification is independently motivated. Failing to find any justification can undermine our commitments (a phenomenon that is often the source of the existential crises that befall people at certain stages of life). The role that our value commitments play in our lives makes this sense of justification essential. We spend a lot of time and energy in pursuit of our value commitments, and we sacrifice other things we may want for the sake of them. We have to be able to conceive of the difficulties in pursuing our ends—the sacrifices and expenditures of time and energy—as worthwhile costs; otherwise when we come to reflect on how our lives are going, we would wonder whether these costly ends should be rejected.[10] As Korsgaard (1997: 250) puts it, I must have something to say to myself about why I have the ends I have, "something better, moreover, than the fact that this is what I wanted yesterday". With Frankfurt, I believe that the "something we say" need not have anything whatsoever to do with rational principles. It may be a story about conviction, emotional certainty, or love. It may even be "I want it" together with the conviction that getting what I want is a good thing in life. But if these value commitments are to provide the basis for a positive self-survey, they must be structured in a way that forestalls doubt and sustains a disposition not to reconsider and reject them. A sense of justification provides this needed structure.

Value commitments could not provide the right kind of basis for assessments of how our lives are going if we did not take them to be justified. This is because the knowledge that what we've done in life has nothing to say in its favor will undercut our endorsement insofar as we are reflective and concerned to live well. Surveying my life and thinking to myself, "I've done really well at tending my garden, but it wasn't worthwhile", will not be an endorsement of my life. The positive feelings that may have accompanied this evaluation will likely be dulled by my lack of confidence that the values I've upheld are in any way important. Further, the judgment that my life is going well *because* I've lived up to a particular value commitment will also

---

[10] As I hope is clear, this is not to say that we must always take our efforts to be justified by some further end. It might be that we take the pursuit of the end to be worthwhile for its own sake.

lose credibility when I cannot find anything good about adhering to that commitment. A well-lived life is one that a person endorses from a reflective point of view, and this endorsement is undermined when the standards that are employed in reflection are arbitrary from the agent's own point of view. Again, I want to emphasize that the kind of justification I am suggesting we need is not a highly intellectualized philosophical defense. Clarity and confidence, in Frankfurt's words, may *be* a crucial part of our justification. So, for example, a person's justification for her commitment to her marriage might give a central place to the feelings that Frankfurt thinks are central to love.

To understand fully the importance of the last two features of value commitments (stability and justification), it helps to understand how they work together. Instability in our value commitments undermines our conviction that we are justified in having the commitments we have, and it therefore undermines our sense that these commitments ever have normative or guiding force. This is because in order to take our commitments to have the authority to guide us, we must have the conviction that there is something good about them. This conviction requires confidence in the value of the commitment, and hence in our justification for it, as well as a willingness to suspend our skeptical doubts about it. But it is difficult for this kind of conviction to develop unless there are some stable commitments to support it. Unstable and fluctuating commitments are not generally conducive to developing conviction, because we become engaged in doubting the value of the unstable commitments, and this undermines our confidence that these commitments provide real guidance. Furthermore, taking there to be a justification for our commitments promotes their endurance by providing reasons to continue to give these commitments weight in deliberation and judgment. There is, therefore, a reciprocal sustaining relationship between the endurance of our value commitments and our taking them to be justified.

The above discussion of the relationship between normativity and stability relies on empirical claims about our psychology. In particular, the key empirical commitment here is that a certain psychological profile—namely, a lack of stable value commitments (in the sense discussed above)—combined with a concern to live well from your own point of view is difficult to maintain. To my knowledge, empirical studies that would verify this claim have not been done, but it is a reasonable assumption.

One might think, however, that there are obvious counterexamples: people who have great but fleeting conviction in the value of their commitments, who float from one project to the next without losing faith in the idea that these fleeting commitments have real worth and provide real guidance. There are three things to say about such counterexamples. First, some people who seem to follow this pattern take themselves to be committed to the value of spontaneity or "living for the moment". If this is true, then these people have different, but nevertheless stable, value commitments. Second, some people who seem not to have stable commitments do have stable commitments to values characterized at a more general level of description. A serial monogamist, for example, may have a commitment to good relationships of whatever duration that transcends the particular relationships and allows her to approve of how her life is going, even though she doesn't make a long-term commitment to any one person. (Notice that there are different types of cases here: some people value long-term relationships and believe that they haven't found the right person to commit to yet, while others value having intense, intimate relationships, no matter how long they last.)

Third, people who genuinely have no stable commitments (not even to spontaneity) will divide into two types: those who really do have the goal of living well from their own point of view and those who do not. As I said in the Introduction to this book, I have no reply to the latter type of person, though I think such people are rare. About the first type of person, I submit that if we think more clearly about the details of such a life, we will see that the lack of stable commitments competes with the goal of successful reflective evaluation of how life is going. As this person with a very strong aversion to commitment goes through life, the next time she thinks about how her life is going, she will remember past reflections that relied on different values. For her current evaluation to sustain her endorsement, she must think that her current values are better than the previous ones. But if her whole history is one of jumping from this to that, she has little basis for confidence in her values, and the pattern will be difficult to sustain.

The kind of justification that our value commitments have does not require foundational values or principles. Instead, given the nature of reflective values and the affective element of endorsement, it requires just support by our other commitments, experiences, and affective responses. In particular, one of the standards that our values can be held to is that we enjoy their pursuit, find them rewarding, and the like. Positive affective orientation is one dimension along which our value commitments can be improved, and experience is the means for this particular kind of improvement. Confirmation in experience, then, is an important part of justification, because positive affective orientation is a crucial component of our value commitments, and experience teaches us what we respond to positively. Further, new experiences, together with other values, can present pressing reasons to reconsider our commitments. For example, the discovery that pursuing a specific commitment is painful or boring would be a reason to reconsider it on the assumption that we value enjoyment or excitement.

Paradigm value commitments, then, consist in positive affective states that have diachronic stability, as well as the conviction that one is justified in having these stable attitudes. Commitments such as these are ones that allow us to judge that our lives are going well. In a thoughtful moment, reflecting on the fact that we have satisfied many of our desires may leave us cold if we doubt that these desires are worth satisfying. Value commitments, on the other hand, provide a foundation for reflective endorsement because of the very features that make them normative. The fact that they are enduring features of our lives that it makes sense to uphold means that when we reflect on our lives and see that we have lived in accordance with them, we will have reason to assess our lives positively, with little chance of unsettling doubt or indifference.

We can now see how there is room for improvement of our value commitments, and hence room between our current values and our reflective values. Our actual value commitments can be closer to or farther from the ideal of a reflective value, because they can be more or less stable, justified, and compatible with our affective orientation. The notion of a reflective value provides a regulative ideal for reflection on our values, even without specifying the precise degree of stability or support. Further, the notion of a reflective value provides the kind of standard that will satisfy the reflective self, the part of us that is concerned with genuine normative guidance.

The fact that there is often distance between our actual value commitments and reflective values—the value commitments we have and those we would have if we were wiser—has implications for the notion of a person's own point of view. A person's own point of view includes a commitment to getting it right: that is, a commitment to reflective success. It is because of this commitment that living well from your own point of view does not simply mean liking how things are going. Without this commitment to an ideal built into the subjective point of view, we would end up with an account that has no normative authority, no capacity to give guidance or to answer our questions about how we *ought* to live. An important implication of this picture of normativity is that the normativity of reflective values does not get reduced to empirical claims. This is because the standards that we use in deliberation about whether our value commitments count as reflective values cannot be employed without thinking in normative terms. In reflecting on the merits of our values, judgments must be made about the relevance of certain kinds of information, the relative weights of the different values at stake, and the appropriateness of prioritizing certain experiences over others. For example, reflecting on the value of your deeply satisfying marriage, it does not make sense to put much weight on small things your partner does that annoy you (forgetting to put the toilet seat down, for instance). This is something that most of us think shouldn't get much weight in your reflections on the value of this relationship. Dwelling on little annoyances can undercut other attitudes that we think are more important and a more legitimate part of the justification of the commitment.

Another important implication of the above picture is that people who are concerned to live a life that they can affirm upon reflection do have some reason actually to do some reflecting. Thinking about what matters to us is a way of bringing our actual values closer to reflective values. This claim might seem to be contradicted by the facts about the limits of our reflective capacities. If our conscious, reflective capacities are not very successful at predicting what our emotional responses will be, and if we don't really know our reasons for valuing what we do, then we should be skeptical about the assumption that reflection will help to make our values more stable and compatible with our affective orientations. Skepticism is warranted, I think, but only if what counts as being reflective does not take account of the weaknesses of our conscious, rational capacities. On my view, what counts as good reflection, and hence which value commitments will count as reflective values, is determined by the account of a person with the reflective virtues or wisdom. And wisdom, on my view, must take account of the fallibility of our reflective capacities.

The nature of reflective wisdom is the subject of Part II. For now, this brief characterization will suffice: a person with the reflective virtues learns from experience, has stable commitments to what she deems valuable, and responds appropriately. She knows when to reflect (on her values or the facts) and when to be absorbed in her pursuits, when to insist on scrutinizing her beliefs and when to live with a picture that is probably somewhat distorted. Reflective values are to be understood, ultimately, as the values we choose insofar as we have developed wisdom in this sense. Since reflective wisdom itself requires stable value commitments, it will be helpful to start out with some general claims about what our reflective values are likely to be.

2.2. REFLECTIVE VALUES

2.2.1. The Implicit Values Argument

If the notion of a reflective value that is central to what it is to live well is a normative notion, then we cannot tell what people's reflective values are simply by asking them. How, then, can we find out about reflective values? I use two methods. The first method, used in this section, is to uncover the value commitments that are already implicit in the starting points of our discussion of how to live well. The second method, a partly empirical one, will be the topic of section 2.2.2. As I mentioned above, a complete understanding of a reflective value requires an account of reflective wisdom, the subject of the next four chapters. In a certain way, then, the following discussion puts the cart before the horse. Because the method I use for defending all aspects of the Reflective Wisdom Account is a coherence method, though, it is difficult not to put one of the carts in front of one of the horses at some point. In this particular case, the difficulty is mitigated by the fact that the claims about values defended here are extremely general, and therefore do not require much detail about the nature of good reflection.

According to the Reflective Wisdom Account, to live your life well is to live in such a way that you approve of how your life is going from your own reflective point of view. Taking this point of view requires giving due consideration to the value commitments that constitute standards for evaluating your life. Life-satisfaction and self-direction are two values that are presupposed by this account. Someone who doesn't care about being satisfied with how her life is going at all, or who doesn't care how well her life succeeds in terms of her own standards, would be a person who has no interest in living well from a reflective point of view. As discussed in the Introduction, this concern is a starting point for my account and, I think, a reasonable one.

To be self-directed is to live in accordance with your own values and standards. While this value may seem individualistic, it is not as individualistic as it sounds. Self-direction is relative to the individual in the sense that the goals a person must achieve to count as self-directed must be *her* goals, shaped by her values. But the content of these goals and values need not be self-regarding or self-interested. For example, a person might think that the most important factor in how her life is going is the well-being of her children. In this case, her children's well-being is a goal the satisfaction of which determines (in part) how well her own life is going. Further, insofar as she acts to promote the well-being of her children, she is self-directed in the sense I intend—that is, directed by her own values. The Reflective Wisdom Account may rule out some extreme forms of communitarianism about the good life, according to which individual values and goals do not matter at all, but it does not exclude people for whom the main sources of satisfaction with life are their relationships with other people and membership in groups.

Life-satisfaction is a positive response to the conditions of your life as a whole. It includes both a cognitive assessment or judgment that things are going well and a positive affective component.[11] Strictly speaking, my account presupposes the value of *reflective* life-satisfaction: a satisfied, affective response to the conditions of your life when you adhere to norms of good reflection. While the kind of life-satisfaction that counts as a reflective value is constrained in this way, it is still true that it corresponds, at least roughly, to something we actually experience. In fact, I will now argue that reflective life-satisfaction is similar to life-satisfaction as measured by psychologists. More precisely, the claim will be that life-satisfaction as measured by psychologists is a good proxy variable, a rough but adequate stand-in for reflective life-satisfaction. This is a claim I will rely on in the partly empirical argument of the next section.

One of the most prominent research programs in positive psychology focuses on life-satisfaction as the main component of subjective well-being.[12] Well-being, on this view, is at least partly constituted by positive self-reports of global life-satisfaction.[13] The most widely used self-report scale for global life-satisfaction is Ed Diener's. Diener's *Satisfaction With Life Scale* (or SWLS) is a five-item instrument that asks subjects to rate their agreement on a scale of 1 (strongly disagree) to 7 (strongly agree) with the following:

• In most ways my life is close to my ideal.
• The conditions of my life are excellent.

---

[11] Here I follow L. W. Sumner's (1996: 145–6) account of life-satisfaction as endorsement.

[12] Other prominent approaches that correspond roughly to the philosophical positions include hedonism (Kahneman 1999) and eudaimonism (Ryan and Deci 2000). See Tiberius 2006 for a comparison of philosophical and psychological theories of well-being.

[13] The philosophical position of the leading positive psychologists seems to be that well-being is pluralistic; it includes positive affect, life-satisfaction, health, and more. This pluralistic view is articulated by Ed Diener and Martin Seligman (2004), who argue that many different measures are relevant to our assessment of well-being.

- I am satisfied with my life.
- So far I have gotten the important things I want in life.
- If I could live my life over, I would change almost nothing.[14]

The main difference between the overall life-satisfaction that psychologists measure with this questionnaire and the reflective life-satisfaction presupposed by the Reflective Wisdom Account is that the latter requires (because of the normative dimension of the account of living well) that our assessments be made from the right perspective: that is, on the basis of reflective values. Despite this important difference, life-satisfaction as measured by psychologists is conceptually close enough to reflective life-satisfaction that life-satisfaction research is relevant to our inquiry.

What psychologists measure when they measure life-satisfaction is at least somewhat reflective, because the questions prompt people to take the long view. Moreover, life-satisfaction responses are not hyper-reflective in the sense of being divorced from feeling; while life-satisfaction is not the same as emotional well-being or positive affect, the two are closely related (Sandvik *et al.* 1993, and Pavot and Diener 1993). Although reporting about life-satisfaction is a cognitive task, because it involves making a global judgment, we make this judgment at least in part on the basis of feelings of satisfaction. This is a plus because, according to the Reflective Wisdom Account, hyper-reflection is not appropriate reflection. Because subjects are asked about their lives as a whole, as opposed to their current mood, a long-term perspective and consideration of what really matters are encouraged. It must be acknowledged that life-satisfaction assessments do not always represent this perspective. It has been shown that life-satisfaction reports are subject to distortion by trivial and temporary conditions like mood and the weather (Schwarz and Strack 1999). Nevertheless, there is good evidence that overall assessments of life-satisfaction are relatively stable, which indicates that the person making them takes up a somewhat reflective point of view.[15]

Furthermore, overall (or global) life-satisfaction is highly correlated with what psychologists call important domains and what we might call domains of value (Schimmack *et al.* 2002). This indicates that overall life-satisfaction is somewhat reflective because it is sensitive to the person's values, rather than

[14] Diener's SWLS is in the public domain and can be downloaded from his website: <http://www.psych.uiuc.edu/~ediener/SWLS.htm>, accessed 9 Sept. 2007.
[15] See Pavot and Diener 1993. See Tiberius and Plakias (forthcoming) for further discussion of the stability of life-satisfaction judgments.

being entirely dependent on irrelevant contingencies. In fact, psychologists explicitly conceive of the SWLS as an instrument that gives information about how a person's life is going from the point of view of what matters to her: "The SWLS items are global rather than specific in nature, allowing respondents to weight domains of their lives in terms of their own values, in arriving at a global judgment of life satisfaction" (Pavot and Diener 1993: 164).

Life-satisfaction and self-direction are action-guiding commitments that are inherent in the Reflective Wisdom Account. Concerns for self-direction and life-satisfaction are just part of what it is to have the relevant concern to live well. This means that whether or not people do value life-satisfaction and self-direction is relevant to the legitimacy of the starting point I have chosen for the Reflective Wisdom Account. If people just don't care about these things, this would be some evidence that the account lacks an appropriate audience. As it happens, though, there is good evidence that life-satisfaction and self-direction (once distinguished from independence from others) are widely valued.[16]

The values of life-satisfaction and self-direction are important, but they are also so broad that they may not (by themselves) lead to many conclusions about practical guidance. Can we go further? Part of the point of the argument above was to pave the way for empirical research on life-satisfaction to guide us in an argument for further claims about reflective value commitments. I turn to this kind of argument in the next section.

2.2.2. The Empirical Argument

In this section I have two main goals. First, I want to make a case for three rather mundane claims about our reflective values: (1) that these values are plural, (2) that they include friendship or other close personal relationships, and (3) that they include moral ends and making some contribution to these ends. For my purposes, "moral end" is a technical term defined as a value that has to do with benefit to others. (I might equally have called them

---

[16] See Diener *et al.* 1998; Diener 2000. Some of the skepticism about the value of self-direction comes from worries about so-called collectivist cultures. It should be noted that while people in collectivist cultures place less value on such things as autonomy, individual freedom, and self-esteem, it is not the case that they do not value them at all (S. Schwartz 2006). Further, Ryan and Deci (2001: 157–60) argue that once autonomy as self-endorsement is distinguished from independence, the evidence that autonomy is valued in collectivist cultures becomes more compelling.

"other-regarding ends", but this is more cumbersome.) I mean to leave it open whether these moral ends would be characterized as such by the people who have them, and whether the reasons for having the ends are moral ones.[17] For example, a person who values world peace because she does not want her grandchildren to be drafted into the army would count as having a moral end. As we will see in Chapter 6, I am particularly interested in goals that benefit society at large and that require coordinated human action for their achievement. The point of isolating these particular claims has to do with the topics on which I focus in the rest of the book; I don't mean to suggest that these are the only claims about reflective values that can be defended by this method.

I doubt that anyone will find these claims about values particularly surprising. The second and perhaps more important goal of this section, therefore, is to illustrate a way of thinking about the relevance of empirical evidence to normative claims about reflective values. Even if the results of this argument are not ground-breaking, there are good reasons for making the effort to articulate and employ it. First, the project of constructing a naturalistic, Humean normative theory must take seriously facts about human psychology. Because psychological research into well-being and happiness is fairly new, it may be that we do not yet find much in the way of new direction from the psychological literature. Still, this literature can provide confirmation of our views, and a responsible Humean should make sure that this confirmation exists. Moreover, exploring the ways in which positive psychology bears on philosophical accounts of well-being *now* will prepare us to learn more from this research as it develops.

The second reason for exploring the psychological literature has to do with the influence that philosophers might have on an important and burgeoning field. Some psychologists are aware that they make evaluative assumptions about the *appropriate* goals of life in order to make decisions about what to measure and what not to. Further, some psychologists have argued that positive psychology ought to become a field that embraces certain normative claims about what goals are worth pursuing (B. Schwartz 2000). Questions about what is an appropriate goal and what ends are worth pursuing in a human life are philosophical questions. Philosophers are in a good position to make a valuable contribution to the future of positive psychology, therefore;

[17] I recognize that this way of characterizing moral ends seems suspicious, but, as I hope will be clear, it is all that is required given the purposes served by the claim about moral ends in later chapters.

but we can only do this if we know what positive psychologists do, and if we have thought about how their work relates to our own.

Third and finally, I think there is a benefit of bringing a reflective method to positive psychology research that has to do with how we as individuals living our lives should regard the sudden abundance of popular books on happiness and well-being.[18] From these books, we can gather all sorts of recommendations for life: we ought to be more grateful and optimistic, we ought to be married, we ought to live in democratic countries, we ought not to worry about money but we should make more than the people around us, and so on. The psychologists and economists who have written such books, while not in the business of recommending conduct in their academic work, seem content to write quite prescriptive books for a general audience.[19] The underlying assumption, insofar as one can generalize, seems to be that prescribing conduct to increase happiness is rather like telling people how to be healthy. It is assumed that we all want it, and therefore that we all have a reason to take the means to it. But individual people reading these popular books on happiness might wonder whether the sense of happiness that is at work in psychological studies is the same sense (or the only sense) of happiness that interests them. Further, even if happiness as measured by psychologists is something desired, an individual reader might rightly wonder whether the generalizations apply to her, or whether making a change in habits is likely to cause her to be happier, given her particular reasons for being unhappy. Information from this new science can be useful to us, but, in my view, this information is best considered reflectively.

Before we begin, a disclaimer. As the preceding discussion indicates, the reasons for making this empirical argument have at least as much to do with exploring the relationship between empirical psychology and normative ethics as they do with establishing particular claims about reflective values. So, those who are willing to accept the three mundane claims about reflective values with which I began this section, and who are not interested in the psychological literature for its own sake, should feel free to skip this section.

To begin, what we'd like to know is the content of people's values or self-directed goals insofar as they are being reflective. We might take a top-down

---

[18] See, e.g., Seligman 2002; Gilbert 2006; Layard 2005; Haidt 2005.

[19] Some psychologists are more sensitive to this issue than others. Martin Seligman (unpublished MS), for instance, is very much aware of, and concerned about, the gap between the descriptive goals in psychological research and the prescriptive enterprise that is becoming part of positive psychology.

approach to this question, which would be to describe an ideally reflective agent and think about what such an agent would value given the ways in which she is ideal. I favor a bottom-up approach, according to which we think about what people value and ask whether these values are likely to pass the test of reflection. The relevant norms of reflection direct us to adopt values that are likely to withstand periodic reflection and unlikely to be undermined by other commitments or new experiences. Norms of coherence and information will be particularly salient. To employ the bottom-up method, then, we begin by gathering data about what human beings tend to value and asking whether these values are based on good information and are compatible with other value commitments.

I favor the bottom-up approach for two reasons. First, insofar as the methodology in the top-down approach is different from that of the bottom-up approach, it is very unclear how it works. We are supposed to imagine a perfectly reflective being and then imagine what such a being would value. During this process of imagining, it seems that we are likely to be strongly influenced by our own values in such a way that our method is no longer free from the commitments with which we begin. Insofar as we can abstract away from our own initial commitments, we have to wonder whether the process will result in any particular set of values at all. Further, the method presupposes that the values of an ideally reflective version of me, or the values she would advise me to have, would be the values that the actual me is better off having. But this is not at all obvious.[20] Even if a particular set of values does result from contemplating a perfectly ideal agent, the relationship of these values to real people is left unexplained.

Second, the top-down method is at odds with our focus on the first-person question of how to live well. The process whereby we question, reaffirm, or change our values is one in which we hold some values constant to use as standards of evaluation for other values. Because the Reflective Wisdom Account is meant to be action guiding for actual people as they are, practical advice for us needs to proceed from the values we already have. Thus, even

---

[20] This point has been made by a number of people using some amusing counterexamples. For example, Thomas Hill (1986) argues that a fully and vividly informed sports fan might lose her desire to cheer for her team because of her sympathetic awareness of the competition's sadness and dejection. His point is that, were this the case, it would still not be obvious that cheering for your team is bad. For related criticisms of full information theories see Gibbard 1983; Rosati 1995; Velleman 1988.

if some of the values we have are not good for us, we need an account that makes clear the reasons for us to change them, where such reasons have as their source something we already value.

So, we will begin with what we value and then proceed to think about how these values stand up to reflection. The kind of evidence I will consider comes from self-reports about values. This requires some explanation, because psychologists have recently given us many good reasons to be skeptical about self-reports.[21] Self-reports are important for my purposes, because this is where we start when we are reflecting on our values from the first-person point of view. In large part, the argument of this section should be seen as a model for the kind of reflection that really matters: namely, first-person reflection about our own lives. From the first-person point of view, there is no getting away from our own reports about what we value. Furthermore, other sources of information about what people value are difficult to investigate on a large scale. To be sure, we might find out important information about what people value by looking for the kinds of attitudes that comprise a value commitment. But to ascertain the objects of a certain pattern of attitudes—positive emotional responses, motivation, a sense of justification, and conviction—would be a daunting experimental task. We begin with self-reports, then, but we will not accept them uncritically.

Psychologists who investigate human values, it seems, have been more interested in tracking changes in values over time and in the effects of social pressures on values than they have been in establishing that there are universal values. In order to track changes, however, it is necessary to establish a comprehensive list of human values to track, and this makes the research relevant to our question. In the 1970s, Milton Rokeach (1973) devised the Rokeach Value Survey, a widely used thirty-six-item scale that divides values into "terminal" and "instrumental". Terminal values such as "a world at peace" or "family security" represent end-goals; instrumental values, such as "honest" or "ambitious" represent the behavioral means to those goals. Rokeach asks people to rank the eighteen terminal values from 1 to 18 in order to compare the importance of various values over time. In four different surveys taken from 1968 to 1981, several values retained a relatively high ranking:

---

[21] See Schwarz and Strack 1999 for a critical discussion of self-reports about life-satisfaction. The situationist literature urges skepticism about self-reports of character traits (Doris 2002).

- A world at peace (free of war and conflict): 1 or 2[22]
- Family security (taking care of loved ones): 1 or 2
- Happiness (contentment): 4, 5, or 6
- Helpfulness (working for the welfare of others): 7 [An instrumental value, according to Rokeach's scale, and therefore on a different list from the others referred to here]
- True friendship (close companionship): 9, 10, or 11
- A comfortable life (a prosperous life): 8–13[23]

Rokeach began the construction of his scale by compiling lists of values from the psychological literature and from survey data. His method has been criticized for being subjective and arbitrary, but further research has found few problems with the scale. Valerie Braithwaite and her colleagues, for example, have interviewed subjects to find out what their values are as a way of validating Rokeach's scale, and they conclude that Rokeach's scale includes the most important items (Braithwaite and Scott 1991: 664). Braithwaite and Law (1985: 260), in a study designed to test the comprehensiveness of the Rockeach Value Survey, again using extensive interviews with subjects, suggest adding a domain of value that "relates to basic human rights such as dignity, privacy, the protection of human life, and freedom" and one that relates to physical well-being. Otherwise, they conclude that Rokeach's scale is comprehensive.

Even if the Rokeach Value Survey is not comprehensive, however, it serves my purposes well enough. It shows that people have a variety of values and that they value relatively highly their own contentment and their relationships with family and friends. On the subject of moral ends, Rokeach's surveys show that people rank "A world at peace" as either their first or second most important terminal value. Because a world at peace is an end that has general social benefit and requires social cooperation, it counts as a moral end on my permissive definition. Rokeach also found that the value of helpfulness was ranked seventh of eighteen instrumental values, above (among others) "independent", "capable", "self-controlled", and "cheerful"; this constitutes some evidence that people value contributing to their moral ends.

The case for universal human values has been made most forcefully in psychology by Shalom Schwartz and Wolfgang Bilsky (1987). In Schwartz's

[22] This value is distinguished from "National Security (protection from attack)", which gets a lower ranking (8–13).

[23] I include this example as one that does not necessarily count as a reflective value, a point I will discuss further at the end of this section.

(2006) most recent work, he proposes the following list of ten motivational domains of values: self-direction, stimulation, hedonism, achievement, power, security, conformity, tradition, benevolence, and universalism. In the Schwartz Value Survey, within each domain of value there are many particular goals, character traits, and states of affairs that count as markers for the more abstract domain (S. Schwartz 1992). For example, universalism is represented by markers such as "EQUALITY (equal opportunity for all)", and "PLEASURE (gratification of desires)" is a marker for the hedonism domain (S. Schwartz 2006: 12). Respondents are asked to rank several markers for each value domain "as a guiding principle in MY life" on a scale from "of supreme importance" to "opposed to my values".

In Schwartz and Bilsky's (1987) work, the hypothesis that these are the basic values of all people is supported by a theory of human needs according to which human beings are biological and social organisms with needs for individual survival, interpersonal communication, and group welfare. While some may be suspicious of devising a list of values on the basis of a theory of human needs that has only indirect empirical support, Schwartz and Bilsky (1987) were open to evidence for values they had not predicted on the basis of their theory, and they eliminated previously predicted domains of value that overlapped significantly with other domains without forming a distinct region.[24] We do not need to accept their theory of human needs, or any claims about innate causes of these values, in order to find the value scale legitimate.

Schwartz and Bilsky hypothesized that certain values were more compatible than others, and they predicted that people's rankings of the importance of certain values as guiding principles in their lives would group into compatible domains. For example, they hypothesized tension between the pro-social and achievement domains of value and predicted that people who give a high ranking to the former would not give a high ranking to the latter (and vice versa).

When people seek personal success or focus on task achievement, it is difficult for them not to overlook negative interpersonal consequences of their actions. Conversely, attending primarily to promoting the welfare of others is likely to interfere with concentration on task achievement. (Schwartz and Bilsky 1987: 554)

---

[24] For example, in Schwartz's later work, spirituality as a possible domain of value was eliminated because the items in this domain overlapped to a high degree with items in the domains of tradition, benevolence, universalism, and security (S. Schwartz 2006: 16).

The opposition between these two domains of value was strongly confirmed in studies done in Germany and Israel.

What this research seems to show is that people have value commitments that tend toward a kind of practical coherence. That said, we cannot conclude that people's values fit neatly into compatible domains. The fact that people ranked more highly values in compatible domains does not mean that they did not value, though to a lesser degree, values in the other domains. In fact (as would be predicted by Schwartz and Bilsky's theory of human needs), almost everyone views most of the domains of values as at least somewhat important.[25] Moreover, in Schwartz's continuing research, he has found that at the societal level, with surveys conducted in countries "across representative samples, using different instruments, the importance ranks for the ten values are quite similar. Benevolence, universalism, and self-direction values are most important" (S. Schwartz 2006: 18). Together with Rokeach's survey data, Schwartz and Bilsky's research lends support to the assumption on which I want to rely: namely, that people have multiple values that include relationships (in the benevolence domain, which includes the values of true friendship and mature love) and moral ends (in the universalism domain, which includes the values of social justice and equality).

There are several features of the psychological research discussed above that render it useful for our purposes. First, the conception of what it is for a person to value something used by Rokeach, Schwartz, and Bilsky is relevantly similar to the philosophical notion with which we are concerned. Schwartz and Bilsky define a value in terms of its desirability and its role in directing one's life:

[V]alues are (a) concepts or beliefs, (b) about desirable end states or behaviors, (c) that transcend specific situations, (d) guide selection or evaluation of behavior and events, and (e) are ordered by relative importance. (Schwartz and Bilsky 1987: 551)

In their study, they ask subjects to rank values in terms of their importance as guiding principles in their lives. In later work, Schwartz defines a value as a desirable goal that motivates action (S. Schwartz 2006: 3). Some value surveys carried out by psychologists are not careful about acknowledging this prescriptive or normative aspect of values, and so they end up measuring something that is closer to desire than to value (Braithwaite and Scott 1991: 694). Rokeach's conception of a value also distinguishes it from beliefs,

---

[25] Shalom Schwartz, personal communication, 31 Jan. 2007.

preferences, and other attitudes. He defines values in terms of the preferable or the desirable and conceives of them as providing goals for life (Rokeach and Ball-Rokeach 1989: 775).

Values are also linked to affect, according to Schwartz, in just the way that the Reflective Wisdom Account presupposes:

When values are activated, they become infused with feeling. People for whom independence is an important value become aroused if their independence is threatened, despair when they are helpless to protect it, and are happy when they can enjoy it. (S. Schwartz 2006: 3)

Furthermore, various studies have shown that values are linked to behavior. For example, people who place higher priority on values in the benevolence domain are more likely to cooperate with others, and people who place higher priority on values in the security and power domains are more likely to vote for center-right political parties that emphasize entrepreneurship and the market economy, as well as family and nationalistic values (S. Schwartz 2006: 28–35). That values are linked to affect and behavior is important, for our purposes, because of the worry that self-reports about values might indicate only the would-be charioteer's inaccurate perception. Insofar as the values that psychologists study are linked to affect and behavior, there is evidence for thinking that these values are value commitments in the full sense described in the first part of this chapter.

Second, conceptualizing values in terms of domains or goals that include various specific values within them is useful. This level of generality is necessary to support claims about shared values. And, as we shall see in future chapters, we can put these general values in context in order to argue for particular norms and virtues.

Another source of data about human values is the European and World Values Surveys. These surveys were "designed to provide a comprehensive measurement of all major areas of human concern, from religion to politics to economic and social life" (Inglehart 2006).[26] Hundreds of questions were asked in face-to-face interviews with people in eighty-three different societies comprising a representative sample of 85 percent of the world's population (Inglehart *et al.* 2004: 1). The surveys took place in four different waves: 1981, 1990, 1995, and 1999–2001. These surveys are designed for investigating the relationship between individual values and social, political, and cultural

---

[26] The World Values Survey questionnaires and data are online at <http://www.worldvalues-survey.org/> accessed 15 May 2007.

phenomena. It is difficult, therefore, to draw inferences about individual values from the available data. Nevertheless, we can find some evidence here for my assumptions about values.

First, the World Values Surveys corroborate the assumption that close personal relationships are very important to people.[27] When asked about the importance of various things to their lives, family and friendship were the first and third items, respectively, given the top ranking ("very important").[28] (Work had the second-placed ranking with 65 percent of people overall counting it as very important.[29]) Moreover, 84 percent and 82 percent of people surveyed spend time with family or friends respectively once a week or once or twice a month. This is significantly more than was reported for as much time spent with colleagues from work (50 percent), people at church, mosque, or synagogue (39 percent), or people at a sport, cultural, or community organization (30 percent).

The case for the claim that people value moral ends and their own contribution to these ends is more difficult to make on the basis of these global surveys. Still, there is some evidence that is worth considering. For example, 69 percent of the people surveyed overall agreed or agreed strongly with the statement "I would give part of my income if I were certain that the money would be used to prevent environmental pollution". "Service to Others" was rated "very important in life" by 45 percent of people surveyed, and "rather important" by 41 percent. Forty-two percent of people reported that "A useful job for society" is an important consideration in their employment. And more than 60 percent of people overall said that they were prepared to help the sick, disabled, or elderly in their country.

Granted, this information is sketchy and confounded by various factors. For example, looking at the results country by country, service to others seems to be a less important value in socialist countries, which may be

[27] All of the data discussed here are from European and World Values Surveys Four-Wave Integrated Data File, 1981–2004, v. 20060423, 2006. The European Values Study Foundation and World Values Survey Association. This file is online at <http://www.worldvaluessurvey.org/>, accessed 15 May 2007.

[28] A four-point scale was used (very important, rather important, not very important, not at all important). Family was counted very important by 88 percent of all the people surveyed, and rather important by 11 percent. Friendship was listed very important by 41 percent, and rather important by 44 percent. Rankings in this study allowed indifference: it was open to people to put more than one value in each category of importance.

[29] Work is related to values in important but complicated ways. I have chosen not to focus directly on the value of work, but I do think that the values of life-satisfaction and self-direction, for most people, closely involve the work they do.

because in these countries there is less of a sense that such service is needed. Nevertheless, the data in these surveys suggest that valuing states of affairs that are conducive to human welfare, as well as one's own contribution to these states of affairs, are not alien values that only a naive Pangloss would attribute to people.

Finally, let us consider the claim that our values are plural. This is a claim that seems well supported by the survey data. It is demonstrated, first of all, by the broad scope of the surveys and the fact that within each domain most people feel strongly about something. For example, as mentioned above, when asked what was most important in their lives, the two items receiving the highest ranking were family and work. Value pluralism is also demonstrated by patterns within certain question sets. For example, in the World Values Survey at least 50 percent of the people surveyed listed the following as personally important aspects of a job: good pay (80 percent); pleasant people to work with (68 percent), good job security (68 percent), a job that meets one's abilities (62 percent), a job that is interesting (61 percent), a job in which you can achieve something (59 percent), and good hours (51 percent). Similarly, when asked what is especially important for children to learn at home, at least 50 percent of everyone surveyed chose good manners (74 percent), honesty (73 percent), feelings of responsibility (68 percent), tolerance and respect for people (66 percent), and hard work (51 percent). These lists reveal endorsement of *different* values, and the fact that large numbers of people assign high importance to them suggests that people value a variety of things.

The fact that people care about a variety of things that might even pull in different directions seems to be a fact of life. Of course, we do not need psychological studies to tell us this—the conflict between the values of work and family is ubiquitous and well known. But the studies provide some cross-cultural support for our potentially biased hunches. Moreover, when we look at specific manifestations of the more general domains of value, pluralism becomes all the more obvious.

To summarize, the three research programs in values research I have examined (Rokeach's Values Survey, Schwartz and Bilsky's work on basic human values, and the World Values Survey) provide strong support for the claim that most people value friends and family. There is also good evidence that most of us value some moral goals or ideals, and that we care about making some contribution to them, though this case is more difficult to make. Finally, the fact that the surveys reveal that people's commitments are distributed across a range of values is good evidence for the claim that our values are plural. Having in hand some assumptions about what people value, we can now apply the bottom-up approach and ask whether these values count as reflective values.[30] Here we will engage in a reflective process that considers our values in relation to each other and to the norms of reflection we endorse.

Looking at the evidence, and reflecting on our own experience, the claim that relationships with family and friends are highly valued by most people is well supported. Not only do people across the world find close relationships to be important, but, historically, many of those reflecting on the good life have listed friendship or family as essential to our flourishing. Is this value likely to withstand reflection? One reason to think it will is its very pervasiveness across populations and over time, which suggests that certain sources of disconfirming experiences will be absent for this value. The fact that the value of close relationships is widely accepted means that we are unlikely to confront social disapproval for having this value, which eliminates one major source of doubt about our values. Values that are socially supported would therefore seem to be more stable, and given the relationship between stability and justification argued for above (section 2.1), this lends prima facie support to the claim that family and friendship count as reflective values.

Another reason to think that this is a value that withstands reflection has to do with its relationship to other values. In particular, one of the most robust findings in life-satisfaction research is the correlation between close social ties and life-satisfaction. For example, in one study Ed Diener and Martin Seligman (2002) divided subjects into three groups: high-, average-, and low-happiness individuals. The groups were divided based on peer reports of affect, self-reports of life-satisfaction, and self-reports of affect both global and daily. What they found was that all members of the high-happiness group reported having good social relationships (reports which were corroborated by informants). They concluded that "social relationships form a necessary but not sufficient condition for high happiness" (Diener and Seligman 2002: 83).[31] Correlations between life-satisfaction and other values give us some

[30] Another source of evidence for these assumptions is Hadley Cantril's (1965) well-being studies, in which he asked people open-ended questions about their personal aspirations and fears. This kind of research would be useful for the methodology I am proposing here, but, unfortunately, further studies along these lines have not been undertaken. Cantril's research and related studies are discussed in Adler and Posner (unpublished MS).

[31] For a summary of the evidence regarding the correlation between marriage and life-satisfaction, see Argyle 1999: 359–62. For evidence regarding intimate friendships, see Reis *et al.* 2000.

reason to think that these other values would withstand reflection, because such correlations reveal mutual support between values. If close personal relationships and life-satisfaction "go together", then our valuing the latter is not likely to give us reasons to reject the former. Further, since life-satisfaction is a value that is implicit in the Reflective Wisdom Account, it occupies a rather central position in our network of values. This makes compatibility with the value of life-satisfaction all the more important, because this is a value we would be hard pressed to reject.

Now, the studies cited above establish correlation rather than causation. Correlation provides *some* support for the claim that family and friendship are reflective values, because it shows that this value will not be undermined by valuing life-satisfaction. But while the correlation studies do show that satisfied people have good relationships, they do not show that having good relationships will increase your life-satisfaction. And in order to conclude that the value of life-satisfaction gives us positive reasons to value close personal relationships, we would need to take this next step. Causation is much more difficult to demonstrate than mere correlation, and, further, studies to establish causation are often deemed worth doing only once a clear correlation has been established. We can expect that as positive psychology develops, there will be more studies designed to establish causation; but even now there are some studies with this aim. Psychologists who have worked on establishing causation argue that marriage (and to a lesser degree other close relationships such as friendship) increases life-satisfaction because it provides an additional source of self-esteem, reduces feelings of loneliness, and provides emotional and material support (Myers 1999). Others have shown that the loss of a significant other has immediate and substantial effects on life-satisfaction levels, indicating a causal relationship (Lucas *et al.* 2003; Clark *et al.* 2004).

If these psychologists are correct, then people who have good close social relationships are more likely because of this to be satisfied with their lives. And if this is so, then anyone who values life-satisfaction (or, we might say, who has an interest in reflective success) has a good reason to value close relationships with others. Even without the claim about causation, those who (like most of us) do value close relationships with family and friends should count this as a reflective value insofar as it is compatible with, and will not be undermined by, the value of life-satisfaction. Lest these claims seem so obvious as to be uninteresting, let me make two points. First, studies that establish causation in this area are not as bland as they may seem. After all, alternative explanations are easily forthcoming: for example, one might think that happy people are more likely to have friends and good intimate relationships in the first place, in which case valuing close relationships would not help unhappy people to be happier at all. Second, there may be a tendency to take certain kinds of studies as stating the obvious even when we do not actually know the results of the studies beforehand. In fact, educational psychologists have studied this reaction, the so-called "so what" reaction, and have collected some evidence that people react this way no matter what the results of the study are.[32]

Life-satisfaction research also gives support to the claim that moral ends and contributing to moral ends are reflective values. For example, there are some recent studies that show volunteer work and other altruistic actions to be correlated with life-satisfaction.[33] Robert Emmons (2003) has shown that pursuit of moral goals makes a significant contribution to having a sense of meaning in life. As for a causal relationship, psychologists have recently begun to study well-being interventions, intentional activities that are designed to increase life-satisfaction and/or other well-being indicators. There is preliminary evidence that other-regarding interventions such as performing acts of kindness have lasting effects on happiness and life-satisfaction (Lyubomirsky *et al.* 2005).

Another reason to think that our moral ends would be included in the set of reflective values has to do with the fact that they are a natural outgrowth of our valuing relationships with other people. People who care about other people for their own sakes have a reason to care about the world being an inhabitable and hospitable place. Similarly, it seems to be a natural outgrowth of caring about the state of the world that we would find it valuable to make some contribution toward that goal. Moreover, interests in other people that stem from self-interest—for instance, concern about other people's opinions and esteem, or about whether other people are likely to help us—also give us good reasons to adopt moral ends and to want to make a contribution to them. People who value moral ends are also more attractive as friends and collaborators. (These are familiar Humean points about the benefits of virtue.) Further, because valuing moral ends and contributing to them

[32] In one study, students were as likely to judge false results as predictable as they were to judge real results as predictable (Townsend 1995). Another study found that "people tend to regard even contradictory research results as obvious" (Gage 1991: 16).
[33] Michael Argyle (1999: 365) reports finding that "volunteer and charity work were found to generate high levels of joy, exceeded only by dancing". He is here reporting a study from Argyle 1996. See also Piliavin 2003; Boehm and Lyubormirsky, in press.

are socially beneficial, these values are not likely to be undermined by the disapproval of others. Indeed, quite the opposite seems to be the case: people who care about others and do their part, morally speaking, are likely to receive approval and support.

Is it reasonable to think that pluralism would be preserved in our reflective values? To answer this question, it will help to distinguish the relevant level of description of values. At a high enough level of generality, it might be that all our values could be subsumed under a single value: say, happiness, interest satisfaction, or the object of reflective choice. I certainly have no argument to prove that philosophical analysis could not bring our values under a single rubric of this kind. If values are to be used as action guides, however, as I take them to be, then we need to think of them at a lower level of generality. And at this lower level, values are plural.

The kind of pluralism I am defending is value pluralism in the context of ordinary reflection. The kind of reflection that we do when we think about how our lives are going seems unlikely to eliminate pluralism given the range of things we value. Indeed, I believe that pluralism in this sense is a deep fact about us, which gives rise to a need for the ability to negotiate our various commitments. For the purposes of constructing a practical theory, then, it is better not to conceive of wisdom and good reflection as aiming at value monism, but instead to think about ways that a wise person copes with plural values. My characterization of wisdom, as we will see, responds to this need.

It is worth pointing out that the above methodology may also be used to argue against certain values as reflective values. In particular, materialistic values such as wealth and luxury goods are not well confirmed by the above method. First of all, income, perhaps surprisingly, is not a strong predictor of life-satisfaction or of other well-being indicators.[34] Therefore, striving to make lots of money is not as well supported by the value of life-satisfaction as is friendship. Further, and more importantly, Tim Kasser (2002) has argued that people whose values are more materialistic tend to lose out in many other dimensions, such as physical health, mental health, and happy marriages, as compared to people whose values are less materialistic. (Materialistic values here include wealth, fame, social status, and material objects that increase status or fame.) Kasser's (2002) research shows that people who value materialistic items highly are more likely to feel insecure (p. 42), get divorced (p. 32), and experience problems relating to other people (p. 62). Valuing

---

[34] See Diener and Biswas-Diener 2002 for a review of the literature.

self-acceptance, affiliation, and community feeling, on the other hand, are correlated with higher levels of self-actualization and vitality and lower levels of depression and anxiety than valuing financial success (Kasser 2002: 7).

Such psychological research lends some support to the claim that materialistic values are not reflective values. A reflective person, thinking about whether the values she has make sense in light of the facts, will take notice of the fact that caring a lot about wealth, for example, will increase her stress and anxiety and decrease her ability to be a good partner or friend. Given other well-supported values we have, the fact that materialistic values make us insecure and anxious constitutes a reason for doubting that such values are good to have.[35]

The bottom-up method I have used in this section leads to well-grounded, defeasible judgments about the normative category of reflective values. It does so on the basis of information about what human beings like and are like, together with the application of norms of reflection that direct us to adopt values that are likely to be well supported by future experience and reflection. Particularly relevant in our discussion were norms that recommend mutually compatible values, values that can be pursued successfully together, and values that will not be plagued by undermining considerations. Other norms, such as a norm that recommends being better informed about relevant features of one's commitments, have also played an indirect role, and may play a larger role in individual deliberation about values. In particular, our emotional responses to the pursuit of our values can be an extremely important source of information in individual deliberation; paying attention to our feelings can inform us both about what we do value and what we ought to value. The argument here does not derive normative conclusions from purely factual premises, because norms are employed in the assessment of which of our actual values count as reflective. It does, however, begin with and take seriously the empirical facts: the facts that we learn from experience, taken together with accepted norms of reflection, provide evidence for and against claims about reflective values. For example, the fact that the accumulation of wealth is not a value that is easily combined with the value of a satisfying life will undermine the former value in someone whose norms of reflection require her to place greater weight on life-satisfaction.

Claims about reflective values must be defeasible for two reasons: first, we do not know all the facts that could be relevant to the reflective success of

---

[35] This is not to say that *wealth* isn't good to have. The point here is that *valuing* wealth is negatively correlated with other well-supported values.

one of our values, and, second, we may not apply the norms correctly. These ways of falling into error are clearest in cases in which an individual person is reflecting about her own particular values. Consider a person reflecting on the value she bestows on her collection of antique cars. If she thinks that her reasons for valuing the collection derive from generally materialistic values, and she knows that materialistic values do not tend to make a person happy, then she may decide that this is not a reflective value. But our car afficionado could be mistaken about her reasons for valuing antique cars. Perhaps she has materialism on her mind because she just read a book about the evils of consumer culture, but her real reasons for valuing the collection have to do with her skill as a mechanic and the joy of fixing up cars, or with her intrinsic interest in the history of the automobile and a delight in partaking of this history. Being misinformed in this way could lead her to judge mistakenly that her car collection is incompatible with her commitment to living a satisfying life.

Before I say more about the case of the individual deliberator, I want to make one final remark about the bottom-up method I have articulated. This method suggests the possibility of an interdisciplinary research program for establishing a normative system of human values.[36] Psychologists who study human values discover what we value, while philosophers who propose theories of the good life defend normative claims about the values we ideally ought to have. The method I have used puts these two projects together in order to discover what values people would have if they were somewhat more reflective, though otherwise more or less as they are.[37] Such a program could have some important advantages. For example, it could provide a defense of human goods that engages people's actual motivations and sensibilities. Further, it could inform us about the kinds of argument that persuade people to reconsider or change their values.

2.2.3. Reflective Values and the Individual Deliberator

In order to articulate a general account of what it is to live well, it is helpful to start with claims about values that are shared by almost everyone; such claims, as we have seen, are very general. When an individual

---

[36] Thanks are due to Dan Haybron for helpful discussion about this possibility.

[37] This is not dissimilar to what Martha Nussbaum (2001) has done as part of her research on the capabilities approach. In her attempt to find overlapping consensus on a list of important capabilities across cultures, she discussed this list with women in many different cultures. What emerged from these conversations is considered together with her *normative* conception of human functioning in order to construct a philosophical justification of the list (p. 76).

thinks about how to live her life, however, the values she considers and articulates must be much more specific. It is surely only in rare circumstances that a person would deliberate about whether to value close relationships with others at all, and it may well be the case that if these circumstances arise, something has gone wrong. But some will be skeptical about the idea that we should deliberate about or explicitly reflect on our particular value commitments, and hence skeptical that the process I have described has any role in individual deliberation. One source of skepticism is that thinking about our commitments and trying to justify them seems to be just as likely to undermine our confidence in them as to secure it. This is an important point, and appreciating it will help illuminate the Reflective Wisdom Account.

Deliberating about and justifying our value commitments is not something we do often; nor should it be. As we shall see in Part II, the account of reflective wisdom I defend acknowledges that too much thinking can undermine our commitments in inappropriate ways. For this reason, a wise person does not deliberate or engage in explicit reflection frequently. Reflective wisdom, on my view, is not a virtue that appears only during practical reasoning; rather, wisdom helps us to live well by making us into the kind of people who have stable and satisfying commitments, and for whom such deliberation tends to go well when we do engage in it.

There are, though, times when it does make sense to reflect directly on our commitments. When we have to make important decisions about whether to change careers, marry, have children, and the like, some deliberation about what we really care about is inevitable and appropriate. At such times, the bottom-up method that I have followed in considering what our reflective values are can be employed by people reflecting on their own values. The facts that particular people attend to will doubtless be different from the facts that interest a philosopher constructing a theory. For example, individual deliberators are unlikely to have much interest in survey data. Nevertheless, some facts are useful for both endeavors; for example, people might find it helpful to know that certain values are more highly correlated with life-satisfaction than others.

Applying the reflective process I used above to the individual deliberator's case, there are two points worth making. First, as with the case of defending general claims, individual deliberators should not take their own reports for granted. For there are times when what we are inclined to say matters to us does not matter to us very deeply, or matters to us only because of influences that we actually want to reject. For some of us, this is the case with materialistic values: we may indeed value having a lot of nice stuff, but this may be something we should reconsider upon discovering that organizing our lives around such values does not lead to life-satisfaction. Second, reflection on our values will not necessarily be improved simply by learning more facts. We must also become better at following other norms of reflection, and this means improving our abilities to gauge our emotional reactions, to weight our various commitments appropriately, and to articulate our reasons for valuing what we do. The importance of paying attention to the motivational aspect of our value commitments (our desires, emotions, and feelings) cannot be overemphasized. By paying attention to what our emotions track, we can increase the likelihood that our pursuits will actually result in positive feelings such as satisfaction and a sense of meaning. (A point that is often reflected in the advice of career counselors and parenting gurus who advise us to pay special attention to what we or our children are excited and energized by.)

2.3. THE JUSTIFICATION OF REFLECTIVE VALUES: SOME CONCERNS

Taking together the implicit values argument and the empirical argument, we can say that reflective values include life-satisfaction, self-direction, close personal relationships, and moral ends. These values are ones that are likely to be mutually confirmed, stable, and resistant to change in the light of new evidence. As will now be clear, there is a significant difference between the kind of justification I mean to invoke for reflective values and the kinds of justification that are at work in other philosophical theories. Certain Aristotelian theories, in particular, rely on the claim that we evaluate people as good or bad members of our species in much the same way that we might evaluate a bee as a good bee or a lion as a good lion (Foot 2001). Such species-based evaluation provides grounds for claims about the human good that are independent of particular people's attitudes towards the goods in question.[38] My interest in this chapter is in what people

---

[38] Hursthouse (1999) also relies on species-based evaluation, but she is more careful than Foot not to claim that human nature makes certain things good for every human being irrespective of individual psychology. On her view, our rationality has a "transforming effect ... on the basic naturalistic structure" (p. 222).

value when they are reflective. Human nature is relevant to this question, because our nature makes certain values more likely to warrant reflective endorsement than others. Nevertheless, human nature does not impose norms on us in the way that some versions of the Aristotelian picture assume.

There is a sense in which the justificatory demands on the account I am defending are weaker than is the case for other theories. I have not argued that reflective values enjoy any particular metaphysical status, or that they are values we must have. The particular reflective values I have defended are, on my view, ones it makes sense for most of us to plan for and act in accordance with insofar as we are concerned to live a life that holds up to reflection from our own point of view. My contention is that acting in accordance with these values, for those of us who are reflective in the sense that my argument assumes, will make our lives go better from our own point of view. I do not contend that everyone *must* have these particular reflective values on pain of irrationality or even imprudence. The burden of proof for me is lighter than it is for someone who wants to make these stronger claims.

Surely some will react to this disclaimer with disappointment. If this is what a Humean normative theory amounts to, they might say, then so much the worse for the Humean project. I will address the special problem of normative authority in a Humean context in Chapter 8. For now let me point out that other approaches to normative theory are, at least in some important respects, in no better a position.

First, if the worry is about the scope of the theory, then it is misplaced. Certainly we can find people who do not value the things that most human beings value, and people for whom the usual reasons to value friendship and so on do not apply. Such people are not people to whom the Reflective Wisdom Account applies. But it is not clear what a theory that relies on natural teleology has to offer that my account lacks. If Aristotelian theories are naturalistic (as their proponents claim they are), then they too must rely on generalizations about human nature, and, to this extent, the Humean and the Aristotelian seem to be in the same boat.

This brings us to a second kind of worry: namely, that the Humean doesn't furnish appropriate grounds for criticism of others, or even of ourselves. The Aristotelian, because she imbues nature itself with normativity, is in a position to make certain criticisms of people who constitute exceptions to the generalizations about human nature. It may seem that a Humean account gives us no resources for critical assessments of our values or our conceptions of a good life because it is tied to what we are, in fact, like.

This concern, however, oversimplifies both what people are like and the resources of the account I am proposing. It oversimplifies the Reflective Wisdom Account, because it ignores the role that the distinction between values and reflective values plays in this account. On my view, a person's values, character, and actions can be appropriately criticized by applying the standards of reflective values and reflective wisdom. Now, since these standards are still relative to people and their interests, one might worry that the room for criticism is inadequate. But this response oversimplifies what people are like. Given that we are complicated creatures with a variety of commitments at various levels of abstraction and generality, and given that our values, plans, and conceptions of the good life are not all transparent to us, making improvements to our values and our capacity for wisdom is difficult. We can (and do) fail to live up to the standards of the reflective life in various ways. There are, therefore, grounds for self-criticism and criticism of others on the Reflective Wisdom Account.

A remaining source of concern about my argument for reflective values has to do not with the kind of justification used, but with the values that result from its application. One might think that the values I have discussed, while universal, are so general as to be useless as a basis for a normative theory. Moral ends and close relationships are open to a variety of interpretations and will have different instantiations for different people in different contexts. I do not think this makes the claims about universal values uninteresting or useless, however, for two related reasons. First, in the context of the Reflective Wisdom Account, these universal values are not the basis for normative theory in a sense that should cause concern. If these general, universal values were taken to be the source of normative authority, their generality would be a problem, because the values would not have enough content to provide a footing for any particular set of norms. On the Reflective Wisdom Account, as we shall see in Chapter 8, the source of normative authority is, ultimately, the complex patterns of attitudes that a person constructs through reflection and experience. Universal values are not the source of normative authority; rather, they are building blocks for constructing a more detailed account of a good life for most people. Second, these general domains of value do have enough content to serve as building blocks, though this certainly remains to be seen. It is the purpose of the next four chapters to make good on this promise.

2.4. CONCLUSION: VALUES AND THE CHALLENGES OF MODERN LIFE

Most of us want lives in which we achieve our goals, have close personal relationships, contribute to moral ends, and feel satisfied with the various things we do. Many of the traditional virtues are necessary traits for living lives like this. We could not pursue our commitments in a focused and directed way without some temperance and courage. Generosity and justice are required for friendship and for doing good. The traditional conception of practical wisdom—the knowledge of the ethically salient factors and the ability to choose rightly—is important given any of the values we have.

The focus in this book, however, is on previously unnoticed virtues: aspects of wisdom that come to our attention when we think about the limits of our reflective capacities. Before we turn to the discussion of these virtues, I want to mention a further motivation for the focus on the virtues discussed in Part II. The human community in contemporary industrialized democracies has some particular features that make it difficult to pursue our values in a way that will lead to living a good life. These features of modern life make it the case that there are ways of developing our character that are important now, but that may not have been so important at other times in other contexts.[39]

Indeed, it makes sense that a Humean account of the good life, tied as it is to people's actual sentiments, commitments, and conceptions of their own good, would allow for virtues whose value is contingent on a particular setting. A Humean account can therefore make a virtue out of contingency by tailoring its normative ideal to local needs and circumstances. Certain traits of character might be vitally important for those of us living with the particular challenges we face here and now, even though these traits have not always been important for everyone throughout time.

What are these challenges? Modern life is demanding in at least four different ways. First, our attention and energy are pulled in many directions. More options are presented to us than people have ever had before; we have (or at least perceive) more choice about who to be, what to do, and what to buy (B. Schwartz 2004). The media present these options in ways that make some of them seem absolutely imperative, even though they may not

---

[39] For lack of a better and less contentious word, I will use "modern" to characterize the post-industrialized, consumerist culture of Western and other developed countries.

in fact be conducive to our happiness or satisfaction. Further, some conflicts between values are exacerbated in a fast-paced, competitive, capitalist society. For example, think of the pull of family and work, each listed as "very important" by more people than any other item in the World Values Survey. The way our society is currently organized, these two features of life pull strongly in opposite directions, each demanding more of our increasingly limited time. The tension between work and family is a notoriously difficult issue for working women, but women are by no means the only ones who experience it.

Second, our culture emphasizes self-direction and the importance of being ourselves and making our own choices, but does not make this easy (Elliott 2003). We do not receive training in developing our autonomy; nor is being ourselves always rewarded or even tolerated by our culture. Moreover, given the pressures of culture filtered through the media, it is sometimes difficult to hear one's own voice in the din. This effect is made worse by clever marketing strategies that use the ideal of authenticity to sell products so that we think we are expressing ourselves by buying the same products that everyone else is buying (Frank 1997).

Third, while autonomy and consumer choice are highlighted, community ties that used to provide meaning and satisfaction in life are being eroded by such factors as job mobility and suburban living. This trend increases our isolation and alienation from our fellow citizens and neighbors.[40]

Finally, those of us who live in relative affluence live in a world in which the moral demands on us are tremendous and apparent to anyone who is minimally informed. Given this era of globalization, we know more about distant people and their problems than we ever have before, and our actions (and especially the actions of our governments) have more effect on those distant others than they ever have before.[41]

These facts of life in modern societies make life difficult in a variety of ways. The options presented to us make it difficult to figure out what we want and what would make us happy. When we do think that we know what we want, we are often confronted by social pressures to do otherwise. Impartial moral demands conflict with our partial attachments to our friends or our personal projects in ways that can make us feel powerless, guilty, or

---

[40] Martin Seligman (1990), a renowned expert on the psychology of depression, regards the erosion of community as one of the main causes of recent increases in the incidence of depression.

[41] There is a large philosophical literature and a growing popular literature on this fact of modern existence. See, e.g., Singer 1972; Unger 1996.

overburdened. While these sources of conflict are relatively new, they do not seem likely to disappear in the near future. We are not likely to return to more isolated societies in which we fill roles that are determined and supported by our social group. These facts of life may be contingent and modern, but they are well entrenched and serious, all the same. How we ought to develop our character in the world as we now experience it ought to reflect these facts of life. The aim of Part II is to explain and defend four virtues that are vital to our living reflective lives given our values, the fallibility of our powers of rational control, and this modern context.

PART II

WISDOM AND PERSPECTIVE

3

Wisdom and Flexibility

A reflective agent has stable value commitments and the ability to take a reflective point of view on these commitments when appropriate. Because our value commitments must have a certain kind of stability, which rules out a pervasive tendency to doubt and reconsider, we can already see that wisdom cannot mean constant reflection. A wise person must be guided by her reflective values in some sense, but being a reflective agent does not mean engaging in deep contemplation and justification of one's projects at all times. In fact, such a life, for most of us, would be far from ideal. In this chapter I begin to develop the characterization of reflective wisdom by exploring the particular way in which reflection should guide us.

3.1. A REFLECTIVE CONCEPTION OF A GOOD LIFE

When we reflect on what it is for our lives to go well, we form a rough conception of a good life. Because our various commitments provide support for each other, a conception of a good life that locates these commitments on the same map ensures that the commitments we have do not undermine each other and can be pursued together in the same life. A reflective conception of a good life, then, situates our individual commitments in a justificatory framework. The need for our own reflective approval of how our lives are going requires a conception of a good life for its satisfaction. Without such a conception we would have no sense of how our various commitments function together as an evaluative standard and no reason for confidence in the justification of the individual commitments we have.

A conception of a good life, then, is more than just a jumbled set of values. The conception of a good life imposes some structure and order on our commitments. In particular, a conception of a good life locates the various commitments we have and reveals how they are related with respect to mutual support and relative priority. For example, a person who is committed to running a marathon, health, and achievement would have all of these values represented in her conception of a good life. Within this conception the particular commitment to running a marathon would be supported by more general commitments to health and achievement. Further, our conception of a good life will include a judgment about the relative importance of the plural values that constitute it. This is not to say that our values will be ranked on a cardinal scale, but insofar as some things are clearly more important to us than others, this fact will be reflected in our conception of a good life.

To say that our conception of a good life must have structure is not to impose constraints on a good life that are external to the agent. Structure can take different forms, and a structured conception of a good life is compatible with a wide variety of contents. There are, however, some features we ought not to require in a conception of a good life that might be confused with structure. In particular, we should not confuse structure with constancy or inflexibility, or with detail or thoroughness, qualities we should not insist on in a conception of a good life, for the following reasons. First, because our focus is on what it is to live well from a person's own point of view, according to her own standards, we cannot impose standards that privilege constancy and detail over other norms a person might take to guide her conception of a good life, such as norms of spontaneity and creativity. A conception of a good life is structured, then, in the sense that it locates the components of a good life with respect to each other in some way, but it need not have a particular structure such as that of a detailed plan.[1]

Second, conceptions of a good life cannot be too rigid or detailed because these conceptions are also informed by experience gained from living life when we are not reflective. As we will see, non-reflective experience is a crucial component of a good life and a vital source of information about what it is to live well. Our conception of how to live, then, must be flexible and open to change. In practice, this openness means that some of our value commitments may not be very well integrated into the framework of our other commitments, and also that there may be tensions between some of

---

[1] For an interesting discussion of the idea that the plan model is not the only way of conceptualizing a life, see Walzer 1994: 23–4. In a chapter entitled "The Divided Self", Walzer distinguishes "divided selves" (which he thinks most of us are) from pathological "utterly fragmented selves" (1994: 98). As will become clearer in this chapter, I am very sympathetic to the idea that we are divided selves. By distinguishing structure on the one hand from constancy, inflexibility, or detail on the other, my account of the good life is meant to be one that is accessible to divided selves. I first read about this discussion in Elliott 2003 (p. 299), which also contains an interesting critical discussion of the plan model of a good life.

our commitments that we cannot see how to eliminate. To say that we are open and flexible in this context is to say that we are willing to discover the ways in which our commitments might gain further support and the ways in which conflicts might be eliminated, eased, or accommodated in the future. Importantly, being open also means that we are willing to learn from experience that there are new commitments that it makes sense to add to our reflective map, even if these new commitments will not be well integrated at first.

3.2. THE LIMITS OF REFLECTION AND THE IMPORTANCE OF SHIFTING PERSPECTIVES

We cannot engage in deep reflection—reflection about the nature and justification of a conception of a good life—all the time; nor is a good life one in which we are always ready to engage in such reflection.[2] We can see that a life dominated by reflection is an undesirable ideal when we recall that part of what it is to have a value commitment is to be disposed not to subject it to criticism in the normal run of events. Furthermore, we have seen that stable value commitments function as evidence that there are things worth valuing and that our own experience can be trusted. The commitments we endorse in reflection are not chosen *ex nihilo*; we must have commitments in the first place, in order to have a reflective point of view on them. Given these facts, we can see the importance of taking a reflective point of view only when appropriate, and of sometimes being unreflectively absorbed by what we value.

But when is it appropriate to be reflective? And how do we know when we should shift away from our reflective point of view? Here we find that if we look to traditional philosophical accounts of practical rationality for answers, we will find that they are not very helpful. Philosophers have tended to recommend that in a reflective moment we think about our conception of the good, make a life plan, deliberate, or decide which ends to endorse, and then we put this plan, these decisions or choices, into action. The direction of rational authority is top down: the plans, choices, and judgments we

---

[2] Henceforth, I will use "reflection" to refer to this kind of deep, critical reflection. The claims I make about reflection in my sense should not be taken to be true of a broader conception one might have that would include any kind of conscious cognitive process.

make when we are reflective determine the rationality of the choices, actions, and feelings we have in practice. Of course, top-down accounts of practical rationality acknowledge the distinction between reflection and practice. But these accounts aim to characterize rationality and the reflective point of view by articulating the principles or standards that govern our practical reasoning. They do not take movement between reflection and unreflective experience, or certainly movement between different ways of being unreflective, to be part of the province of a theory of practical reason.

In the remainder of this chapter I argue that the top-down picture of practical rationality is incomplete, and that this matters for how we characterize the virtue of wisdom and the reflective agent.[3] To do this, I will begin in the next section by describing the phenomenon of shifting perspectives and explaining the value that these shifts have for us. A *perspective*, as I intend the term, is a pattern of attention that highlights a subset of our values and brings the associated beliefs and emotions in to the foreground.[4] Because we have many different commitments, and because each commitment is comprised of a pattern of attitudes that can wax and wane, we can be in different perspectives at different times. We can, for example, take a reflective perspective when we are feeling contemplative and we want to think about how our lives are going. Alternatively, when we are absorbed in a project, we take a perspective that focuses on this project and excludes almost everything else. The things that change when our perspective changes are what is most salient to us, which facts are deemed relevant considerations, and what motives are most available.

When we think about the phenomenon of shifting perspectives, we find that reflection is crucially informed by the practical perspectives we take up and that shifts between such perspectives are vitally important. We also see that negotiating changes in perspectives, while a part of practical wisdom, is not accomplished by a straightforward, top-down application of the plan or set of judgments arrived at in reflection. Rather, knowing how and when to

---

[3] Wisdom and practical rationality are not the same thing, but I take it that the capacity for practical reason is one part of wisdom. Note also that the claim here that wisdom does not always require being rational or reflective (where this implies a detached perspective) does not mean that the calm, cool, deliberative moment is never the right perspective to have. The capacity to disengage from our passions and deliberate calmly is an important one, but I will argue that it is not the only capacity that comprises wisdom.

[4] I intend the notion of a perspective to apply to different kinds of value (moral, aesthetic, and so on) and to values we have to various degrees. The notion is meant to be fluid, so that it can capture a variety of different attitudes we might take, to different degrees, toward different value commitments.

shift our perspective requires the capacity to make quite local judgments about the character or values that are demonstrated by our occupying a particular practical perspective. In section 3.4, I discuss the lessons to be learned about the nature of reflective wisdom from our discussion of the value of shifting perspectives. The wise person, I argue, makes judgments about the values and character traits that are manifested in her having a particular perspective, and she does this without direct appeal to her conception of the good. The wise person, then, negotiates the various perspectives that make life satisfying without engaging in intellectual or abstracted reflection. As we will see, this means that wisdom includes more than the construction of a coherent conception of the good for a person and the application of this conception to real life choices. A kind of attentional flexibility is also a part of reflective wisdom.

In the novel *Bel Canto*, the Vice-President of a small Latin American country and about fifty others are held hostage in the Vice-President's mansion. They have been cooped up in the living room for months, and many believe they will not survive the ordeal. When their captors finally let them outside for some air:

Vice President Ruben Iglesias, who thought he would not live to feel once again the sensation of grass beneath his feet, stepped off the shale stone walkway and sank into the luxury of his own yard. He had stared at it every day from the living-room window but now that he was actually there it seemed like a new world. Had he ever walked around his own lawn in the evening? Had he made a mental note of the trees, the miraculous flowering bushes that grew up around the wall? What were they called? He dropped his face into the nest of deep purple blossoms and inhaled. Dear God, if he were to get out of this alive he would be attentive to his plants. (Patchett 2001: 281)

Ruben Iglesias undergoes a change in perspective on his life and his values as a result of the highly unusual circumstances in which he finds himself. Instead of a myopic focus on the value of success in his career and working for the sake of that goal at the cost of many other possible pursuits, as he had done for many years, he begins to see the importance of stopping to smell the roses—in his case, quite literally. Several of the other characters in Ann Patchett's novel experience similar changes in perspective, as they come to appreciate the value of things they previously took for granted or did not have time to notice at all.

I suspect that many of us, reflecting on Ruben Iglesias's change of perspective, will think that this is a valuable experience, one that it would be good for many of us to have if we could have it without the risk of death. Acknowledging the beauty of our everyday surroundings and appreciating the wonders of nature are good things to do, and sometimes invaluable tonics for the materialistic or accomplishment-focused perspectives that can easily absorb us. Nevertheless, it would not obviously be a good thing for Ruben to keep his attention focused on his plants, to the exclusion of other interests and concerns, especially once he is released from being a hostage and his duties as Vice-President resume. It is good to stop and smell the roses, but not so good to smell them all the time.

Ruben Iglesias is not the only example we can find to illustrate the value of shifting perspectives on life. Nor is it necessary to have one's life under the imminent threat of death in order to experience such shifts. There are many life events that can cause us to see life in a different way, to change our priorities or our values, even if only temporarily. The death of a loved one can have this effect, as can other major life changes such as being fired from a job, recovering from a major illness, or having a child. Changing one's physical surroundings by traveling or getting out into nature can trigger changes in perspective, as can an encounter with great art. There are also ways in which one can try to bring about such a change intentionally—for instance, by meditating or just going for a walk.

Further, the two perspectives that Ruben Iglesias's case draws to our attention—one focused on career success and the other on natural beauty—are not the only two perspectives one can have. The unexpected death of an acquaintance can make us take the perspective of "living for the moment" in which short-term pleasures seem paramount, whereas the arrival of a child can make us take a perspective that emphasizes the long-term benefits of our actions to a wider circle of people. Perspectives are defined by what values we attend to, what is more or less salient to us, which facts are deemed relevant considerations and which are not. Because the notion of a perspective is defined very broadly, these shifts can be more or less significant; some might be so insignificant as to be not worth talking about. Only certain of the changes in our focus and attitudes of salience are important for how our lives go.[5]

None of the perspectives just mentioned is a paradigm of the rational or reflective perspective recommended for making normative judgments. Ruben

---

[5] Nevertheless, I do not want to impose a content restriction that would rule out these insignificant shifts, because which shifts are important will differ from person to person and perhaps also within the same person over time.

Iglesias is not focused on evaluating his reasons for valuing nature in light of the facts. Rather, he is in the grip of a set of attitudes and dispositions to act. He is, I will say, absorbed in a particular *practical perspective*. From a particular practical perspective one set of values plays the role of a goal for action and appropriate feeling, and critical scrutiny of these values is suspended. From a *reflective point of view*, on the other hand, the point is to engage in critical scrutiny about some of our values. The result of taking a reflective point of view is not (at least not immediately) action or emotion, but considered judgments about our conception of a good life. Notice that reflection here does not mean intellectual engagement in general. Being intellectually engaged, say, by a puzzle or a philosophical problem, is being in a practical perspective that emphasizes the value of truth, intellectual achievement, or mental challenge. The kind of reflection I mean to exclude from occupying practical perspectives is the much more specific kind of critical reflection that concerns the justification of one's values or projects.

In this section I want to make the case for the claim that shifts from one practical perspective to another, and between practical perspectives and reflection, are a valuable and important part of living life well. As we shall see, these shifts are important in two related ways. First, shifting perspectives is necessary for the full realization or pursuit of the values they highlight. Second, this realization of values informs our reflection about the shape that our conception of a good life ought to have.

The first point is nicely illustrated by the case of Juan and Linda from Peter Railton's (1984) seminal paper on alienation and consequentialist moral theory. Juan and Linda are a happily committed couple who live in two different states. Linda is depressed, and Juan knows that an extra visit from him would help. So he goes, even though the money he spends on this visit could be much more helpful to others if he were to give it to Oxfam. Because Juan is a "sophisticated consequentialist", Railton argues, he will not try to perform the most beneficial action; rather, he will act on the disposition he has cultivated for consequentialist reasons; namely, his love for Linda. According to Railton, "in thought and action we shuttle back and forth from more personal to less personal standpoints and both have an important role in the process whereby identity, meaning, and purpose are generated and sustained" (1984: 164–5). Juan's reflective, moral point of view is consequentialist: he thinks that he ought to do whatever will produce the best consequences for all concerned. But Juan also thinks that a world without loving relationships would be unbearable, and so he fosters dispositions in himself that allow for real loving relationships even though they may cause him to violate his own criterion of right action. In order to have a truly loving relationship (to meet that goal of his), Juan must be able to shift from his consequentialist moral perspective to a perspective from which Linda's happiness is most important.

Railton's move to sophisticated consequentialism is supposed to explain the way in which consequentialism is less alienating than critics have charged.[6] His own view is that this move does not result in multiplying perspectives or points of view for the subject. Rather, he seems to think that there is one unified point of view that comprehends both the value of maximizing objective goods and the value of Linda's happiness. But I think this is only partly true. While Railton may be right that the philosophical perspective from which Juan grasps the consequentialist criterion of right action and the justification for his partial dispositions toward Linda, the perspective from which he decides whether to take the flight is not all-encompassing in this way. When he decides to take the flight, his love for Linda takes over, and he does not, as Railton says, "even try to do the most beneficial thing" (1984: 159). A comprehensive reflective point of view may be available to Juan, but he cannot stay in this perspective and hope to achieve the values that it recommends.

Railton points out that Juan's motivational structure, which includes his love for Linda, meets a counterfactual condition: "while he ordinarily does not seek to do what he does simply for the sake of doing what's right, he would seek to lead a different sort of life if he did not think his were morally defensible" (1984: 151). But this counterfactual condition cannot impose itself on the perspective Juan takes when he decides whether to visit Linda. If it did, it is hard to see how Juan could still decide to go. After all, by hypothesis, more good can be done by spending the money in some other way, and Juan could decide not to go if he tried. It *isn't* morally defensible to fly to visit Linda. Rather, what is morally defensible is having the dispositions that cause him to go.

Note that the above is not intended as an argument against Railton's solution to the problem of alienation. I think Railton is correct that one can be committed to consequentialism and yet not use the consequentialist criterion to make decisions. My point is that when Juan makes these decisions on the basis of the values and dispositions that may conflict with the

---

6 For such criticism see Williams 1973; Stocker 1976.

consequentialist criterion of right action in particular cases, he has a different perspective on his values. Moreover, he must take up this perspective if he is to succeed in having a genuinely loving relationship with Linda. Again, this is not to say that his love for Linda must be blind, or that he may never wonder whether his life with her is morally defensible. Rather, the point is that when he makes decisions about how to treat Linda, he cannot *at the same time* and in every case be wondering whether his life is morally defensible. If he does this, he has retreated to the kind of consequentialism that is truly alienating, and he has missed out on an important element of a good human life.[7]

One might think that it is only if the reflective point of view in question is consequentialist that one needs to become absorbed in particular practical perspectives. But this is not the case. Juan's case is just one example of the way in which avoiding deep reflection can be a good thing for a person's life. To see that the point has broader scope, consider the case of someone whose reflective perspective is, more or less, virtue-ethical, centered around the notion of a flourishing life for a person. Let us imagine that Ruben Iglesias is such a person. From a reflective point of view, Ruben has a comprehensive conception of a good human life that includes a variety of worthwhile goals, each of which emphasizes a different aspect of his nature. This conception of the good life includes judgments about the reasons for developing particular virtues and pursuing particular ends such as friendship, health, and mental cultivation. From the reflective point of view, Ruben can see that the justification for pursuing the particular ingredients of his conception of the good life has to do with what it is for him to flourish as a human being.

Now if Ruben is going to have the kinds of attachments to his wife and children that are necessary for his flourishing, his attachment to them needs to transcend this perspective. He needs to be devoted to them in a way that has nothing to do with his flourishing. Of course, virtue ethics does not claim that people should value friendship and other important ends *for the sake of* their own flourishing; on the contrary, part of what it is to have the virtues relevant to friendship, for example, is to love friends for their own sakes. But virtue ethics also typically maintains that developing the virtues is part of what it is for an individual to flourish. So, far from eliminating the divide between perspectives, the fact that virtue ethics says on the one hand that

---

[7] Railton calls the kind of consequentialism that is truly alienating "subjective consequentialism" (1984: 152).

74   *Wisdom and Perspective*

we ought to pursue friendships for their own sake, and on the other hand that friendships are necessary for our flourishing, highlights the existence and importance of multiple perspectives. The perspective from which Ruben can grasp a comprehensive conception of the good is not the perspective from which he can realize the particular values that comprise this conception. To be an effective and dedicated politician, he has to be absorbed by his job, so devoted to it that at certain times it seems the most important thing in the world to him. Similarly, to be a good father, he must respond lovingly, without stopping to reflect on his other roles and commitments or the reasons for which being a good father is valuable. Moreover, the pattern of dispositions to action and emotion that make Ruben thrilled to be in politics is not likely to be the same one that makes him a devoted father. To gain all that he can out of each part of his life, he needs to shift between different practical perspectives.

Notice also that Ruben's change in perspective, brought about by the threat of death, is very much engaged with certain specific values. He does not take a broad view, does not try to understand the reasons for which appreciating nature might be good for him; nor does he try to fit this value into a larger conception of a good human life. Rather, he simply appreciates the beauty and finds himself motivated to continue to do so. Here we can see that changes in practical perspectives are important for appreciating a full range of values. If Ruben were to see his life from the perspective in which accomplishment in his career has priority, which he must do sometimes if he is to be successful, he would never stop to notice the beauty of the flowers in his yard. But the peaceful and appreciative perspective from which natural beauty has priority, while necessary for the awestruck experience he has in his garden, is not likely to be the perspective from which he should make decisions about his career.

The case of virtue ethics makes it easy to see how even deep reflection on the good life is not a point of view we can occupy all the time. In short, taking a reflective point of view on our values is not the same as being engaged by them, and we cannot be fully engaged by everything that has value for us at once. Because reflection is concerned with justification and putting together a whole, coherent ideal, it is necessarily disengaged and detached to some degree. There is nothing wrong with detachment, in its place. Taking a reflective point of view is important in its own right: it is from this perspective that we can address our concerns for justification and that we can think about the overall shape our lives should take. But if we were reflective and detached all the time, we would never experience the things that have value in the way we need to. Practical perspectives in which we focus on the particular and ignore the whole are vital to living a good life, because it is through these practical perspectives that we really discover and achieve what is valuable in them. Further, if the values that constitute a good life are many, we must be able to take different practical perspectives at different times. Sometimes we should be focused on friendship, sometimes absorbed by our careers, and sometimes overwhelmed by the beauty of nature.

Consider again the example of the personal and global perspectives that Juan and many others move between. In a reflective mood, we can see that a commitment to the overall good is compatible with being the kind of person who has partial love toward another person. But being a good friend, husband, or politician requires at some points an unquestioned commitment and undivided energy. A shift to a more personal perspective while one is helping a friend or tending one's garden is just what is needed for these commitments to flourish and to add to our flourishing. A global or less personal perspective is what we need, so that we do not lose sight of our own moral values and commitments to larger causes. And a reflective perspective on our own good gives us a reasonable set of standards that make possible the satisfactory review of our own conduct that is part of what it is to live well.

To illustrate the importance of this kind of absorption, think about activities such as rock climbing, dancing, playing the guitar, or solving a philosophical problem. These activities, when done well, absorb us and demand all of our attention. We won't get a feel for what is exciting, beautiful, or intellectually invigorating about doing these things if we are at the same time reflecting on their value. "Being in the moment", although now a cliché, has much to recommend it.[8] Experiences such as the awe of nature, the physical exhilaration of dance, sex, or sport, or the mental exhilaration of a great conversation are not experiences we can really have while wondering what the point of them is and how they fit into our lives. Moreover, examples such as these reveal that it would not be desirable, even if it were possible, to occupy many practical perspectives at once. Of course, some values can be pursued or appreciated together to mutual advantage. For example, the physical exertion of mountain climbing may enhance one's appreciation of

---

[8] There is empirical evidence for this claim in the extensive literature on "flow". Flow experiences are a kind of absorption in a practical perspective, and such experiences have been shown to have many good effects for the people who have them (Csikszentmihalyi and Csikszentmihalyi 1992).

natural beauty. Still, not all practical perspectives are mutually supporting in this way. Trying to enjoy sex while appreciating the beauty of nature seems likely to frustrate both aims, and a great conversation can distract one from an appreciation of art or nature if the conversation is about something else (or sometimes even if it isn't).

The point alluded to above that we discover what is valuable through practical perspectives brings us to the second claim I want to make about shifting perspectives: practical perspectives inform the reflective perspective in an important way. Practical perspectives inform our reflection because it is (at least in part) by being a friend, daughter, sibling, or parent that we discover what is valuable about these relationships. It is by absorbing ourselves in a hobby or career that we experience the value of accomplishment. It is by losing ourselves in the moment that we experience the value of pleasure, peace of mind, or fun. Thinking abstractly about what has value and what ends are important to human life, we may very well be able to acknowledge intellectually all the various important ends and values. My point is not that there are truths about value that are impossible to articulate or grasp in any way from the reflective point of view. Rather, the point is that we learn from experience and that, often, the right kind of experience is one in which we are absorbed in a way that excludes being reflective.[9]

The informative role played by shifts in perspective can be seen by considering the phenomenon of being stuck in a rut. It seems that we can get stuck in a practical perspective in such a way that we are prevented from living well. When this happens, we need to discover or be reminded of other important values and goals. Sometimes reflection helps us in this, but sometimes we need to take a different practical perspective that reveals other values to us. This was the experience of Ruben Iglesias: a new perspective taught him something that will be relevant to future reflection on life, but reflection did not help him to make this discovery. This experience of taking a new perspective and finding it instructive is familiar to most of us. Sometimes a reflective point of view from which we see the real value of each thing, and do not get carried away by any one thing, is helpful. As we will see in more detail in the next chapter, this reflective point of view can help us to put things in the *right* perspective by revealing that what we are distressed about is not important enough to warrant our reaction. But sometimes a completely different practical perspective that immerses us in other values is

---

[9] I am grateful to Jimmy Lenman for helpful discussion on this point.

more valuable than measured reflection. For example, another character in Patchett's novel, a reserved and responsible businessman, discovers the joys of romantic love when threatened with the possibility of imminent death. This new perspective could not have resulted from reflection because he did not know that romantic love was something he was missing; the new perspective teaches him something vital about life that he could not have discovered by thinking about it. In Jonathan Haidt's terms, a new perspective can inform our reflective selves about the needs of the elephant.

To sum up, we cannot at the same time occupy the reflective point of view and be fully absorbed in a practical perspective; nor can we occupy many practical perspectives at once. One of the conclusions of Chapter 2 was that, for most of us, reflective values are plural. This means that living well includes the realization and appreciation of many different values in addition to deep reflection, and if this is so, then shifting perspectives is necessary for living well. Furthermore, it is because practical perspectives allow us to discover what is valuable or deeply satisfying about various human activities that they can inform reflection about the nature of a good life. Being absorbed in practical perspectives prevents our reflective capacities from becoming disconnected from experience and leading us to do things that we are unable to endorse. Moving between various practical perspectives and shifting from the practical to the reflective is an important part of life. Eliminating these shifts would leave us with vastly diminished resources for learning about what has value and for achieving the ends that we already value.

3.3. ATTENTIONAL FLEXIBILITY

We need to be able to shift from one practical perspective to another, and to take a reflective point of view on our life as a whole when appropriate. Importantly, we need to be able to make these shifts without the top-down application of a reflective conception of a good life. First of all, the choice to shift perspective cannot be the result of applying the reflective conception to practice in any rigorous sense, because one of the things that needs to be judged is when to take up that reflective point of view. In other words, we cannot decide when we need to shift perspectives by becoming reflective and judging that our model of a good human life implies that we ought to make a change. This mode of change assumes that we have already decided to become more reflective. The basis for this original shift in perspectives cannot be a direct application of a reflective model.

Second, even when it comes to shifts between practical perspectives, we cannot always decide about these shifts by adopting a reflective perspective and standing in judgment. This is because of the way in which practical perspectives have us in their grip. To be in a particular practical perspective is for our emotional responses and dispositions to accord with the values that define that perspective. Practical perspectives also shape the "everyday" practical reasoning, planning, and decision making that we do on the basis of (temporarily) fixed goals or values. Practical perspectives have a certain life of their own, an inertia that is the result of these emotional and dispositional patterns. When Juan is living his life, being a good husband and not engaging in reflection about the permissibility of his projects, his love for his wife makes certain courses of action seem obvious, and it crowds out other options and other ways of responding to her distress. Juan can distance himself from this pattern of responses, but not immediately. The reflective perspective, then, is not always available to us when we could most benefit from a shift in perspectives. So we need to be able to judge that we should try to see things differently without already having taken up a reflective stance. One could, of course, stand perpetually ready to engage in deep reflection, always aware of the way in which one's practical commitments are contingent on reflective approval, always ready to evaluate one's commitments from the reflective point of view. But a person who lives this way does not gain what there is to gain from being absorbed in practical perspectives.

Reflecting on our examples, it might seem that shifts in perspective are caused by changes in external circumstances. In Ruben Iglesias's case the shift is forced by drastic changes in his situation. In many other cases, shifts in perspective seem to be the natural result of ordinary shifting circumstances: the rock climber does not have to make an effort to focus her attention on the rocks and forget about her job. Similarly, coming home from the office tends to shift a person's attention away from values associated with his job and toward the values associated with family and with being a father or partner.

This explanation makes it seem that shifting perspectives is not something we do, but something that happens to us. This may make it seem unlikely that there is anything to say about how we shift perspectives without taking up the reflective point of view, and even less likely that shifting perspectives has anything to do with wisdom. It is true that perspective shifts can be caused by external changes, but dismissing the role of agency and the virtue of practical wisdom is unwarranted. We can see why if we think about two kinds of failure with respect to perspective shifts. First, there are cases in which people's perspectives do not change, despite changes in their external circumstances. Some people who come home from work do not stop thinking about the office. And some people who hike, play music, or sit on the beach watching the sunset never become fully absorbed by the experience. Second, there are cases in which perspective shifts occur inappropriately. Sometimes a shift in perspective is really a way of avoiding or retreating from something important. People sometimes become reflective when they ought to be enjoying the moment due to fear or self-doubt, and others avoid reflection when it would be appropriate, due to a desire to avoid a difficult decision.

What takes wisdom is shifting perspectives at the right time, in the right way, and for the right reasons; this is the kind of attentional flexibility that counts as a reflective virtue. The wise person is open to perspective shifts and the reasons for them and, consequently, shifts perspective when it is appropriate to do so. We can understand what it is to be open to shifts in perspective as a capacity to grasp reasons or values, quasi-intuitively, without engaging in any reflection on how they are justified. This openness to reasons and values is a capacity that can be more or less developed. It can vary in its tendency to grasp the right things and in its tendency to grasp them at the right time. The fact that our power to grasp reasons and values can be better or worse makes room for reflective wisdom. The person with the virtue of attentional flexibility grasps the right reasons and values at the appropriate time and changes her perspective accordingly.

This notion of shifting perspectives for the right reasons creates a problem, because the obvious way to understand notions of *right* here is by appeal to a person's reflective conception of the good life. Now there are some ways in which a person can appeal directly to her conception of a good life in order to effect changes in her perspective.[10] For example, from a reflective point of view, recognizing our tendency to get stuck in a certain practical perspective, we can engage in self-manipulation or pre-commitment to effect changes at a later point in time when we are no longer being reflective. Consider the person who recognizes her tendency to bring her work home with her and plans to have a long bath and a cocktail when she gets home to put her in a different frame of mind. In this case the plans she makes while reflective have some influence on perspective changes later.

---

[10] I thank Elijah Millgram for drawing my attention to this possibility.

Self-manipulation and pre-commitments are sometimes foiled, however, as, for example, when we cannot see the reason for following the plan we adopted from a reflective point of view once we are out of that point of view. Moreover, these strategies are not available for every kind of desirable shift. Sometimes the conditions that give us a good reason to change our perspective are not predictable and are not anticipated from the reflective point of view. The wise person, therefore, must sometimes make such shifts using only the resources available from within a particular practical perspective, without referring to her reflective conception directly. And this presents a problem, given that it is from the reflective point of view that we consider and evaluate the relevant reasons.

The answer to this problem consists in two claims. First, other normative considerations are available from within particular practical perspectives to some degree. While it is true that a fully reflective perspective intrudes upon an engaged practical perspective, a person within a practical perspective is not entirely blind (or at least not for long) to considerations that present reasons for shifting out of that perspective.[11] Considerations that are not the focus of attention can nevertheless be on the periphery of one's attention, or they can be considerations that one is disposed to acknowledge in certain triggering conditions. Whether these considerations are on the periphery of awareness or out of awareness but potential candidates for our attention will depend, in part, on how much a particular practical perspective has us in its grip. Even when we are deeply absorbed in an experience, the particular pattern of attention that comprises a practical perspective waxes and wanes; this means that while there may be a moment during which not much could shake us out of our particular focus, other considerations will be available to be triggered in due course. A wise person, then, can recognize the force of other values from within a practical perspective when her focus loosens somewhat and these other values come into her peripheral view, or when external circumstances change in such a way as to trigger the disposition to see them.

The second part of the answer is that we can grasp and act on these normative considerations without taking up a reflective point of view.[12] The

---

[11] As David Velleman (2002*b*: 322) argues, motives that are not part of the story on which the agent is acting at the time "are nevertheless present". For further discussion of Velleman's view, see Ch. 7 n. 11.

[12] I am grateful to Jennifer Whiting and George Sher for helpful discussion of this section of the chapter.

person with attentional flexibility does consider the reasons there are for shifting perspectives, but not by applying a decision procedure or model to the circumstances. Rather, the wise person is open to the intuitions, feelings, and perceptions that draw her attention to the relevant reasons without fully engaging her rational capacities. Being open to reasons from within a practical perspective means being able to appreciate what is at stake in considerations that are not at the center of attention from that perspective. Since considerations may appear to us as reasons without bringing along the justificatory background that makes them reasons, our acknowledgment of these reasons need not invoke a reflective conception of the good life or require that we take up a reflective point of view. This appreciation of reasons is not an explicit rational acknowledgment, but something more like an intuition or impression.

Some shifts in perspective are habitual, natural, or instinctive in such a way that no judgment is required at all for the shift to take place. For many people, the shift in attention that happens when we stop working and come home to our families or our hobbies is like this. But needed shifts in perspective are not always this easy, and so wisdom sometimes requires a person to make more explicit judgments about perspective. Such judgments, I suggest, are assessments of one's perspective based on the normative considerations that are available from within that particular practical perspective. Because these judgments are based on an intuitive grasp of reasons, we do not need to be engaged in deep reflection in order to make them. To see how this is so, let us consider an example of a particular type of judgment, one that has a natural role in shifts of perspective: namely, judgments about the character manifested in having a particular perspective.

Imagine a person who is *very* devoted to his dog. Frank believes that his relationship to his dog is valuable and important. Caring for another entirely dependent being has taught him compassion and has allowed him to extend his sympathetic capacities.[13] Observing the dog's way of being in the world has also encouraged him to enjoy life in ways he did not before. Moreover, Frank feels a real commitment to the dog, and he takes his relationship with Rex to have value in itself, independently of what the dog can teach him. While Frank's relationship with his dog is, by and large, healthy, he has a tendency to become obsessed with concerns about his dog's welfare

---

[13] Lori Gruen (2004) argues that because animals are so different from us, our relationships with them help to develop and extend our capacities for sympathy, empathy, and compassion.

to the point of distraction. During one of these times, Frank worries so much about Rex at work that he can't get anything done, and he declines invitations he would like to accept because he is so worried about leaving Rex alone. We might say that if Frank were wise, he would recognize that being stuck in this perspective where Rex has taken complete priority is obsessive, self-indulgent, or melodramatic. He may think his perspective is obsessive because it is preventing him from achieving many of his goals. He may think it is self-indulgent if he recognizes that he is using it as an excuse to avoid social engagements or challenges at work that he finds intimidating. He might assess his perspective as melodramatic if he realizes that he is really looking for attention and that his concerns for Rex have not translated into any actions that are particularly good from the dog's point of view. Or Frank might find that his having this perspective too exclusively, or for too long, suffers from a combination of these vices or other vices we have not considered.

Here it is natural to say that it "registers with" or "dawns on" Frank that he is being obsessive. Or we might say that Frank grasps, quasi-intuitively or impressionistically, that his attention to his dog has become pathetic or unhealthy. In these cases the wise Frank is *open* to the reasons for shifting from his "dog-centric" perspective, and they come to him through intuition and feeling rather than explicit thoughts about reasons. His judgment that his perspective is obsessive, melodramatic, or the like is based on his not fully reflective grasp of these reasons. Of course, his intuitive assessment may ultimately lead him to deeper reflection, but the shift in perspective is not itself brought about by reflection on his life and values.

Similarly, Juan recognizes that letting his personal perspective crowd out the global perspective from which his wife's needs diminish in importance would be uncompassionate or blind. He can see this even when he is focused on his wife's needs, during the normal ebb and flow of attention; this is what keeps him from becoming obsessively devoted. Losing the personal perspective altogether, though, would be insensitive or unloving, and this can be grasped from other points of view. Notice that these virtue evaluations capture the ways in which perspective shifts are valuable and that the same considerations might represent themselves in terms of the values that are at stake. To call something obsessive is, in part, to say that you have focused on it to such an extent that it is preventing you from paying attention to the other things you value. To say that you are being insensitive, blind, or narrow-minded is, in part, to say that your current perspective prevents you from noticing other ethically salient features.

A wise person shifts perspective when there is reason to do so. Because the resources for shifting perspectives must be ones that are available from within a particular engaged practical perspective, the wise person must have the ability to appreciate reasons for shifting perspectives that do not require reflective engagement or explicit rational thought. To have attentional flexibility, then, is to be open to considerations that are not the focus of our current practical perspective (perhaps not at every moment but eventually), and to be able to make judgments on the basis of these considerations about our current perspective.

Having emphasized the non-inferential shifts in perspective that are a part of wisdom, I do not mean to deny that wisdom also includes explicit reflection. If we are committed to having reflective values, as discussed in Chapter 2, we should sometimes reflect on our conception of a good life and think about how our various value commitments fit into this conception. This kind of thinking shapes a person's overall conception of a good life, which in turn influences what reasons to shift perspectives are (indirectly) available to her, as well as what constitutes having the appropriate emotions and actions given her reflective values. The point of emphasizing the importance of perspective shifts is that they are a previously unnoticed aspect of wisdom that comes to our attention when we consider the shortcomings of our reflective capacities working alone.

3.4. WISDOM AND RATIONALITY

The wise person, according to Aristotle, is able "to deliberate well about what is good and expedient ... about what sort of things conduce to the good life in general" (*Eth. Nic.* 1140ª26–9). If shifting between the reflective point of view and different practical perspectives that focus our attention on different values is part of a good life, then wisdom includes the capacity to make such shifts appropriately. I have argued that appropriate shifts do not employ inferential practical reasoning. Given the tendency to conceive of wisdom as being closely related to practical reason, this may be jarring. In this section I take up some objections to the association of wisdom with the quasi-intuitive process I have described.

First, some might be concerned that the admission that judgments about shifting perspectives are not directly inferred from one's conception of a good life introduces too much looseness into the picture of practical wisdom. After all, if the guidance provided by the conception of a good life is indirect, the mapping between that conception and how one actually lives will admit of gaps. Notice, though, that these gaps cannot be eliminated if we are going to learn what practical perspectives have to teach us. There is no way of life at which we can aim that is a perfect mapping of reflection onto practice. Or, at least, such a life would not really be ideal. Rather than practical life being a smooth and steady realization of an ideal conception of how to live, then, it will be a journey roughly guided by an ideal or goal that will itself change in response to the steps taken in that journey. The point of discussing the value of taking up different perspectives is that this is how it has to be. A neatly mapped life in which we realize our ideal conception of how to live well is a life in which we are always somewhat detached, always ready to check ourselves against an ideal model—a life in which we do not get lost in experience and therefore do not learn from it.

A more serious concern has to do with the justification of the intuitive grasp of reasons that provides the basis for judgments about the need to shift perspective. That is, one might be concerned that if these judgments about one's practical perspective are not made in accordance with a rational process, if they are not directly inferred from one's conception of a good life, then they will not be justified at all. But this concern ignores the reason-giving force that such impressionistic judgments have. Given the coherence pictures of justification at work in the Reflective Wisdom Account, our ordinary normative judgments, made without full reflection, do have some authority. The authority of these judgments increases as they become integrated into a more reflective point of view and become part of a refined set of judgments. As we develop as agents, we learn and accept a variety of normative judgments, including judgments about character and about the values that are important for a good life. Such judgments have some authority as inputs to the justificatory process of reflection. Ideally, as we develop and continue to reflect, our reflection has more influence over the judgments we make when we're not being reflective. For example, as one's judgments about what counts as selfish change in response to more mature reflection on the needs of others, the automatic judgments one makes about what counts as selfish without engaging in reflection will also change. In addition, the justification of a conception of a good life gains force when it changes in response to new experience. The process of justifying our conception of a good life and our particular normative judgments is a dialectic process that takes seriously the verdicts of critical reflection and the teachings of experience.

Judgments about the character traits or value commitments that are manifested in occupying a particular perspective, insofar as they are justified, must at some point be grounded in a reflective conception of a good life. Nevertheless, making the judgment that in some particular circumstances one is being self-absorbed or uncompassionate does not require taking up a reflective point of view from which one understands the justification for thinking that these are vices. Given these facts about normative judgments (and judgments about the character traits manifested in taking a practical perspective in particular), we can see that recognizing reasons to shift perspectives does not require any explicit attention to one's reflective conception of a good life. Rather, we make judgments about such reasons automatically, without the aid of critical reflection. Granted, these "automatic" or impressionistic judgments about reasons would not have much force if they were entirely divorced from reflection and justification, however, this is not the case. Intuitive judgments about reasons are tied to reflection and justification, albeit indirectly.

Finally, one might be concerned about the fact that the aspect of wisdom I have described does not seem to involve any rational *process*. If we have a picture of practical rationality according to which reasoning proceeds from premises about values, goals, or desires via practical syllogisms to conclusions about actions or intentions, then the non-inferential aspect of practical wisdom I have described will appear to be irrational or at least non-rational. Since wisdom and practical rationality are closely related, this seems undesirable.

The first thing to say in response to this problem is that while practical wisdom and practical rationality are related, we need not take them to be one and the same. If we understand practical wisdom as Aristotle did as including an understanding of the good and an ability to procure it, then we might say that wisdom includes, but is not limited to, practical rationality. The capacity for practical reason, on this view, is a capacity to adapt means to ends, to draw out the conclusions of practical syllogisms or the implications of various commitments. This capacity, the capacity to follow a rational procedure, is just one of the capacities possessed by the wise person.

The second strategy of response is to reduce the worry that the non-inferential capacity I have described is non-rational by drawing an analogy to theoretical rationality. In matters of theoretical rationality we can see a need for a quasi-intuitive grasp of principles that is not itself supported by the application of an inferential process. Lewis Carroll's (1895) dialogue between the tortoise and Achilles shows that there must be rules of inference that have a different status from the premises to which the rules apply. One way of putting the point is that for us to be able to reason our way to conclusions, there must be some rules of inference that we grasp without reasoning to them.[14] The fact that a non-inferential capacity to grasp principles is necessary for theoretical rationality should make us more comfortable with the idea that a non-inferential capacity to grasp reasons is a part of practical wisdom.

This picture of practical wisdom as including a non-inferential capacity stands in contrast to top-down conceptions of practical rationality according to which rational choices are the choices made in explicit accordance with a life plan or a coherent system of values.[15] Granted, the wise person does need to have a larger perspective that encompasses all her values; she needs some comprehensive (though perhaps not very detailed) conception of a good life in order to have a basis for judgment that sticking with one perspective would be insensitive, narrow-minded, self-indulgent, or the like. But many of the choices that require wisdom are not direct inferences from this ideal conception. Having a reflective conception of a good life is one part of wisdom, but another important part of wisdom is being able to set this conception aside, to allow one's reflection to be informed by experience and at the same time to maintain the capacity to see one's weaknesses from within the experience. Furthermore, given the impossibility of taking up numerous practical perspectives at once, and given the importance of being open to the lessons of experience, a reflective conception of a good life is unlikely to be the kind of detailed plan or map that would allow direct inferences about what to do in any circumstances.

Aristotelians have been better about not assuming a top-down picture,[16] but even Aristotelian conceptions of wisdom could benefit from an acknowledgment of the role of shifting perspectives in a good life. When we acknowledge this role, the resulting picture of reflective wisdom differs from the Aristotelian picture of wisdom as a kind of comprehensive perception that takes in all the ethically salient facts and sees the virtuous thing to do in the context of all the other virtues (McDowell 1979). On my view, practical perspectives are partial takes on the ethically salient features of life, and a

---

[14] I thank Chris Hookway and Roger Crisp for drawing my attention to this point and for helpful discussion of the Lewis Carroll example.

[15] See, e.g., Rawls's (1971: 395–424) discussion of rational life plans.

[16] Martha Nussbaum (1986: 299), e.g., emphasizes the fact that practical reasoning for Aristotle is not a science and that it is concerned with "insight through experience". Sarah Broadie (1991: 198–202) argues against the top-down or, as she calls it, the "Grand End" picture of practical wisdom. See also McDowell 1996.

person can make a wise choice without perceiving everything that is ethically salient. In other words, there is real wisdom to be found in choices that are made with less than complete awareness, less than full perception. One could insist that wisdom is exhibited only in choices made from a totalizing perspective, but this would amount to denying the value of practical perspectives as I have described them.

Further, the ideal of the unity of the virtues in the practically wise implies that everything we need to grasp in order to act well can be appreciated from the reflective point of view, and this is an assumption we might challenge. Sabina Lovibond's (2002: 27–9) characterization of practical wisdom, for example, includes both a grasp and an ordering of all that matters in life.[17] If I am right that we learn about what makes for a good life from our unreflective engagement with our values, then an overarching point of view that specifies the relative value of each constituent of a good life may not be the right goal. While there is a sense in which we can acknowledge a plurality of values from the reflective point of view, this point of view may not be the one from which we have the kind of appreciation of values that allows us always to act in a way that is conducive to a good life.

The preceding discussion points to an advantage of my account of practical wisdom which is that it makes wisdom more accessible than some critics have charged. Julia Driver (2001), for instance, accuses Aristotelian virtue ethics of being overly intellectual in its emphasis on practical reason and wisdom. If wisdom is as I have described it, then there is at least one important part of it that is importantly unlike a technical skill or highly intellectual capacity. Instead, practical wisdom's intellectual demands on us are like those of the other virtues: it requires that we make judgments (about character or values) that are informed by a conception of what is good for a person, but it does not require—in fact, it may sometimes preclude—a full and reflective knowledge of this conception while we are making these judgments.

3.5. CONCLUSION

The person with practical wisdom should have a conception of a good life that guides her in reflective moments. But this conception of a good life is

---

[17] I take Lovibond's (2002: 24) account of wisdom to be sympathetic to mine, however, insofar as she emphasizes what she calls "the openness to the layout of reality" or what I would call an openness to evaluative perspectives.

also shaped by the person's engagement with the world, the experience and practice that come from having different practical perspectives. An important part of wisdom, then, is the capacity to use what we learn from experience and to judge when our being engaged in a particular way manifests a problem with our character or with our ability to pursue other values. Such judgments are, in turn, informed by a reflective conception of how to live, but the wise person makes these judgments without directly appealing to her ideal.

In this chapter I have emphasized the importance of learning from experience and not thinking too much. In part, these are important aspects of wisdom, because it is by way of unreflective experience that we learn what our values should be. Of course, having the right values is not sufficient for living well, or for wisdom. The wise must also be *guided* by these values. One obstacle to being guided by our reflective values is that we may not have a very good idea of what they are. Another obstacle is that we may not have the ability to pursue them fully because we are plagued by doubt or excessive reflection. Attentional flexibility helps us with these problems. But these are not the only obstacles we face. Sometimes we are prevented from responding appropriately to what matters by things we don't really care as much about, but which commandeer our attention all the same. This problem and the aspect of wisdom it gives rise to are the subject of the next chapter.

4

Perspective

In the previous chapter, we saw that when we use our reflective capacities to think about our values, we should take our motivations and unreflective experiences into account. Once we have standards for our lives that do take these experiences into account, it would be good if we could live up to them. We need not only to *have* appropriate standards, we need to be able to use them when we are called upon to make plans for the future, as well as to act in accordance with them. If our actions are not in keeping with our standards, our lives will not be ones that uphold them and earn our approval. But now we confront a problem with our reflective capacities, which is that they are sometimes very weak motivators. Even when our reflective values are an excellent fit with important emotional predispositions, other aspects of our personalities (short-term desires, competing emotional responses, emotionally insensitive reasoning, and rationalization) may lead us in different directions.

To solve this problem, we need the ability to bring our thoughts, feelings, and actions in line with our values. I call this aspect of reflective wisdom the virtue of perspective. In this chapter I first provide two examples of perspective in order to give an intuitive sense of the nature of the virtue. Sections 4.2 and 4.3 contain an account of perspective as a virtue. I discuss the ways in which perspective as characterized contributes to living well in section 4.4.

4.1. HAVING PERSPECTIVE: SOME EXAMPLES

In her advice column, "Tell me about it", Carolyn Hax advises one of her readers to "get some perspective". The reader had written to Carolyn complaining bitterly about the pain and suffering she was enduring after being "dumped" by her boyfriend. The relationship with this boyfriend had lasted only about three months. Carolyn did not think the woman's complaints were entirely unfounded, but rather that they were out of proportion to the value this relationship should have for her, given its short duration. Carolyn suggested that the letter writer take up some volunteer work for a worthy cause as a way both to meet other people and to help her gain some perspective.

Phrases such as "Get some perspective" are probably familiar to most people.[1] We do advise people to do this, and it seems that there is some wisdom in this advice. Part of the wisdom is that there are things not worth worrying about, and that to expend time and energy worrying about these things leads only to unhappiness. The person who is emotionally devastated by something that is not actually all that important lacks perspective. For her to gain perspective, it seems, would be for her to develop a better sense of what is worth worrying about and an ability to bring her thoughts, feelings, and actions into accordance with this better sense.

A more complex example is to be found in Barbara Kingsolver's novel, *The Poisonwood Bible*. Leah Price is one of four daughters who was taken to the Congo by her fierce, missionary father. While in the Congo, Leah's youngest sister, Ruth May, is bitten by a snake and dies. The day that Leah's sister dies happens to be the same day that the newly elected leader of the Congo is murdered, an event that has very tragic consequences for the Congolese people. Later, Leah marries a Congolese revolutionary. On the day that Leah mourns her sister's death, her husband, Anatole, mourns his country's loss of independence and the thousands of people who have been taken political prisoner, beaten, and killed. Leah reflects on the differences between their griefs, and she remembers an incident from the village in which her father was a missionary.

I can recall, years ago, watching Rachel [Leah's older sister] cry real tears over a burn hole in her green dress while, just outside our door, completely naked children withered from the holes burning in their empty stomachs, and I seriously wondered if Rachel's heart were the size of a thimble. I suppose that's how he [her husband Anatole] sees me today. Any other day I might pray ... to lose my self-will in the service of greater glory. But January 17, in my selfish heart, is Ruth May's only. (Kingsolver 1998: 430)

Most readers will be inclined to think, with Leah, that Rachel is completely lacking in perspective: clothes are not valuable enough to warrant serious distress even at the best of times. Leah, however, does have perspective. Leah

---

[1] There might be other ways of putting the same point or giving the same kind of advice. For example, "Don't sweat the small stuff" is closely related.

recognizes that her sister's death is worth grieving, and she allows herself to grieve. At the same time, she sees that she must not lose herself in grief to such a degree that she cannot appreciate or be motivated to act on other value commitments she has, such as the commitment to the cause of the Congolese people.

4.2. PERSPECTIVE AND REFLECTIVE VALUES

When we advise people to get perspective, we are usually advising them to get perspective on some particular thing or things they value. Carolyn advises her reader to get perspective on the relationship she had with her boyfriend. Had Leah advised her sister Rachel to get some perspective, she would have wanted Rachel to gain perspective on the value of her dress. Leah seems to have perspective on her love for her sister and her commitment to the Congolese cause. Getting perspective is something we do with respect to commitments we have.

Part of what it is to be committed to something, or to find it valuable, as we discussed in Chapter 2, is to have certain affective dispositions. To be committed to a friend is to care about her well-being, to want to spend time with her, to feel angry when she is wronged, and to take her into account in our plans. To be committed to one's career is to want to succeed in it, to give it weight in one's plans, to feel anxious when it is threatened, and proud when one gets a raise or promotion. The thoughts, feelings, and dispositions that make up our commitments play a vital role in planning and action. We plan to act in accordance with our value commitments, and we succeed in acting in accordance with these plans when we are motivated by the desires or other motivational states that are constitutive of these commitments.

As discussed in the previous chapter, a perspective is defined by which value or values we are focused on, what we attend to, and what we take to be salient at the moment. Perspective shifts can occur in varying degrees because our attention can be more or less focused, other values can be nearer or farther from the current view, and the relevant values can demand more or less of our attention. *Having a perspective* on something we're committed to, we can say, is a matter of that commitment's playing a particular practical role in our life due to the pattern of attention that constitutes the perspective. To take a *new* perspective on a value commitment is to change that practical role. For example, if the lovelorn writer to the advice column were to take a different perspective on her failed relationship, she would no longer be inclined to write letters to advice columnists nor to wallow in her own misery. She would instead be focused on other things, no longer dwelling on her feelings of rejection.

Taking different perspectives (or changing one's perspective) on a value commitment is possible because of fluctuations in the components of such commitments and the interaction among our various values. Although one might remain committed to something one values, the various thoughts, feelings, and dispositions to action that make up a particular value commitment do not remain constant. Variations in the intensity, duration, and vivacity of our thoughts and feelings, and in the immediacy and gravity of relevant action, seem to be part of normal life.

One cause of these variations is the interaction between different value commitments. The dispositions that make up our commitments are expressed in different ways and have different roles in planning and action depending, in part, on the other attitudes we have. For example, consider Percy's disposition to feel disappointed when he fails to get a deserved promotion, which is part of his commitment to his career. This disappointment will be expressed and experienced in different ways, depending on other facts about him. Because Percy has normal moral convictions, he does not express his disappointment by murdering his boss or sabotaging the career of the person who did get the promotion. Similarly, the character of the experience of disappointment can change because of other attitudes Percy has. If on the same day that he gets the bad news about his job Percy also learns that the lump in his neck is a benign cyst rather than cancer, the disappointment about his career might be much less intense than it would otherwise be.

The fact that a particular commitment is located within a web of values means that we can try to alter our thoughts and feelings about it, and thereby to change the role it will play in planning and action. This is not to say that we can always change our attitudes when we want to. Emotional responses—particularly emotional responses to people or projects we once held dear—can persist despite our wishing they would go away. Nevertheless, in such cases we can often change the ways these dispositions are expressed in action and cause them to lessen over time.

What we seem to be recommending when we advise someone to "get perspective" is to bring her thoughts and feelings in line with what really is important. In Chapter 3 we saw that the ability to shift between various *appropriate* perspectives is an important part of wisdom. Now we are considering the aspect of wisdom that contends with attentional patterns that are not appropriate. This aspect of wisdom I will call *right perspective*, or *the virtue of perspective*.[2]

Perspective as a virtue would seem to require having the right perspective on one's commitments, the right dispositions of thought, feeling, and action in the right strength. That is, the virtue of perspective seems to consist in taking our commitments to be no more and no less important than they really are.[3] But we might mean different things by "what is really important". To clarify this point, we need to consider the theoretical work that the virtue of perspective is meant to do. As a reflective virtue, right perspective is meant to facilitate living a life that we will endorse from a reflective point of view. It does so by bringing life into line with our reflective survey. A person who has perspective, then, will be more likely to judge that her life is going well from a reflective point of view because her actions and feelings are more in line with the values that make up this point of view. So, "what really matters" in this context is defined in terms of reflective values. This claim about the virtue of perspective and its value raises three worries. I discuss them briefly here, but two of them will require more attention in the remainder of the chapter.

First, given the concerns about reflection discussed in Chapter 1, one might worry about the idea that perspective makes us better off by bringing life in line with reflection. If reasoning and reflection can lead us in the wrong direction because of implicit biases, inadequate introspection, poor capacity for predicting our future responses, and a tendency to confabulate reasons, then bringing life in line with reflection will seem misguided. This worry loses its sting, however, when we recall from the previous chapter that the reflection recommended by the Reflective Wisdom Account corrects for the problems with our reflective capacities by emphasizing the importance of experience

---

[2] It is somewhat awkward to use the word "perspective" to describe the virtuous state as well as the various attentional patterns we can be in with respect to our values. Nevertheless, there seems to be no better term for the virtue, and other terms for the attentional pattern—outlook, point of view, stance—are either stylistically awkward or fail to capture the meaning. I have therefore chosen to use "perspective" in both contexts and to clarify when clarification is needed by referring to the virtuous state as "right perspective" or "the virtue of perspective".

[3] There is, then, a mean to be reached in attaining perspective on a particular commitment. It is not obviously helpful, however, to characterize perspective itself as a mean. One might say that perspective is the mean between obsession and indifference, but this seems to make perspective into a static state according to which there is one correct attitude to take toward any and every commitment. As will become clearer in the following sections, this is not how perspective ought to be understood.

and our affective responses to it. A person who has perspective is not someone who tries to keep her emotions in line with a highly intellectualized conception of what her emotional responses should be. Rather, a person with perspective tries to bring her emotional responses in line with what she takes to be important on reflection, which is profoundly influenced by how she feels.

A second concern arises from the fact that the claim that perspective makes it more likely that we will achieve reflective endorsement seems to be an empirical claim. We should be clear, though, about what kind of empirical claim it is. The point here is that, given our goals, limited knowledge, and limited control over many aspects of life, cultivating the virtue of perspective is a good strategy for living a life we can reflectively endorse. Of course, even the "good strategy" claim is an empirical claim, and more needs to be said to support it. This discussion will be more fruitful when we have a richer description of the virtue of perspective on hand, so I will defer it until section 4.4.

A third concern has to do with the use of reflective values to capture the idea of "what's really important" that seems to be central to the notion of perspective as a virtue. Having the virtue of perspective, I have said, requires the capacity to bring thoughts, feelings, and actions into line with our reflective values. While it is true that reflective values are not just whatever one happens to like at the moment, it is also the case that reflective values are subjective in the sense that which values appear in the set and how these values are ordered is determined, ultimately, by the attitudes and judgments of the person whose values they are. Reflection on the priorities that one's core commitments have operates against the background of a person's prior commitments, and therefore different people will make different judgments about what matters most upon reflection. Some will judge that traveling the world is as important as their careers, while others will judge that their careers are more important than anything except their families. Different reflective judgments about the importance of various commitments will yield different standards for appropriate related dispositions.

There may be some resistance to characterizing the virtue of perspective in this subjective way. One might be inclined to think that a person whose thoughts, feelings, and actions are perfectly in line with her crazy values lacks perspective. But this claim is not available to us if we are trying to give an account of how to live well from a person's own point of view. More will be said in the next section to address these concerns about subjectivity.

4.3. REFINING THE ACCOUNT OF PERSPECTIVE

To advise a person to get perspective is to advise her to bring her thoughts and feelings into line with her reflective values, rather than reacting to her circumstances by succumbing to the most powerful thoughts or feelings of the moment. Our reflective values entail standards of appropriateness for our attitudes, choices, and actions. The advice that one ought to have some perspective amounts to the recommendation that one bring one's attitudes, actions, and choices into line with what is appropriate given one's reflective values. The first thing to notice about the person with perspective, then, is that she must have commitments that count as reflective values from her point of view because she takes them to be stable, justified, and supported by her experience. Without this, there are no standards of appropriateness for her thoughts and feelings; there is no sense in which she can "get it right".

If the ultimate goal for the person with perspective is to achieve this kind of alignment, we can see that having perspective for normal human beings will also require having certain skills or abilities that help to bring us closer to this ideal. First, because acquiring perspective occurs in the context of the temptation to become absorbed by something trivial, the wise person must have some habits that allow her to "get perspective". In particular, she must have cultivated a habit of seeing her distress from a different point of view, one that tells her whether her response is reasonable or disproportionate. One relevant point of view, I suggest, is the point of view of other people whose values are threatened in different, more serious ways. Given this, the person with perspective needs to be capable of sympathizing with the experiences of others at least to the minimal extent that would allow her to be reminded of her own reflective values. She must be open to experiences that remove temptations to lose perspective. To have such experiences, a person must be capable of taking threats to someone else's important interests to remind her of her own. Notice that this is the kind of habit one can consciously adopt: we can set ourselves to think about the ways in which we are fortunate as compared to others (to "count our blessings"); we can habitually remind ourselves of what others are experiencing in the world; and so on.[4]

---

[4] Counting blessings is a sustainable exercise that has been shown to increase life-satisfaction and other aspects of well-being (Emmons and McCullough 2003; Lyubomirsky *et al.* 2005).

In the case of Rachel, one reason why we want to say that she lacks perspective is that she fails to take the suffering of children outside her door to remind her of what is important to her. Similarly, we are inclined to think that Leah does have perspective, in part, because she recognizes the significance of other people's suffering. Perspective may not require compassion or empathy, but it does seem to require sympathy enough to identify the values that are at stake in others' experiences. This minimal sympathy, as we might call it, allows the person with perspective to remember her own important values, and therefore to see that she is succumbing to the temptation of obsession with the trivial.

Moreover, if one cannot identify the values at stake in others' experiences, one lacks more than a resource for remembering one's own values. This is because the capacity for minimal sympathy is the interpersonal expression of understanding the importance of one's own values. There is, then, a part of minimal sympathy that is an indispensable feature of perspective. Minimal sympathy includes the ability to abstract away from one's current experience in order to identify what is at stake beyond what currently seems most pressing. So, the person who lacks minimal sympathy lacks the capacity to distance herself from the immediate in order to grasp the true importance of any experience, whether it is her own or another's.[5]

Second, the person with perspective has the ability to modify her attitudes in response to what she learns from experience. She can shift her attention away from what does not matter, and, importantly, she can actively appreciate those things that she really does value. Having the appropriate attitudes does not simply mean refraining from becoming engrossed in inappropriate reactions, it also means experiencing the thoughts and feelings appropriate to finding valuable what one thinks is important on reflection. The person with perspective, therefore, will not be passionless or perpetually moderate; as we saw in the previous chapter, it *is* often appropriate and important to be wrapped up in a project, emotionally charged, excited, and sometimes even carried away. The virtue of perspective, then, consists in the ability to reflect on one's values, to learn from the experience of others when one's attitudes are inappropriate, and to bring one's attitudes and actions into line with one's reflective values. Acquiring the virtue of perspective is a matter of developing

---

[5] This claim would not be plausible if minimal sympathy included a disposition to feel tenderness or compassion for the person in question. But the kind of sympathy I mean is truly minimal: it is only the ability to identify what others really value and how their experiences are affecting these values.

habits that move us away from obsessive dwelling on trivial problems and toward more appropriate responses to our circumstances.

To say that a particular constellation of dispositions is a reflective virtue is to say that it is needed by human beings in usual circumstances for making positive judgments about how life is going over the long term. Given human tendencies to obsess about immediate but relatively trivial concerns and our receptiveness to the experience of others as relevant evidence, the virtue of perspective is best characterized as including the above two kinds of capacities: the capacity to distance oneself from distress over things that don't matter through minimal sympathy, and the capacity to modify one's attitudes in light of what one really cares about. We should say, then, that the virtue of perspective consists in these two capacities aimed at bringing one's attitudes and actions into line with one's reflective judgment.

The person with perspective has appropriate attitudes, given the standards she endorses, toward the objects of her value commitments. We might think that the standards that people would endorse if they reflected on the matter would form a fairly inclusive, ordinal ranking of possible experiences in terms of the appropriateness of various emotional responses. The torture or painful death of our loved ones would be at the top of the list, holes in our clothes and hangnails would be much closer to the bottom, and our emotions would track the incremental changes in degrees of importance. It does seem that if we were to set about to create such a ranking, there are many occurrences that we would judge more worthy of sadness, grief, fear, etc. than the experiences toward which we often feel these emotions. If we reflect vividly on the variety of experiences to which people around the world are subject—starvation, torture, severe oppression—then anxieties about our careers, vacation plans, taxes, and the like pale in comparison. Those of us who live in developed countries in relative affluence do very often gain perspective on one of our own problems by thinking about how lucky we really are relative to the state of most of the world's population.

Nevertheless, there are some worries about the assumption that we can or should construct a ranking of all relevant events and experiences in terms of their importance. First of all, the task is daunting. While it is not difficult to decide that torture is worse than a hangnail, other comparisons are less obvious. Moreover, there are so many comparisons to make that the task of ranking them all would be overwhelming.

Second, making sharp distinctions between some experiences can impoverish our own value commitments by preventing us from honoring them in the required way. For example, if a person were to judge that it is far worse to be the victim of torture than it is to be diagnosed with an often curable form of cancer, then it would seem to follow that the perspective she ought to take on her friend's cancer diagnosis is one according to which she does not react very strongly because, after all, things could be much worse. But to take this perspective does not seem to be a good thing for her to do if she loves her friend. To react to the diagnosis of a friend's serious illness by proclaiming that things could be worse does not seem to leave room for the appropriate fear, sympathy, and compassion that are required by real friendship in this case. If achieving one's own good requires not only having good experiences and feelings, but also valuing important things to one's fullest ability, and if valuing entails the disposition to feel negative emotions when what one values is threatened, then judgments about appropriate emotional responses must take this into consideration.

Finally, even if we could provide a detailed ranking of experiences in terms of the degree to which they warrant certain emotional responses, our attitudes do not seem to be fine-grained enough to track small changes of this kind. So, even if we were to judge that torture is, in some sense, worse than cancer, our emotional responses to either would be powerful. While it is certainly true that our emotional responses to different circumstances are qualitatively distinct from each other in subtle ways, emotions do not seem to come in units of seriousness that would allow for precise quantitative distinctions.

A person with perspective must make comparative judgments about the appropriateness of emotional responses. But, given the above concerns, we should say that these judgments should make room for indifference among items that are more or less equally valued. The person with perspective need only make rough divisions among different events or experiences. She groups these events according to their relevance to similar, not identical, degrees of value. Events that make a profound difference to the quality of one's life will be at the top of the ranking, and the measure of profundity will, by necessity, be rather imprecise. Further, she must allow herself to experience the thoughts and feelings required by her own value commitments, provided that these values are ones she really thinks are important, without diminishing her commitment to other similarly important values. A return to the example of Leah Price will help us better understand these complexities.

On the one hand, there is a sense in which Leah believes that the grief she feels for her sister is less appropriate than the grief that her husband,

Anatole, feels for his people. But on the other hand, despite the fact that she at one point labels her emotion "selfish", there is a certain righteousness in her attitude. If she really thought she was behaving wrongly, we would expect her to feel ashamed of her reaction, but she does not. Rather, she appears defiant and even a little bit proud.

Most likely, the truth is that Leah makes two different value judgments from two different points of view. From her own point of view she judges that her sister's death is of profound importance to *her*. Leah cared deeply about her sister, and therefore her grief is entirely appropriate. But from another point of view—the point of view of the world, or of morality—Leah judges that the tragedy of the Congolese people is more important than the death of her sister. She judges that the suffering of thousands is more important from a global point of view, and this is a point of view with which she herself identifies. But the fact that the suffering of the Congolese matters more according to the impartial morality that Leah endorses does not imply that her sister's death is unimportant to her. The facts about the world that Leah recognizes do not make her value her sister any less.

Given all of Leah's values, she is concerned to express her grief in such a way that she honors her love for her sister without losing her ability to sympathize with the plight of others. Leah's wisdom is displayed in two facts about her: first, that she allows herself to experience grief over her sister's death, thus honoring that commitment without allowing this grief to overshadow and prevent the appreciation of other value commitments; and second, that both of the values she is responding to are really, on reflection, important to her. Leah's commitment to her sister and her commitment to the cause of the Congolese people surely differ in terms of their appeal to others (people who don't know her sister, for instance), but they are similar in terms of the depth of commitment and the bearing on her happiness. To have the virtue of perspective, then, Leah is not required to rank the importance of her sister and the cause of the Congolese people. For Leah, these values might both be in the category of values of the highest importance.

At this point we should consider an objection to the account of perspective I have defended. One might observe that, given the notion of perspective above, according to which a person has perspective if she responds in accordance with *subjective* standards of appropriateness, even Rachel might count as having perspective if her green dress happens to be what is most important to her on reflection. Given my account of the virtue of perspective, it seems that Rachel would count as having perspective if, even in a reflective moment, she cannot be made to see the relative unimportance of her green dress. This will seem quite unintuitive: first, because there is something seriously wrong with Rachel's reaction to the hole in her dress, and second, because Rachel seems to be a paradigmatic case of someone who lacks perspective. Given these two claims, why should we accept an account of perspective that allows someone like Rachel to have it?

The primary reason to accept an account of perspective according to which Rachel might have it is that our focus on a person's own point of view requires us to do so. A person's judgments of how well her life is going from her own point of view will be responsive to her value commitments, not to objectively correct values to which she has no commitment.

There is more we can say about Rachel, however, to explain our reactions to her behavior. First, regarding the claim that there is something wrong with Rachel's reaction to her dress, we can still criticize her, from the moral point of view, for having the wrong values. Moreover, Rachel might very well lack other moral and non-moral virtues. She certainly lacks deep compassion that would allow her to grasp what is important to other people from their own points of view. The fact that her own values are trivial and shallow implies that she at least lacks imagination. That she has all these shortcomings should make us less uncomfortable with the possibility that she has perspective: she is still not a paragon of virtue by any means.

Nevertheless, the possibility that Rachel does have perspective is unpalatable. Here too there are things we can say to reduce the counterintuitive implications of the account. The first thing to notice is that Rachel does not have perspective if she is entirely unreflective. The virtue of perspective presupposes a set of reflective values, with which one's attitudes can be consistent, and to have a set of reflective values, one must at least be committed to norms of improvement for one's actual value commitments. If Rachel does not see her commitments as subject to standards of better or worse, if she cannot entertain and consider criticisms of her values, then she is not a candidate for reflective virtue at all. Second, given the role of minimal sympathy in perspective, if Rachel is to count as having perspective, it cannot be the case that she does value the satisfaction of her own basic needs more than she values her clothes but she simply cannot be reminded of this by the hunger of others. Such a person would lack perspective because she lacks the capacity to distance herself from her current emotional stance. She therefore also lacks the main capacity by which she can be reminded of her own reflective values in times of temptation.

The version of Rachel who would provide a problem for my account of perspective would have to find the condition of her clothes more valuable than the satisfaction of her *own* basic needs on reflection. So the critic would have to be thinking of a Rachel who has very strange values, who is capable of sympathizing with threats to those values in the experience of others, and who is reflective. But this person is an unusual character. First, it is unusual to find people who are reflective, yet care more about clothes than their own basic needs. Second, it is unusual to find people who can sympathize with others enough to take their experiences as reminders of their own reflective values, yet who do not appreciate in the slightest that these others care most about entirely different things. The capacity for minimal sympathy is not easily contained: once we appreciate others' experience enough to see its relevance to our own decisions, the natural tendency is to begin to see and appreciate what the others value, rather than just seeing their experiences through the framework of our own values.

It does follow from the present account that someone who is reflective and minimally sympathetic would count as having perspective even if she has the wrong values, as long as her thoughts and feelings are appropriate given these mistaken values. The point of the preceding discussion has been to show that this implication of the account of perspective is not as problematic as it might have seemed at first glance.

4.4. THE VALUE OF PERSPECTIVE

Perspective includes the capacity for minimal sympathy and the capacity to make one's values play an appropriate practical role given the judgments arrived at in reflection. What can be said in defense of the claim that perspective is a virtue that is necessary for living well from one's own point of view?

First, since living well requires, in part, the pursuit of values that pass the test of appropriate reflection, we can see that perspective is a constitutive part of living well. Perspective presupposes the ability to reflect on one's values, and requires the capacity to bring one's thoughts, feelings, and dispositions to action in accordance with these reflections. Insofar as a person has the virtue of perspective, then, she just is disposed to act in accordance with her reflective values and, hence, is disposed to live well from her own point of view. Furthermore, when a person with the virtue of perspective thinks about her life from a reflective point of view, she is able to bring her reflective values to bear without being distracted by less important pushes and pulls. Without the virtue of perspective, therefore, she could not have the kind of self-survey that will bring reflective success and satisfaction.

Second, perspective has an instrumental role in bringing about a person's good. I take claims about the instrumental value of the virtues to be claims about the best strategy for living one's life, and such claims are, at least in part, empirical claims.[6] At this point, those of an empiricist bent might hope for psychological experiments to show that having perspective causes life-satisfaction, or something in this vein. While there have been some psychological studies on wisdom (defined in such a way that there is some overlap with my notion of perspective), there are no studies that show just what we would like to know.[7] Perspective, as I have characterized it, is a difficult virtue to measure, because a person who lacks perspective is precisely in the wrong position to know that she lacks it. Self-reports, therefore, will not be a good way to sort out who has the virtue and who does not. Reports of friends and family may be somewhat more reliable, but a good deal of training would be required to get these observers to be responsive to the particular skills and habits that constitute perspective. Moreover, even if we could identify the people with perspective, in order to establish causation rather than mere correlation, we would need an intervention that changes how much perspective people have, and we would need to be able to measure relative degrees of perspective before and after the intervention. None of these steps have yet been taken. This program of research is certainly not impossible, but to do it well would be tricky, time-consuming, and expensive.[8] At least for now, therefore, we must turn to other kinds of evidence and observations about human nature and behavior.

It will be helpful to begin thinking about the instrumental value of perspective by considering Philippa Foot's (1978) characterization of a virtue in terms of a corrective for common human weaknesses. There are three weaknesses that perspective helps us overcome: first, the tendency to become

[6] Rosalind Hursthouse (1999) argues for the best strategy view in her *On Virtue Ethics*. There are some views about the value of the virtues for their possessors that do not rely on empirical claims in this way. Michelle Mason, e.g., argues that possessing a virtue benefits you by giving you a certain normative standing. See her "Living Well and Faring Well" (unpublished MS).

[7] See Peterson and Seligman 2004b, and Baltes *et al.* 2002 for overviews of the psychological literature on wisdom.

[8] Thanks are due to John Walker, and to psychologists Marty Gonzales and Mike Steger, for discussing with me the possibility of conducting such a study and impressing upon me the various difficulties.

excessively distressed when things we care about are threatened; second, the fragile nature of our ability to appreciate certain values; and third, the tendency in deliberation to be overly influenced by violent emotional responses or vivid but ungrounded thoughts that are out of proportion to the actual value of that to which we are reacting (the motivational weakness of our reflective capacities). These weaknesses and the ways in which perspective corrects for them to promote our good are the topic of the remainder of this section.

The Stoics noticed that we are made miserable when the things we value are threatened. We suffer painfully when we lose our health, when our friends and loved ones are sick or hurt, or our reputations are tarnished. The Stoics' advice was to care very little about anything except that over which we have control: our character. While we might think that the Stoics' notion of what really matters was too limited, we can appreciate their advice if we reflect on the fact that we are made miserable by our attachments to things that do not matter, as well as our attachments to things that do. We frequently become overwrought and unhappy when our projects are not going smoothly, even when we know that these particular projects are not as important to us as other things we value that are not threatened. Living in a consumerist society, we are strongly encouraged to put more weight on our possessions than we might do reflectively, and this too affects our stress and distress. If perspective is, in part, the disposition to respond in proportion to the value one attaches to one's reflective commitments, then perspective can prevent some of the misery we have over things that do not matter.

Another lesson to be learned from the ideal of the Stoic sage is that our natural tendencies to form attachments and respond emotionally do not always correspond to our reflective judgments of what is important. The Stoic sage is an ideal because he or she really does care about things in proportion to the value they have. This is something that needs to be achieved; it is not the natural state for most people. Part of the problem here is that we care too much about things that matter least (money, power, material goods), and, as we have discussed, we are disposed to become miserable when these things are threatened. But this is not the end of the story. Just as the non-Stoic tends to fail to appreciate the value of her own character, so too we tend to fail to appreciate the value of things that we judge on reflection to be most important. This brings us to the second way in which perspective compensates for human weaknesses.

As we saw in Chapter 2, when you ask people what really matters, they say that the things that are truly important are things such as their friends and family. But then if we observe the practice of these same people, we find that their behavior and their emotional responses do not correspond to their judgments that these are the things that really matter. The well-being of our loved ones is something we do not even notice until it is in jeopardy. Many of us are prone to take for granted the values that we *are* realizing; we get caught up in other things, and we do not take the time to appreciate our friendships or the successes we have had.

There seems to be a human tendency to worry about the things that are not going smoothly, and to ignore the things that are. Of course, this tendency makes a certain amount of sense. After all, if we were to ignore the things that really need our attention, we would certainly be frustrated in our pursuits. But this tendency makes our ability to appreciate the value that is available to us somewhat fragile. Consider the fact that when one spends a long time not appreciating the good in things, one can become depressed and unable to find anything pleasant, fun, stimulating, or in some other way worthy of a positive response. The capacity to find value in the world is one that must be cultivated and engaged, or else it is at risk of deteriorating.

Since having perspective requires *appreciating* the value of what we care about on reflection, the person with the virtue of perspective has, to some extent, overcome the weakness in her ability to appreciate the good things in life. Overcoming this weakness requires making an effort to turn one's attention to things that are not demanding that attention. It requires, in other words, a commitment to appreciating value. The connection to living well from your own point of view is not difficult to see: finding and appreciating good things, in general, prevents misery and makes people happy with how their lives are going.

This point about appreciating what has value highlights the way in which the virtue of perspective is like a skill, because the ability to appreciate value is an ability that one can cultivate. To see this, we must think about why it is that some values do not demand our attention and require an active effort on our part to appreciate them. First, as already mentioned, these values are by hypothesis ones that are not threatened: nothing dramatic is happening to them that commands our attention. Second, it is also true that many of these values are subtle and require some training to appreciate. For instance, the aesthetic value of some kinds of natural beauty is quiet and delicate; it is not as imposing as the aesthetic value of a dramatic film, or as entertaining as the value of enjoying fine wine with a good friend. The value of a peaceful moment, a painting, a long walk, or the sensation of one's health are what we might call "quiet values" insofar as they do not demand strong responses.

The ancients thought that virtues were similar to skills in two respects: both require practice and habituation, and both require intellectual grasp, or "some level of understanding what it is that you are doing in exercising your skill" (Annas 1993: 66–70).[9] Unobtrusive or "quiet" values take skill to appreciate in the sense that we can train ourselves to appreciate them. We can practice achieving the peace of mind that enables us to appreciate a walk in the woods. We can cultivate the habit of noticing the value of a peaceful moment rather than allowing the moment to be filled up with mental clutter. It is not as clear that appreciating value requires understanding of what one is doing, but there is a comparison to be made here too, at least with respect to certain kinds of values. Notice that we can deepen our appreciation of the kinds of quiet values mentioned above by learning about the value in question. We can develop a greater appreciation for works of art, for example, when we know something about the art form. Although we can appreciate the value of nature without knowing much about it, we might think that some knowledge of the ecosystem we encounter can help to foster or sustain our appreciation and keep us from becoming bored by it.

The skill of appreciating quiet values and the commitment to appreciating the value that is available can promote a person's good in several ways. First, appreciating the value of nature, for example, can add to our happiness and deflect misery precisely because of its relative serenity. If, as Mill thought, tranquility and excitement are complementary constituents of a satisfying life, then achieving some serenity by appreciating the value of nature might be an important part of living well (1979 [1861]: 13). Furthermore, these quiet values are often available to appreciate when other things are not. A person who has the ability to value what is around her, and to take pleasure in the more permanent features of her environment, is less likely to be miserable and unhappy than those who do not have such abilities. Finally, the ability to appreciate value and the commitment to find it can overcome the psychological inertia that makes us continue worrying about what we do not have rather than cherishing what we do.

The emphasis on serenity and calm appreciation of nature (or any quiet value, for that matter) that is part of the virtue of perspective recalls the

---

[9] As Annas points out, different philosophical schools disagreed about how closely virtues resembled skills. The Stoics thought that the virtues simply were a type of skill, while Aristotle thought that the virtues were like skills in some respects but unlike them in others.

advice that is often given to practical reasoners to deliberate in a calm, cool moment. This brings us to the third way in which the virtue of perspective conduces to living well by compensating for a weakness. Having perspective can help us to deliberate better about how to live our lives.

Why is the common wisdom that we can make better decisions in a calm, cool moment? Making good decisions, whether these decision are moral or prudential, requires (among other things) appreciating the facts and giving each consideration the right amount of weight. When moral philosophers, such as Bishop Butler, invoke the notion of a cool reflective moment, the intention seems to be to compensate for fleeting and violent passions that can distract our conscience, or our faculty of reason, from the facts that are actually relevant and important.[10] Butler's point in invoking this notion is not that we make our best decisions when we feel no emotions or sentiments at all. On the contrary, Butler thinks that we need to be guided by cool self-love and benevolence.[11] His point, rather, is that there are certain passions that distort or conceal the facts about what is really at stake in our choices.

We can see, then, how perspective would aid us in making better decisions about our lives. The person with perspective has emotional responses that are in proportion to her hierarchy of values. This means that the psychological forces that sometimes distort our sense of what is important are, instead, counteracted by perspective.[12] The person with perspective is not misled by inappropriate emotions or distracted by disturbing thoughts, because her emotional responses are appropriate to the various values that are at stake in her decisions. For example, consider a graduate student who is distraught because he has received some insulting and vituperative comments from one of his professors. In the midst of feeling most hurt by the comments, and most insecure about his own abilities, he considers whether he ought to stay in graduate school. Most conscientious teachers would advise such a student

---

[10] See, e.g., Butler 1983 [1726]; Darwall 1983: 93–8; Falk 1986.

[11] Bishop Butler (1983 [1726], 30) characterizes conscience as the ability to reflect "coolly" upon one's actions, which corrects for our tendency to focus on consequences to ourselves.

[12] The assumption that we are capable of changing our perspective in a way that counteracts distortion receives some support from a recent study on reflection on negative emotions (see Kross *et al.* 2005). In this study, subjects were caused to have either a "self-immersed" or a "self-distanced" perspective by experimental manipulation following the recall of an anger-eliciting interpersonal experience. Subjects who had the self-distanced perspective were better able to face and reflect on their negative emotions without becoming overwhelmed by them. The techniques used to change the person's perspective in the experiment are ones a person could probably use on herself. For example, subjects were instructed either to "relive the situation as if it were happening to you all over again" or to "take a few steps back and move away from your experience ... watch the conflict unfold as if it were happening all over again to the distant you" (Kross *et al.* 2005: 711).

to postpone deliberating about major life choices until the immediate sting of the experience subsides. We do this because we do not think that one set of nasty comments warrants such a drastic response, and we think that the student's perception of the facts is distorted by his immediate, inflated reaction. Importantly, it is not always our emotions that lead us astray in this way. We could imagine a similar student who responds with (appropriate) anger at the professor, but who dismisses his anger as inappropriate because he has constructed an elaborate system of (unwarranted) beliefs about his lack of ability. Violent passions, as Butler realized, and, I would add, inappropriate or emotionally obtuse reflection, can lead us astray from good judgments about how to live just as they can lead us astray morally. The person with perspective is disposed to recognize that nasty comments from one person are not worth the kind of despair that would move him to reevaluate a commitment or project that is central to his life.

One might think that a person could achieve these three benefits of perspective without actually possessing the virtue, or that one could, unluckily, fail to achieve them despite possessing the virtue. This is true; but it is not an objection to the present account. First, we can point out, as I did above, that a commitment to having perspective follows from a commitment to living in accordance with our reflective values; perspective therefore has a kind of value that is independent of its likely consequences. Second, as explained in Chapter 1, a defense of the virtues should not be required to establish that each virtue is necessary and sufficient for living well. Virtues must be shown to be a good strategy for living life well from your own point of view, and this, given the above argument, is not an unreasonable view to have about perspective.

4.5. CONCLUSION

The virtue of perspective includes the ability to relate others' experience of their values to our own, and the ability to bring our thoughts, feelings, and actions into accord with these reflections. Perspective thus defined helps us to live well from our own point of view because a person with perspective can be reflective about her values and can allow the reflective moment to guide her life in important ways.

According to the picture of reflective wisdom we have drawn so far, a wise person has a set of relatively stable value commitments, the ability to take a reflective perspective on these commitments when needed, the ability to shift appropriately between reflection on and engagement with her values, and the ability to bring her emotions and actions into line with the value commitments she has. The person with reflective wisdom is well positioned to judge that her life is going well: she has commitments that provide the standards for this evaluation; she is able to direct her life so that these commitments are indeed the ones that shape her actions and life choices; and she knows when to engage in reflection and when not to. In these ways wisdom is a great benefit to those of us who are concerned to live a life that goes well according to our own standards.

Given this benefit, it makes sense for those of us who are concerned to live well to cultivate the reflective virtues by training our habits of thought in accordance with them. We can do this by attending to the values that are highlighted by these virtues: having a conception of a good life, learning from experience, having an awareness of what is really important, and being totally engaged by particular practical perspectives. We can use our knowledge of the reflective virtues and the values they embody to change our own behavior and to shape our way of thinking in the future. The methods we might use to inculcate other virtues can also be used to encourage the development of reflective virtue: habituation, emulation of others whose character is better developed than ours, and simply making an effort to attend to what we have previously neglected.

5

Self-Awareness

As a young man, Sam Clay, the comic-book writer in Michael Chabon's (2000) novel *The Amazing Adventures of Kavalier and Clay*, lacks self-awareness in a way that profoundly affects his ability to live well. Although Sam is vaguely aware of his warm (and sometimes romantic) feelings for his male friend Tracy Bacon, he does not really know that he is gay. He certainly does not know or does not admit to himself that he would be much happier if he allowed himself to acknowledge this part of himself. Not fully realizing the nature and importance of their friendship, Sam lets Tracy slip out of his life. Because of his lack of self-awareness, he was unable to categorize this friendship as something worth sacrificing for; nor could he communicate to Tracy its importance to him. When Tracy leaves, Sam is lonely and grief-stricken, but still not sure why the departure of a "mere friend" would have this effect. In Sam's example we see the way in which self-awareness can be crucial for living well.

Less tragic examples of a lack of self-awareness are perhaps more common. We criticize people for a lack of self-awareness when they fail to apply standards of criticism to themselves that they apply to others, or when they refuse to admit to or "own" an attitude that is evident from their actions. Jane Austen's Emma displays a lack of self-awareness of this kind when she insists to Harriet Smith that she is not advising her about whether to marry the farmer Mr Martin (whom Emma regards as beneath Harriet). After Emma has described at some length how to reject Mr Martin's proposal, Harriet asks Emma whether she is recommending refusal. Emma replies, "I certainly have been misunderstanding you, if you feel in doubt as to the *purport* of your answer. I had imagined you were consulting me only as to the wording of it" (Austen 2000 [1816]: 32). When Harriet presses for advice, Emma demurs, "I shall not give you any advice, Harriet. I will have nothing to do with it. This is a point which you must settle with your own feelings." Emma does appear to believe that she is not advising Harriet, and, further, she seems committed to thinking that it would be wrong to give this kind of advice. Nevertheless, it is clear that she is doing exactly what she claims not to be doing. Emma's lack of self-awareness is a mark of her immaturity in the novel and one of the grounds on which the greatly admired Mr Knightly faults her.

In both the above examples we can see the way in which our social lives make self-awareness so important. Emma's lack of self-awareness causes problems for her friendship with Harriet and difficulties in many of her social relations. Sam's case is more complicated: Sam marries a woman, a good friend of his who is pregnant and in need of a husband, and becomes a good father and family man. He finds this role fulfilling and valuable in its own way, but that there is something missing from this relationship is evidenced by the secret relationships he has with various men on the side. For Sam, living in denial of his true feelings prevents him from having and enjoying the kinds of intimate relationships that are, for most of us, so important to living well.

Sam's example also reveals a society that encourages self-expression and individual achievement while at the same time imposing serious restrictions on what one may express. Such social strictures are not new by any means—one might even argue that they are on the decline—but when these strictures are combined with the modern media's messages of conformity, they have renewed power.[1] Having self-awareness does not remove social pressures, but without it one does not even know what needs to be resisted. Self-awareness gives a person a sense of what would make life go well and, therefore, of the need to resist damaging social pressure.

It is not difficult to see the ways in which self-awareness helps us to live well, given the values discussed in Chapter 2. Cultivating habits that result in the acquisition of self-knowledge can help us to make choices that are more likely to be satisfying, and it can help us to pursue our goals in more effective ways. In addition to its instrumental value, I will argue that self-awareness benefits us as an essential part of the process of self-direction. We will also see that the vigilant and relentless pursuit of *self-knowledge* is not good for us. I use the term "self-awareness" to characterize the virtuous disposition, which includes some self-knowledge but is distinct from a complete understanding of the facts about oneself. It would, in fact, be more accurate to call the virtue

---

[1] For an interesting discussion of the media's mixed messages about authenticity and conformity, see Elliott 2003: 112–15. On the modern media's ability to co-opt the ideals of individuality and authenticity and sell them to the public, see Frank 1997.

"moderate self-awareness" (though I won't usually add the qualification explicitly). The virtue of self-awareness comprises knowledge about features of oneself that are relevant to one's reflective values and one's conception of a good life. It also includes the skills and commitments that are necessary for acquiring this knowledge and for constructing a self-conception that befits one's own view about how to live without destroying the harmless illusions we have about ourselves that make life better.

5.1. THE SCOPE AND LIMITS OF SELF-KNOWLEDGE

Surprisingly little has been written by contemporary philosophers about self-knowledge as a state of intellectual character or virtue.[2] This is particularly striking given our Socratic heritage, and given the ways in which self-knowledge seems to be important to successful practical reasoning, life plans, and other topics that have been of central concern to philosophers. The reason for this may be that the resurgence of virtue ethics has focused on moral virtues, and neither self-awareness nor self-knowledge is obviously a moral virtue.

There is, of course, something to be learned from those who have thought about self-knowledge in the context of moral virtue. Among those who have examined self-knowledge in this context we find agreement that this knowledge is not knowledge of just any facts about ourselves (such as our height, weight, and eye color); rather, it must be about something important to the practical matter of how to live our lives. This claim about the content or object of self-knowledge seems to be just as true when we are thinking of self-knowledge in the context of reflective virtue as it does in the context of moral virtue.

We might start by acknowledging the importance of knowing the possibilities that are open to us, what we are capable of, and what we might do. This is an important element of self-knowledge for our purposes, since people are more likely to pursue projects that will be satisfying in the long term if they have a good sense of their options and abilities. Iris Murdoch (1970: 39–40) emphasizes the knowledge of what we cannot do: that is, the way in which our commitments, emotions, and personality make it impossible for us to

---

[2] A search on "self-knowledge" in *The Philosopher's Index* turns up dozens of articles on the debate about the privacy of our own mental states, but very little on self-knowledge as a virtue.

take some apparently available options without having a breakdown or a crisis of identity.[3] Again, this kind of knowledge would seem important to living well, given that the person who has it knows what her deepest commitments are and can therefore plan and act accordingly.

A sensible position is that self-knowledge requires knowledge of both our capacities and our limitations; the object of self-knowledge is, on this view, our character.[4] But knowledge of our character in this sense is just one part of the knowledge necessary for making good choices about our lives. We also need to know in very basic terms what we like and what we *are* like.[5] To make choices that we are likely to find confirmed by reflection and further experience, we need to know about our desires, interests, tastes, aversions, and emotional predispositions. A reflective person, we will recall, is a person who has value commitments that constitute a reflective survey of how life is going, perspective on the relative importance of these commitments, and the flexibility needed to shift perspectives when a change in the degree of absorption in experience is required. A person who does not know her own tendencies to distraction, exaggeration, and obsession with trivialities may lack perspective on her commitments. A person who does not know about herself what is required in order to maintain her commitments can easily fail to shift perspectives when she needs to, perhaps becoming overly reflective at the very time she needs to "be in the moment". And a person who pays no attention to what grabs her emotionally will be less likely to pursue activities that are deeply satisfying. Moreover, given the importance of social ties discussed in Chapter 2, and given that a lack of self-awareness can result in treating others in objectionable ways, self-knowledge is important to the maintenance of the personal relationships that are a vital component of a good life. The scope of self-knowledge, then, needs to be quite broad.

At the same time, self-knowledge must have limits; knowing oneself is important, but it is possible to go too far. The effort to acquire self-knowledge can veer into a narcissistic preoccupation with oneself or an unhealthy

---

[3] Frankfurt's (1994) discussion of volitional necessity would also lead us to think that this is an important object of self-knowledge. See also Frankfurt 2002*a*.

[4] This is John Kekes's view. According to Kekes (1995: 115), self-knowledge is knowledge of one's own character, which is comprised of an enduring pattern of motivation and action. On Kekes's account, "self-knowledge has as its objects both the moral possibilities and limits set by our conception of a good life, and personal possibilities and limits, set by our character as it is formed by permanent adversities and our own efforts" (1995: 158).

[5] D. W. Hamlyn (1983: 250) emphasizes this point when he says that a person who knows himself in this way "knows, without obscuring the fact from himself, where his values lie, what he truly wants, and where he stands in relation to those wants".

self-consciousness. The idea that it is virtuous to possess self-knowledge also seems at odds with the claims of psychologists that some positive illusions about oneself are beneficial. Such concerns about self-knowledge can help us to see the nature of the virtue of self-awareness more clearly, and they can bring out the point that different ways of thinking about one's life are appropriate at different times. Appreciating that there are limits to self-knowledge reminds us of the importance of seeing things in different ways for different purposes.

The psychological literature on positive illusions reveals that, in fact, we are systematically biased creatures who tend to see ourselves as better than we are. In particular, psychologists have found that people have positive illusions about themselves of the following sorts:

(a) They view themselves in unrealistically positive terms; (b) they believe they have greater control over environmental events than is actually the case; and (c) they hold views of the future that are more rosy than base-rate data can justify. (Taylor and Brown 1994: 21)

For example, in a study about people's perceptions of their driving skills, 80 percent of respondents rated themselves in the top 30 percent of all drivers (Svenson 1981). The phenomenon of exaggerating our own abilities is widespread; it has earned the name "The Lake Wobegon Effect" because of Garrison Keillor's description of his fictional town, "where all the women are strong, all the men are good-looking, and all the children are above average".

There are a number of ways in which such inaccurate self-perceptions are good for us. First, having an exaggerated sense of our own abilities and prospects can actually help us succeed. These illusions are correlated with contentment, positive attitudes toward the self, the ability to care for and about others, openness to new ideas and people, creativity, the ability to perform creative and productive work, and the ability to grow, develop, and self-actualize, especially in response to stressful events (Taylor 1991; Taylor and Brown 1988).

Second, examination of our feelings and values can undermine our preferences and value commitments in undesirable ways. For example, in one study two groups of people were allowed to choose an art poster to take home with them. The first group was directed to analyze their reasons for liking and disliking their various options before making their choice, the second group made the choice without such reflection. Two weeks later, the second

group was significantly happier with their choices than the first (Wilson *et al.*
1993). As Wilson and Dunn (2004: 505) explain, numerous studies have
been done in support of the claim that introspection about the reasons for
our preferences is harmful to us in a variety of ways:

Analyzing reasons has been shown to lower people's satisfaction with their choices
(Wilson *et al.* 1993), lower people's ability to predict their own behavior (Wilson
and LaFleur 1995), lower the correlation between people's expressed feelings and
their later behavior (Wilson and Dunn 1986 and Wilson *et al.* 1984), lower the
correlation between people's evaluations of a product and expert evaluations of it
(Wilson and Schooler 1991), and lower the accuracy of sports fans' predictions about
the outcome of basketball games (Halberstadt and Levine 1999).

We can imagine that many of the negative consequences listed by Wilson
above (though probably not the last) will affect our ability to live well.

Wilson argues that the explanation for at least some cases of detrimental
self-analysis is that we cannot access the unconscious processes that are really
responsible for why we prefer one thing to another, and so we make up
reasons that are inaccurate. (I will say more about this in the next section.) If
this is the explanation, it is not so much an indictment of self-knowledge as
an indictment of relying on introspection to achieve it.

There are other explanations of detrimental self-analysis, however, that
do indicate that the pursuit of self-knowledge itself should be limited. In
some cases close examination of our commitments is detrimental because
the value commitments in question are fostered by perceptions that are just
plain distorted. Amélie Rorty (1975: 22) claims that a certain amount of
self-deception is necessary for romantic love.[6] And psychological studies have
shown that the happiest people in intimate relationships are those who have
various false or exaggerated beliefs about each other.[7] In other cases, as we saw
in Chapter 3, the act of reflection itself can undermine our commitments by
preventing us from being fully absorbed in the activities from which we learn
what has value for us. For example, consider the final scene of Bergman's film
Scenes from a Marriage: Marianne wakes up from a nightmare and laments
to Johan that she doesn't know if she has ever loved or been loved. Johan

---

[6] Hamlyn (1971: 59–60) makes a similar point about self-deception and personal relationships.
[7] One study demonstrated that the happiest people are those who think that their partners are
very much like them, whether these similarities exist in reality or not (Murray *et al.* 2002). Another
showed that people are happier in relationships when they idealize their partners and their partners
idealize them (Murray *et al.* 1996).

replies that he loves her in his imperfect, selfish way and that he's quite sure she loves him too: "We must not harp on love", he says, "or it will dissolve."

The third way in which a lack of self-knowledge can benefit us is that sometimes self-deception looks to be a necessary coping mechanism. Self-deception seems acceptable when we simply must deceive ourselves in order to maintain the motivation to go on at all. These cases typically involve a person whose situation is dire, and who would be paralyzed or incapacitated by facing the truth. Take the example of the father who deceives himself about the damage to his health caused by extra work taken on to support his family. Because his family would be upset if they knew the extent of his sacrifice, the father deceives himself so that they will be unable to detect his sacrifice from his behavior.[8] Similarly, the person who deceives herself about the real causes of a nasty divorce so that she can get beyond her grief and anger long enough to put her life back together seems similarly justified in maintaining her self-deception.[9]

Knowledge of all sorts of things about ourselves seems to be helpful for making choices that are likely to win our reflective approval. Yet, too much self-examination and self-knowledge in many contexts seems to have some serious disadvantages. I believe that even when we take seriously the evidence against self-examination and self-knowledge, there is still a case to be made for a virtue that I will call *(moderate) self-awareness*. In the next section, I characterize the virtue of self-awareness in more detail, taking account of further empirical evidence about our capacity for self-knowledge. After we have a better sense of what self-awareness is, we can return to the question of how self-awareness is both valuable and compatible with helpful gaps in self-knowledge such as positive illusions about ourselves.

5.2. ACQUIRING SELF-KNOWLEDGE

Thinking about the objects of self-knowledge might suggest that acquiring it is a simple matter of learning a bunch of facts. To gain self-knowledge, we investigate and discover the features of our character and our motivational dispositions as we might investigate and discover facts about the solar system by reading a book. But this simple picture is false in at least two respects.

---

[8] The example is King-Farlow's (1973: 82).   [9] This example is from Baron 1998.

First of all, if we merely acquired a bunch of facts about ourselves, we would not necessarily have acquired self-knowledge. Really, this is true of other kinds of knowledge as well; even learning about the solar system is not a simple matter of acquiring a bunch of facts. To acquire knowledge, these facts have to be integrated, absorbed, and processed. When we acquire self-knowledge, we organize the facts we learn into a self-conception or self-image. A self-conception is not just the set of facts we might learn about ourselves; it is an interpretation of these facts within which values are prioritized, emotions are labeled, and attitudes are endorsed or rejected. Importantly, the process of organizing what we know about ourselves into a self-conception is partly a creative or constructive process. This is because the objects of self-knowledge come to us in a disorderly fashion and are in need of interpretation. Value commitments, for instance, are complex patterns of attitudes that do not come labeled with their place in our conception of a good life. Our various commitments may be in tension with each other, and the particular commitments we take to instantiate our basic values may change over time in response to experience. They may not even come labeled with their exact objects, as in the case where you might be unsure what it is that you value about something that you do. These features of our value commitments render interpretation and organization a necessary part of forming a self-conception.

Further, the process of acquiring knowledge about our emotions, attitudes, and commitments may lead us to new understandings of them or the patterns of which they are a part. This is the phenomenon that Richard Moran highlights in his argument that self-knowledge includes an aspect of what he calls *avowal*. According to Moran (2001), knowing oneself is partly a process of discovery; but engagement in such a process can transform the objects of knowledge. Sometimes when we come to understand one of our emotional responses and the reasons that we have for it, that emotion changes character. Moran gives the examples of acknowledging one's guilt and coming to see it as false, or of recognizing one's anger and seeing it as childish. In these cases, he says, "there is indeed a dynamic or self-transforming aspect to a person's reflections on his own state, and this is a function of the fact that the person himself plays a role in formulating how he thinks and feels" (Moran 2001: 59).

To see Moran's point in an example closer to our topic, consider a case of increasing self-knowledge in someone who begins to examine the value she assigns to luxuries and material goods. Imagine someone who claims to value having designer clothes, jewelry, and a fancy car. She has some sense of the reasons she has for valuing these things: she likes the status they give her, the admiration of peers, and the sense these possessions give her of being successful. As she thinks about it, though, she comes to see that while it is true that these items give her a certain status, that status infuses her with anxiety: she is worried about losing it, she senses envy and competitiveness from her friends, and she is always frantically trying to keep up. As she reflects more on the ways in which her values are related, and the real implications of the value she assigns to her possessions, her attitudes toward these things will change. She may still value them, of course, but there will now be a layer of complexity that was previously absent. Instead of thinking that these are truly important components of her happiness, she may conceive of herself as valuing them despite herself, or she may come to think that while she likes and takes some pleasure in her possessions, she needs to find ways of including them in her life without taking her well-being to depend on them. (To put the point in terms of the analysis of value commitments in Chapter 2, we could say that her sense that her values are justified is shaken by the conflicting attitudes, and this undermines her confidence in them as normative for her.)

Because our commitments are disorderly, uninterpreted, and changeable in these ways, there is an inevitable element of creation in the process of acquiring self-knowledge. To emphasize, my point here is not that reason triumphs over feeling to determine our *real* values.[10] Rather, the point is that reflection can change the character of our affective responses, and in so doing, it creates the need to decide which of our various conflicting commitments to side with. To come to see some of your commitments as harmful in the light of other commitments is not (at least not necessarily) to lose the feelings for the former. But seeing things in this new light does change the character of our responses: "guilt affected for the sake of appearances" is different from "deserved guilt", and "passion resulting from a successful advertising campaign" is different from "passion for something I've loved since childhood". Deciding what place these attitudes will have in our self-conception—choosing what to avow—necessarily involves both passions and reflection; it is, after all, because of our other emotions and commitments that an attitude under a revised description looks healthy or unhealthy, fitting or distasteful.

---

[10] Here I am sympathetic to David Velleman's (2005, 2002*a*) work on self-narrative. Velleman rejects the idea that there is an essential or "real" self that gets reported by the narrator. He also argues persuasively against the view that there is a single narrative that contains all the important aspects of a person's self-conception.

The second way in which self-knowledge is different from other kinds of knowledge has to do with the unique obstacles to investigating and discovering many things about ourselves. We are complicated creatures who hide things from our conscious attention by self-deception and rationalization. That we are not open books is painfully obvious and, perhaps, not in need of demonstration. But recent psychological research has begun to make useful distinctions among the various kinds of obstacles there are to self-knowledge. According to this research, we are creatures with minds that include unconscious mental processes to which we lack introspective access.[11] This fact about us causes us to be ignorant of the reasons for our feelings, how we will feel later, and sometimes even how we feel at the moment. Because such findings have important implications for self-awareness as a reflective virtue, it will be useful to discuss them in more detail.

First, according to current psychological research, we are not very good at predicting what our feelings and emotions will be in the future (Gilbert 2006; Gilbert *et al.* 2004; Gilbert and Ebert 2002). According to psychologists who study affective forecasting, when we make predictions about how we will feel in the future, we have a tendency to focus narrowly on the particular change that is at issue, not realizing that how we will feel has many other determinants. Further, we do not take into account the psychological defense mechanisms that help us adjust to negative changes. For example, in a study that may be particularly surprising to academics, assistant professors predicted that their tenure decision would greatly affect their long-term happiness; yet interviews with those who received tenure and those who did not revealed both groups to be equally happy after a few years (Gilbert *et al.* 1998).

Second, there is evidence that we are poor at ascertaining by introspection the reasons why we have the particular emotions, feelings, and preferences that we have. According to Timothy Wilson, a leader in this area of research, we lack introspective access to the reasons for our feeling whenever these reasons are the product of unconscious processes. When this happens, we fabricate explanations that seem plausible. "People who analyze the reasons for their attitudes, for example, often focus on incomplete information and construct new attitudes that are inaccurate" (Wilson and Dunn 2004: 507).[12] The studies that aim to establish this kind of lack of awareness typically manipulate subjects into having certain preferences by stimulating

---

[11] For an excellent overview and discussion of the research on unconscious mental processes, see Wilson 2002.

[12] For more detail see Wilson *et al.* 1995.

an unconscious process. Then subjects are shown to have beliefs about their preferences that reveal a lack of awareness of the true causes of their attitudes.

For example, in one study male subjects were approached by an attractive female assistant who asked them to participate in an unrelated psychological study. On conclusion of the interview, the female assistant gave the men her phone number and invited them to call her to discuss the interview if they wanted. The men were divided into two groups: the first group was approached while they were sitting on a park bench, the second group while crossing a scary elevated footbridge. Researchers kept track of how many of the men called the female assistant to ask for a date. The hypothesis was that the men who were on the footbridge when approached by the woman would attribute their elevated heart rate and breathlessness to physical attraction and be more likely to ask the woman out. This indeed is what happened: the men who were approached on the footbridge were more than twice as likely to call as those who were on the bench when approached. The idea again is that a lack of awareness of the real cause of certain physical symptoms led the subjects to fabricate reasons for these feelings. Studies like this support the claim that our motivations are sometimes the result of processes that are not accessible to consciousness, and when this is the case, we lack introspective access to important facts about ourselves.

Finally, and most controversially, there is some evidence that we sometimes do not even know what we feel at the moment.[13] Some of the research that has been done to establish this claim has focused on racist attitudes. For example, some studies aim to show that while people disavow racist attitudes explicitly, they nevertheless have implicit racist attitudes that affect their performance on various tests (Wilson *et al.* 2000).

One might think that the psychological studies are too contrived, or too specific, to support claims that are relevant to our thinking about how to live in broad terms. I would suggest, however, that we can also learn from literature and from experience that the phenomena of poor affective attribution and prediction are widespread and important. People who are mistaken about their own romantic feelings, in particular, are very familiar in life and in literature. Captain Wentworth in Jane Austen's *Persuasion* is a good example of such a character. Having had his proposal of marriage

---

[13] This phenomenon seems to be related to the fact that we do not always know the reasons for our feelings. For example, one thing we might say about the men standing on the footbridge in the study discussed above is that they did not know that they were feeling fearful, and so took the reason for their physical symptoms to be sexual arousal.

rejected by Anne Elliot many years ago, Wentworth is sure that he is over her, even going so far as to court another woman. The reader is made aware that Wentworth is not being honest with himself, however; we are told that "Anne Elliot was not out of his thoughts, when he more seriously described the woman he should wish to meet with. 'A strong mind, with sweetness of manner', made the first and the last of the description" (Austen 1995 [1818]: 42). Captain Wentworth eventually figures out for himself that he still loves Anne, and the novel ends happily; but there is a significant period during which Wentworth does not really know his own mind.

The process of acquiring self-knowledge, then, is complicated by the fact that reflecting on our psychology can change the objects of this reflection and by the fact that certain parts of our psychology are opaque to us. These two features of the process of acquiring self-knowledge make it the case that we cannot see this process as one of simple introspection and discovery. Rather, the process by which we gain self-knowledge must be thought of as including a set of ongoing commitments that acknowledge the transformative power of self-examination, the importance of taking an external point of view on oneself, and the possibility that there are things we simply cannot or should not know. Further, because one of the most important targets of self-knowledge from the standpoint of living well is the set of value commitments we endorse on reflection, and because this target changes over time, the process of acquiring self-knowledge must be conceived, at least in part, as a creative and transformative process. Finally, because a lack of self-knowledge is sometimes beneficial, this process must include awareness of when it is appropriate to acquire self-knowledge. It is because of these complexities that I suggest we distinguish between self-awareness (the virtuous state) and self-knowledge (one of the things the person with self-awareness aims to have). I will say that a person with the virtue of moderate self-awareness has an adequate self-conception, appropriate self-knowledge, and, in addition, those habits and skills that are necessary for the process of constructing a self-conception and integrating it into one's practical life.

5.3. MODERATE SELF-AWARENESS: HABITS AND SKILLS

Socrates had the view that the most important aspect of self-knowledge is the knowledge of one's own ignorance. The importance of Socrates' teaching was his insistence on a kind of self-criticism or self-inquiry in service of discovering the truth. Socrates was particularly concerned to bring us to appraise critically our understanding of morality; but applying his wisdom to the case of a more pedestrian kind of self-knowledge gives us a good place to start. The self-aware person is disposed to be critical of herself in the sense that she does not take every apparent fact about her at face value. She is committed to arriving at a better and more complete picture of her own motivations, talents, and interests by whatever are the best methods for achieving this goal.

What are these methods? A helpful source of information is the literature on self-deception, our penchant for which is one of the main obstacles to self-knowledge.[14] Bishop Butler gives us a starting point for thinking about the habits or skills necessary for overcoming self-deception: at the end of his sermon on self-deceit he gives some practical advice about how to avoid self-deception. Butler suggests, first, that we assume we are self-deceived in some respect, because it is almost inevitable that self-serving passions have influenced our judgments. Second, he suggests that we become acquainted with our real character by keeping our eye out for the suspicious part of it. He gives us a thought experiment to help us imagine what the faulty parts of our character are:

Suppose then an enemy were to set about defaming you, what part of your character would he single out? What particular scandal, think you, would he be most likely to fix upon you? And what would the world be most ready to believe? There is scarce a man living but could, from the most transient superficial view of himself, answer this question. (Butler 2006 [1726]: 108)

Butler (2006 [1726]: 109) also suggests that we try to take up the perspective of an outside observer by imagining what judgment we would pass on another who exhibited our behavior.

Butler is right that self-deception can be revealed by an investigation that aims to discover those motives that have an undue influence on our beliefs

---

[14] I mean "self-deception" in its broadest sense here. We are self-deceived when our coming to have inaccurate or inadequate information is caused by our underlying motives. Here I follow Martin (1986: 3) and Erwin (1988). Philosophers have been particularly interested in self-deception narrowly conceived so that it requires that a self-deceiver believe p and, at the same time (perhaps subconsciously), know that not-p, have evidence contrary to p, or engage in thoughts that p is false. See, e.g., Audi 1993; Mele 1983. This may very well be the right way of thinking about self-deception when trying to distinguish it from other failings. For my purposes it makes sense to think of self-deception defined so as to include misinterpretations of information that are not volitional, or that differ from self-deception (strictly defined) in other ways.

about ourselves. But his narrow focus on self-examination misses the two distinctive features of self-knowledge discussed above. An appreciation of these features will lead us to a better picture of the virtue of self-awareness.

First, Butler was likely unaware of the degree to which introspection and explicit conscious evaluation are inadequate to reveal the right information about us. Given the inadequacy of introspection, we need other tools: an openness to evidence, including the vital information we get from those who know us, a sensitivity to hidden desires, beliefs, and emotional responses, and a willingness to let them surface. We also need to be able to observe our own behavior as another person might do to make discoveries about our inner mental life: that is, the ability to infer what our mental states must be from our behavior.[15] This feature of the self-aware person is a specific instance of the more general willingness of the reflective person to learn from experience.

Since our motives are sometimes opaque to us, it can be very helpful to get a third-person point of view either by taking that perspective ourselves or, literally, by asking another person. Butler does rightly highlight the importance of the third-person point of view, but he does not recognize that sometimes it must be literal.[16] Here Socrates was a step ahead; his preferred method for revealing ignorance, the interpersonal method of elenchus, seemed to recognize the limits of introspection.[17] Taking seriously the perspectives of others who know us well and whom we respect may be the only path to understanding certain features of ourselves. Emma, we will recall, learns about her own vanity and hypocrisy by taking in Mr Knightly's criticisms and seeing herself through his eyes, not by turning her attention inward. Sometimes, by observing your behavior, other people see things about you more accurately than you can yourself, either because they do not know the rationalizations you have created for your choices and conduct, or they can see through them.

In the same way that perspective requires the ability to let the experiences of other people inform our sense of the appropriate response to circumstances,

[15] This is the strategy favored by Timothy Wilson. See Wilson 2002; Wilson and Dunn 2004.

[16] Butler is also incorrect to suggest that we should concentrate only on ways in which we might be worse than we seem. In the passage cited above, and elsewhere, Butler supposes that self-love or a desire to maintain a good opinion of one's character is the only motive to self-deception, and therefore the only motive that needs exposing. Self-awareness needs to be broad enough to pick up on all the ways our beliefs can be distorted. For further discussion of this point see Tiberius 2000*a*.

[17] Thanks to Michelle Mason for reminding me of this point and its connection to my discussion of self-awareness.

so, too, self-awareness requires the ability to let others' views of us inform what we think of ourselves. This point about the role of friends in the development of character is an important piece of practical advice, but it also has more theoretical significance. First, social pressures greatly influence the traits of character we have and can develop (Merritt 2000). If this is true, then it is important to show how the virtues that are part of a well-lived life can be socially encouraged and sustained. Second, if friends are among the things we value, then we have revealed a way in which pursuing our values contributes to the development of our character. This adds support to the coherence justification of the Reflective Wisdom Account, because it shows that the elements of this conception of a well-lived life are mutually supporting and sustaining.

The role that other people play in a person's acquisition of self-knowledge is not without complications, of course. Wilson and Dunn (2004) argue that there are formidable obstacles to using others as a source of information about ourselves, for two reasons. First, we are not very good at figuring out what other people think of us; we generally operate on the assumption that others see us as we see ourselves. Second, other people are not necessarily better judges of our psychologies than we are. Just as we ourselves have unacknowledged motives that can distort things, or hide them from our conscious attention, so too others can have agendas that make them inaccurate mirrors for us. Moreover, friends and family members may purposely distort their feedback to us, hiding negative assessments for the sake of politeness or avoiding confrontation.

A further problem is that certain social institutions such as forms of oppression may make the usual third-person sources of self-knowledge unavailable or systematically distorted. We might think that this is true in Sam's case. Sam had no friend with whom he could talk about his feelings for Tracy Bacon (not even Tracy himself, it seemed). Given the taboo about sexuality in general, and homosexuality in particular, it would have been extremely difficult for any of his friends or family to suggest to him directly that he might be gay.

These objections must be taken seriously, but there is reason to think that other people can still provide an important source of information about ourselves, within appropriate limits. First, given the importance of relationships with others to our well-being, one of the things it is useful for us to know about ourselves is how others feel about our treatment of them. If what we need to know is how our behavior is perceived, then our friends can be good sources of information regardless of whether they accurately perceive our inner mental life. Others do not have to be good at ascertaining our deepest motives in order to be a good mirror for the effects of our actions on them. Second, as far as our ability to detect how other people see us is concerned, it seems that being on guard against self-serving bias can go at least some way toward correcting this problem. If we know that we have a tendency to assume that others see us as we see ourselves, then when we are trying to discover something about ourselves, we can try to compensate. Granted, we may not be able to change our automatic tendency toward such a bias, and changing this bias in general may not be good for us anyway, but we can try to counteract it when it is important to do so. We can also pay special attention to the friends who will be honest with us. The person with the virtue of self-awareness must be prepared to evaluate which opinions are trustworthy and therefore deserving of being integrated into her self-conception. Finally, regarding the point that others are not necessarily more accurate about our psychologies than we are, if others make *different* errors, then we can hope to home in on a more accurate picture of ourselves by a process of triangulation.

The second feature of self-knowledge that Butler's advice misses is the creative or transformative aspect of the process of acquiring it. The transformative power of self-reflection indicates that part of the virtue of self-awareness consists in what we do with self-knowledge once we acquire it. Whatever the source of information about oneself—whether it is gained from introspection, therapy, or trusted friends—one cannot be concerned only with accumulating facts. We must also take the stance of avowal, and decide which attitudes to identify with and which to reject. Often this will happen quite naturally.[18] Consider Emma's reaction to Mr Knightly's criticisms of her. At first she is defensive and denies that she is as he says. But as she matures, Emma comes to believe Mr Knightly's judgments and at the same time to endorse the normative aspect of the judgment. She sees that she has indeed been cruel to Miss Bates, regrets her behavior deeply, and vows to change. We would not think that Emma had grown at all if her reaction to Knightly's judgment had been to think, "Oh, yes, I was cruel to Miss Bates and how deserving she was of that cruelty too, tiresome old woman." The aim of a person with the virtue of self-awareness is to take the truths she discovers

---

[18] Though not always. Sometimes the process that leads to avowal may be complicated, as Richard Moran's (2001: 120–4) discussion of the therapeutic context suggests.

about herself and allow them to inform a self-conception she can endorse as a basis for making decisions about how to live.

Reflecting on the empirical evidence, one might think that the claim that introspection is unreliable, and that we create false stories in order to make up for lack of information, creates a problem for the creative aspect of self-awareness. But creation and fabrication are two different things. Self-creation, as discussed above, is not making up feelings we don't have; rather, it is a kind of affirmation of certain aspects of ourselves and a rejection of others as a part of our self-conception. The creative aspect of self-awareness is transformative in the sense that it changes our self-conception on the basis of accurate information about how we feel. Self-fabrication, on the other hand, tries to make something false fit the facts.

The language of affirmation and rejection should not be taken to imply that we have so much control over our feelings that we can accept or delete them at will. It is important that affirmation and rejection pertain to our self-conception, where a self-conception is at least partly something to which we aspire. We may not be able to rid ourselves of the feelings of childish anger or unwarranted guilt, but we can take a different attitude toward these feelings upon seeing them as inappropriate. Similarly, we may not be able to stop ourselves from caring about certain things that are detrimental to our happiness, but we can change the role they play in our reflection about our lives. Instead of seeing these values as goals on a par with other goals, we can see them as impositions that we should wean ourselves away from, insofar as this is possible. Taking this disapproving attitude toward a passion for consuming, for example, probably won't eliminate the desire altogether, but it may incline us to look for other sources of pleasure and to feel differently when these desires are frustrated. Alternatively, if the goal we disapprove of is not terribly harmful, we can decide to see it as an occasional indulgence, part of our personality that doesn't quite fit with everything else, but which makes life interesting when prevented from taking over. Seeing the questionable goal in this way may make it less likely to frustrate our happiness.

The skills of self-awareness, then, cannot be just the skills needed for the discovery of facts. What is required, in addition, is the ability to step back to a more detached viewpoint and an openness to the information given by one's emotional responses, other psychological reactions to circumstances, and the observations of trusted others. We also need an enduring commitment to constructing a self-conception that is responsive to the truth and to our ideals. Without this commitment, we might settle too easily on conclusions that are still the product of self-deception, or we might allow our self-conception to become stagnant and unresponsive to change.

Our discussion of self-awareness has emphasized a set of skills that are self-consciously critical and reflective. How does this emphasis square with the worries about self-knowledge and self-examination that I raised earlier in this chapter? We see how when we recognize that insofar as self-awareness is virtuous, it is a part of reflective wisdom, and a person who has this kind of wisdom will not be someone who is always reflecting and scrutinizing her own motives.[19] The self-aware person is committed to discovering her real motivations, and has the ability to see herself from a third-person point of view. This does not mean that she is a person who is constantly seeking self-knowledge, or that her life is pervaded by a vivid awareness of the facts about herself. Being self-aware will sometimes require that we pay particular attention to ourselves, think very seriously about our real motives, and closely examine our behavior. But we must not lose sight of the point that the virtue of self-awareness is supposed to be developed in the context of living well overall, which includes other practical problems, virtues, and strategies.

Drawing on the account of reflective wisdom that we have so far, we can say that the virtue of self-awareness constitutes a perspective focused on the importance of close attention to one's motivations and a commitment to get at the truth about oneself. This perspective fulfills the need to discover certain facts about oneself and to formulate a self-conception that can sustain a positive reflective survey. To live well, we need to know when it makes sense to assume this perspective (that is, be attentive to oneself), and when it makes sense to be entirely unselfconscious. Sam Clay needed greater awareness about his emotional life to be happy, but it would not have made his life better to engage in relentless self-examination even during the times (such as while he was engaged in creative work on his comics with his cousin Joe) when he was really enjoying life. As I argued in Chapter 3, this is just the kind of knowledge that a wise person has: the wise person knows when to shift in and out of various perspectives when it is beneficial to do so. Research in social psychology seems to support the idea that this kind of selective awareness is possible. For example, there is some evidence that people's illusions are more modest when they are contemplating a decision (Gollwitzer and Kinney 1989).

---

[19] For a similar solution to the problem posed by positive illusions see Elga 2005.

As to the question of when we should engage the skills of self-awareness, we are unlikely to find any rules or decision procedures here, although we can formulate some rough guidelines. First of all, when you are in the middle of enjoying an experience of something that you have previously decided is valuable, engaging in critical self-reflection is probably inappropriate. Second, engaging the skills of self-awareness is likely to be appropriate as part of the preparation for making certain kinds of decisions.

With these two points in mind, let us return to the three kinds of problematic cases that were distinguished at the end of section 5.1: (i) cases in which an unrealistic assessment of our abilities and prospects helps us succeed; (ii) cases in which examination of our reasons undermines our commitments to values; and (iii) cases in which self-deception is an indispensable coping mechanism. Notice that the third case is less common than cases of the first two types, and that it doesn't present a serious problem for self-awareness as a virtue. This is because these are cases of extreme circumstances, in which one might just say that ordinary imperatives of virtue do not apply. For example, we can say that the distraught father is in dismal enough circumstances that he is unable to cultivate or benefit from the virtue of self-awareness.

The first two types of cases are cases in which lack of self-awareness seems to be beneficial in all sorts of ordinary circumstances. Notice, however, that neither is a case in which distortion of the facts that are directly relevant to a person's deliberations is beneficial.[20] There are two clarifications to be made here. First, to say that self-awareness is a virtue that has particular importance in the context of decision making is not to say that when we are on the brink of making a choice we ought to marshal all of our reflective skills and approach the choice steeped in the facts about ourselves. The decision-making context, as I suggested in Chapters 3 and 4, is larger than the very point at which we make a decision, and it may be that appropriate reflection and self-awareness are most important as background conditions for making good choices.

Second, self-reflection and the attempted acquisition of self-knowledge can be bad for a person in the context of decision making if they aren't done well. A person who doesn't recognize the limits of introspection, the potential to fabricate stories that don't fit, and the need for transformative self-creation, may be worse off by trying to be self-aware. The important

---

[20] Psychologists, including Wilson, have acknowledged this point. For example, the point has been made that it is important to acknowledge facts about health risks in the context of making decisions about various behaviors. See, e.g., Peterson and Chang 2003; Weinstein 1989.

point here is that such a person does not have the virtue of self-awareness. She has, rather, some harmful habits and a misguided conception of how to attain self-knowledge.

To summarize, the characterization of the virtue of self-awareness that I have given is compatible with the negative effects of self-knowledge and self-examination for two reasons. First, evidence of these downfalls is compatible with self-awareness being a good thing at certain times, in certain contexts. Second, a person who has the virtue of self-awareness, as well as the other aspects of reflective wisdom, will preserve the useful positive illusions that help make life go well.

We can now see how self-awareness has the elements of a reflective virtue outlined in Chapter 1. First, it consists of habits of thought that can be cultivated, whether alone or with the help of one's social group. Second, the habits of thought that make up self-awareness are organized around certain practical needs: namely, the need to make decisions based on accurate information about oneself and (as will be discussed further in the next section) the need for a self-conception that can provide the basis for endorsement of one's life. In the next section I will discuss the ways in which self-awareness is good for its possessor, the third feature of the characterization of a reflective virtue.

5.4. THE VALUE OF SELF-AWARENESS

To live well from one's own point of view is to live in accordance with the evaluative standards that one endorses from a reflective point of view. As we saw in Chapter 2, for most people, this means having friends, contributing to our moral ends to some extent, and finding enjoyment and achievement in our chosen projects. If we begin with a conception of living well as living in accordance with our deeply held value commitments, it should not be surprising that self-awareness turns out to be helpful in several ways.

5.4.1. The Instrumental Value of Self-Awareness

The self-aware person knows what her reflective values are, and can therefore shape her life in a way that is appropriate to them. Through the process of self-discovery and construction of a self-conception, the self-aware person develops a sense of who she is that informs her choices. This self-conception will include values that are more specific than the general reflective values defended in Chapter 2; in becoming self-aware, we partly discover and partly decide what particular shape these general values should have for us. Further, the self-aware person knows enough about herself that she can tailor the particular ways she chooses to pursue her values to her own talents, interests, and inclinations.

Self-awareness can also help us live well by letting us see when we undermine our own values or frustrate our own goals. For example, had Emma been more self-aware, she would have been a better friend by her own standards. Emma's case is not tragic because her lack of self-awareness is due largely to her youth. We do not expect her to be terribly self-aware, and we are pleased to see her mature as a result of Mr Knightly's direction. What would have happened had Emma never become aware of her failings? We can imagine Emma's circle of friends withdrawing as her youthful charm no longer compensates for her insensitivity. In particular, we can imagine those who are good judges of character—the people Emma seems most concerned to please—not inclined to maintain their friendships with her. If this were to happen, then when Emma reflects on her life, she would have to admit that while she values certain friendships and the good opinion of others, she has not succeeded in maintaining them.

Moreover, the case that self-awareness is important to friendship does not rest on the assumption that an insensitive friend will eventually be rejected by others. Since Emma values *being a good friend* (not *feeling like she is a good friend*), it makes sense from her own point of view to develop habits that are likely to make her a better friend, period. From her own point of view, what matters is being a good friend, and she won't be a good friend if she is unaware of her negative effects on others. This point is independent of whether or not her friends ultimately reject her. Emma's friends may stick by her because of her social standing, but she will not have succeeded in being a good friend, which is, after all, one of the things she cares about. The point here can be generalized to other value commitments. As long as we are committed to attaining a goal (as opposed to merely thinking that we are doing so), it will matter to us whether we have actually achieved it or not. When we have commitments like this, which most of us do, it makes sense for us to be committed (at least to some degree) to knowing how we are doing with respect to these goals.

The case of Sam Clay reveals another way in which self-awareness is instrumentally valuable. Sam would have been better off with greater self-awareness, which might have allowed him to do what he wanted to do, and love whom he wanted to love, with less inner conflict and doubt. He is surely hindered by his lack of self-awareness, which deprives him of the ability to create a path that minimizes that conflict. Sam Clay is a much sadder figure than Emma, though, in part because he is genuinely conflicted between pursuing intimate relationships that would bring him an important kind of happiness and fulfilling his familial and societal duties. The tragedy for Sam is that his circumstances give him no way to realize both important parts of himself. Now, I want to suggest that even if there is no way for Sam to achieve everything he wants, self-awareness could still do him some good. To see this, we need to think again about the way in which emotional residue from frustrated parts of oneself influences reflection on one's life. When Sam thinks about how his life has gone, as long as he refuses to admit his romantic preferences, there will be things that do not fit: a feeling that there is something missing in his marriage, sexual desires he cannot satisfy, and so on. Absent self-awareness, these feelings will be alien and unexplained, which makes them a hindrance to a satisfying review of his life.

Self-awareness, then, is instrumental to living well. When we are aware of our desires, emotions, and so on, we are better poised to make choices that accommodate them. When we are aware of our effects on others, we are able to be better friends. Further, an accurate self-conception facilitates a satisfactory review of one's life by removing one source of unexplained conflicts.

5.4.2. Self-Awareness and Self-Direction

Our discussion of self-awareness as a virtue highlights the fact that a person's conception of a good life and the values that comprise it are relative to the person herself in important ways. Our conception of how to live needs to conform to important facts about us if it is to stand the test of experience, and it needs to take account of the norms and values we accept if it is going to withstand further reflection. While the conception of a good life for almost anyone will include values that are deeply social (friendship, community, moral ideals, and so on), these values are, in an important sense, one's *own* values. The Reflective Wisdom Account, then, presupposes the value of self-direction or authenticity (as we discussed in Chapter 2); since it is an account of how to live well from one's own point of view, this should not be surprising.

Self-direction, authenticity, or being true to one's values, is one thing that is sometimes meant by autonomy in the philosophical literature, and one of the puzzles in this literature is how to distinguish what is authentic from inauthentic in light of the fact that mere possession of a desire or commitment does not seem sufficient for authenticity.[21] The need to distinguish between desires we happen to have and authentic desires stems from an interest in describing the nature of authenticity in a way that captures its value.[22] The mere fact that a desire belongs to our psychology does not seem to make it authentic in a normatively interesting sense, because any particular desire can be one that the agent herself rejects as a motive that *should* direct her.

A popular solution to this problem is to say that authentic first-order desires or values are ones that are sanctioned by second-order attitudes. On Frankfurt's (1988) view, for example, it is wholehearted identification with a first-order desire or value that makes it an authentic one. One question that has been asked about hierarchical models such as Frankfurt's is: "What is special about second-order volitions?" (Watson 1975). Why think these second-order volitions are more closely tied to whatever it is about the self that we think *ought* to direct? Behind the hierarchical theories is the idea that the second-order attitude—whether endorsement or identification or something else—expresses something important about the person that might not be present in a mere first-order desire or feeling of approval. But it has proved difficult to articulate precisely what it is that distinguishes this normatively significant part of the self. The Reflective Wisdom Account suggests an answer to this problem, along the following lines.

What matters from the point of view of living a life that you can regard with reflective approval is how much your life has taken account of things about you that will invariably be part of the process of reflection on how your life is going. The importance of the self in living well, then, has to do with the possibility of reflective success.[23] Reflective success, and hence a positive evaluation of how one's life is going, depends, in part, on the compatibility

---

[21] As Nomy Arpaly (2003: 117–48) has pointed out, "autonomy" is a word that does too much work. Self-direction as I intend it is closest to what Arpaly calls "authenticity" in her helpful taxonomy of senses of autonomy. The distinction between autonomy as self-control and authenticity as being true to one's values is Velleman's (2002*b*).

[22] Insofar as the subject is autonomy in the sense of self-control, the aim is rather to define a notion that supports an intuitive division between free and unfree action. I am not talking about autonomy in this sense.

[23] Another way of explaining this importance is by reference to what is essential to the self. This seems to be the view that Frankfurt came to have, in which motives are authentic to the

of the values and norms that make up a person's point of view with the other aspects of her self-conception (her desires, emotional predispositions, talents, and so on). One way to help ensure this compatibility is by constructing the right kind of self-conception. So, the Reflective Wisdom Account makes self-direction a matter of being directed by a self-conception that can support a positive review of one's life.

Authenticity (or self-direction), then, is a matter of being directed by the *right* part of yourself. And the right part of yourself is the self that is the appropriate measure for how your life goes: the features of you that will be part of your reflective self-conception either because you are committed to them on reflection (your values, for example) or because experience will make them salient (your talents and passions). Now we can see the important role that self-awareness plays in distinguishing the authentic from the inauthentic. The virtue of self-awareness allows a person to construct a self-conception that is responsive to all the aspects of the self: judgments, aspirations, emotions, and wants. And, further, by constructing a self-conception, the self-aware person decides what is important to her. In other words, from the point of view of the person herself, the distinction between authentic and inauthentic choices is made by employing the skills of self-awareness and "avowing" what matters to her. The self-aware person does this with some authority because of her relatively high degree of self-knowledge, her acknowledgment that she may yet not have everything right about herself, and her openness to the evidence from various kinds of experience. This story about the nature of authenticity is not in conflict with the hierarchical picture; rather, I take it to provide an explanation for the authority of a particular kind of second-order attitude: namely, the avowals or endorsements of a person with self-awareness. (In fact, we might say that self-awareness is the characterological precondition for wholehearted endorsement.)

Importantly, if we think of self-awareness as *moderate*, as I have been suggesting, so that the self-aware person is not obsessively self-critical or free of positive self-illusions, then we do not make reason the source of authenticity. As long as self-awareness is moderate, a reflectively constructed self-conception will not be a self-conception that prioritizes thought over feeling, or beliefs about oneself over information received from emotional

---

self when they are part of the self's volitional nature. The account of self-direction that follows from the Reflective Wisdom Account does not presuppose the existence of an essential or "inner" self. For a compelling skeptical discussion about the idea of an essential self, see Velleman 2002*a*.

experience. Nor will an appropriate self-conception be an unrelentingly accurate picture, if this means abandoning useful positive illusions.

I have argued that insofar as a person possesses self-awareness, her choices and expressions of approval count as more self-directed or authentic. To summarize the argument: to be self-directed is to be guided by an appropriate self-conception. Self-awareness is the virtue that guides the construction of our self-conceptions. Therefore, self-awareness is part of the process of living a self-directed life. If this is so, and if self-direction is a constitutive part of living well, then self-awareness is not merely instrumental to the well-lived life, it is part of what it is to achieve it.

5.4.3. Some Problem Cases

It is worth considering some apparent counterexamples to the argument that self-awareness, as I have characterized it, is good for us. First, there are various cases of people who seem to be virtuously self-aware, yet very miserable. Second, there are people who have very little self-knowledge (and hence not much of the virtue of self-awareness) but are extremely happy. Literature and life abound with examples. Silas Marner, George Eliot's miserly loner, seems to know exactly what he values (his gold), yet is entirely unhappy until a small girl enters his life and his values change. Silas's self-knowledge seems stultifying rather than helpful. Then there is Mr Collins, the obnoxious and obsequious pastor in Jane Austen's *Pride and Prejudice*.[24] Mr Collins seems blissfully lacking in self-awareness, and it is easy to predict that an increase in his self-awareness could only make him less happy. Finally, there are those for whom self-awareness arrives too late in life. A good example here is the butler, Stevens, in Kazuo Ishiguro's *Remains of the Day*.[25] Late in life, Stevens seems to lose confidence in his past choices and values; for example, he realizes how nice it would have been to have been able to pursue the woman he loved. But self-awareness at this late stage seems only a cruel twist.

The first point to make in addressing some of these cases is that self-awareness is not sufficient for living well. Assuming that Silas Marner does indeed have the virtue of self-awareness, he is miserable because his values are not deeply satisfying and give him no happy experiences. So we might say that his problem is that he lacks other requirements for living well; another part of

---

[24] Thanks to Frances Howard-Snyder for suggesting the example.
[25] Thanks to Julia Driver for the example, and to her and Dan Jacobson for helpful discussion of it.

living life well, after all, is cultivating values that are supported by emotional experience in such a way that we have some foundation for a positive reflective survey. Of course, we might also wonder whether Silas Marner really possesses self-awareness. On my view, paying attention to our emotional responses and integrating this knowledge into our practical lives is crucial, and Silas does not seem to have done this. People who are miserable because of their self-proclaimed yet crippling values may actually lack self-awareness precisely because they pay no attention to their emotional lives.

The other cases present the more difficult challenge to the necessity of self-awareness for living well. It seems that Mr Collins is doing quite well without any self-awareness, and that Stevens was better off without it. To answer this challenge, we need to recall what the Reflective Wisdom Account is meant to be and the kinds of questions it is meant to answer. Imperatives to develop virtues such as self-awareness are directed at people who are concerned to live lives that they can regard with reflective approval. The account aims to answer the first-person question of how to live and to articulate a process for living, rather than a substantive account of a good life. For current purposes, what this means is that we need to ask whether there are reasons to develop the virtue of self-awareness from the first-person point of view insofar as one is concerned to live a life that one can reflectively endorse.

There is a sense in which Mr Collins himself has reasons to develop the habits of moderate self-awareness. Insofar as his inflated sense of his own merits and his complete lack of awareness of his defects are part of an overall strategy to avoid reflecting on others' feelings about him, this is a problematic strategy. Following it requires him to limit his society to those who maintain his illusions, a requirement which is indeed quite limiting. Moreover, if Mr Collins really is committed to living a life that can bear his reflective survey, he cannot deliberately follow this strategy; rather, he will just have to be fortunate enough never to be forced to think about the things that reflect poorly on him. It is one thing to be willing to live happily with helpful positive illusions about yourself, but quite another to adopt the policy of never being self-critical at all. The latter seems inconsistent with a commitment to living in accordance with your own standards (as opposed to merely thinking that you are).

None of this is to say that Mr Collins could be brought to see these reasons as reasons to change the way he is living his life. Most likely, he believes that he has sufficient self-knowledge and that his positive illusions are no more egregious than anyone else's. When his proposal of marriage to Elizabeth results in a reaction that flatly contradicts his positive view of himself, he quickly explains it away. But when we put ourselves in Mr Collins's shoes and ask whether it makes sense for us to cultivate the habits of self-awareness, we cannot choose massive delusion and still maintain a commitment to living a life we could reflectively approve. This point also applies to the case of Stevens, to which I turn next.

It is clear that Stevens is concerned to live a reflective life; the novel is a first-person narrative portrayal of Stevens's reflections on his life and choices. Yet, it seems unfortunate that Stevens should come to doubt the value of his choices and look back on his life with uncertainty and (muted) regret. The larger point here is that when people make bad decisions, commit to unsuitable values, or have seriously flawed characters, suddenly acquiring the virtuous habits of self-awareness may make them miserable and less likely to regard their lives with reflective approval in the short term.

The first thing to say here is that while it is true that increasing self-awareness can make such people miserable in the short term, if we accept my argument for the value of moderate self-awareness, then we should accept that self-awareness is also instrumental to making better choices in the future. The value of self-direction is most evident in the context of a whole life in which earlier self-directed choices lead to later consequences for a person's self-survey. What is tragic about Stevens is that he came to his self-knowledge too late to change much about his life: the reflective survey he reports in the novel is implied to be one of his last. Interestingly, avoiding the cultivation of habits of self-awareness earlier in his life did not prevent him from having to confront his honest reflections on his choices in the end.

Second, as discussed above in the case of Mr Collins, Stevens does have some reasons to develop moderate self-awareness from his own point of view, insofar as he shares the concerns presupposed by the Reflective Wisdom Account. In fact, once a person considers the reasons he has for trying to be more self-aware, it is difficult to see how he could reject them. This is because of the close relationship between self-awareness and self-direction. The imperative to cultivate self-awareness is, in essence, a demand that we define our own point of view, review the values that make up our reflective survey, and decide whether to endorse or reject them. Seen this way, a person who considers whether to be self-aware or self-deceptive, and chooses the latter, is sacrificing his attempt to guide his life by his own values.

Of course, such a choice does not usually confront people in such stark terms; these options are usually presented in confusing ways. Moreover, the choice between moderate self-awareness and self-deception is further complicated by the fact that *moderate* self-awareness includes some positive illusion and self-deception. Therefore, the kind of choice we must be thinking about here is a choice between general policies: cultivate the skills of moderate self-awareness or adopt a policy of widespread self-deception. What this means is that, in particular cases, there may be reasons stemming from other concerns or extenuating circumstances that override the reasons to seek self-knowledge at the time. For instance, we might think, compatibly with the Reflective Wisdom Account, that if Stevens had been able to consider the fact that his late arriving self-awareness could do him no good, then he would have had a reason not to develop this virtue.

5.5. CONCLUSION

Moderate self-awareness is a virtue that helps us to live self-directed lives that we can endorse from a reflective point of view. It consists in the capacity for self-criticism, an openness to various sources of information about oneself, and humility about what one can find out. Tempered by wisdom, self-awareness comprises a set of skills that operate within certain boundaries and are particularly relevant to the context of decision making. Having the virtue of self-awareness requires some success in applying these capacities and actually achieving some knowledge of facts about oneself that are important to one's practical life. Those with the virtue of self-awareness are likely to make choices that better reflect their values and fit their own interests and talents; in particular, they are better suited to having valuable friendships and being good friends. They are also better constituted to live self-directed lives, because self-awareness is essential to constructing a self-conception that represents the important aspects of the self.

Importantly, self-awareness is not self-absorption or narcissism; nor are the habits of mind that constitute self-awareness ones we should employ all the time. Reflective virtues are to be developed in the context of living well overall, which means that the perspective of self-awareness that emphasizes discovering facts about oneself must coexist in a person's life with other perspectives that emphasize other aspects of living well and wisely.

6

Optimism

In the previous chapter we saw that a reflective person needs to compromise between seeking the facts and living with illusions when it comes to forming a self-conception. Some self-knowledge is important for living a reflective life, but the virtue of self-awareness does not require a relentless purging of every useful fiction. In that chapter, I tried, somewhat artificially, to constrain the topic of our discussion to facts and illusions about oneself. Of course, one might point out that awareness of the facts in general seems to be a candidate for a reflective virtue.[1] Certainly, knowing the facts about the world is important to making good choices, and this is reflected in the account of reflective values in Chapter 2. Appreciating the facts (in general) is important to living a reflective life, because our ability to reflectively endorse our lives will be hindered if we are frequently contradicted by our actual experiences with the world.

Might there also be a reason to tolerate some deviation from the facts about the world, as there is reason to tolerate positive self-illusions? One reason comes from research in positive psychology: there is mounting evidence that positive future-directed attitudes such as hope and optimism (conceived so as to include more than positive illusions about oneself) are correlated with, and sometimes a cause of, various components and indicators of well-being. Hope and optimism predict achievement in many domains, freedom from anxiety and depression, good social relationships, and physical health.[2] Given the emphasis in the Reflective Wisdom Account on social relationships, enjoyment, and accomplishment, the empirical data suggest that optimism or hopefulness might be important for living a life that one can reflectively endorse.

There is reason to think that conclusions similar to those we reached in the previous chapter can be reached in other domains of knowledge; knowing the

---

[1] Julia Driver and Simon Keller pressed this question at SPAWN, the Syracuse Philosophy Annual Workshop and Network, Syracuse University, July 2006.

[2] For a useful summary of this research see Peterson and Seligman 2004*a*. See also Seligman 1990. I will say more about the relationship between my definitions of cynicism and optimism and the definitions used by psychologists in section 6.5.

facts is a good thing, but we shouldn't go overboard. I also think, however, that we must be cautious; other domains of knowledge raise different issues, which warn against drawing general conclusions without considering the details. In this chapter, I consider our beliefs about and attitudes toward humanity. In this domain, I argue that it does make sense for us to develop certain optimistic patterns of thought, but we should not abandon reality entirely. The goal here is to define a kind of optimism that is compatible with a reflective life. To do this, we need to articulate a more specific attitude or set of attitudes than simply a general belief that things will work out for the best. We also need to be clear about the reasons we have for trying to be more optimistic or hopeful. The general empirical case for hope and optimism lumps together many correlates not all of which are relevant to living a reflective life. I propose to develop an account of realistic optimism as a virtue by paying attention to the connections between our optimism or cynicism about human nature and certain of our reflective values.

The aim of this chapter is to characterize cynicism and optimism, and to argue that cynicism (properly understood) is a vice, and optimism (properly understood) is a virtue. An important part of the argument for establishing cynicism as a vice will be to distinguish cynicism from what we might call "being realistic", which is often beneficial. The argument for considering optimism to be a virtue requires locating the appropriate mean between cynicism and a kind of foolish optimism, or being a Pangloss, which is often harmful. We will see how cynicism hinders both the cognitive and the affective components of our capacity for endorsement by influencing our views about what is worthwhile and by dampening (or precluding entirely) our positive attitudes toward others.

6.1. PRELIMINARIES: ENDORSEMENT AND VIRTUE

As discussed in Chapter 2, valuing is a special attitude, different from desiring, liking, or judging. To value something in the fullest sense is, in part, to have a positive affective response, and in part to take our attitudes toward what we value to be justified. To live life in accordance with our own reflective standards, we need values in this sense, because such values provide the standards for our assessment of how our lives are going. We can call the attitude we ideally have towards our values "endorsement", where this includes both affect and judgment. In this chapter I argue that there are important internal factors that affect our capacity for endorsement in general, and our ability to endorse friendship and moral ends in particular. Cynicism impairs our ability to endorse what we find valuable. It impedes both aspects of reflective endorsement mentioned above: it hinders critical reflection, and it influences the motivational stance that accompanies the intellectual component of endorsement. The virtue of optimism, or what we could more precisely call "realistic optimism", facilitates these abilities.

To avoid confusion later on, it will be helpful to make two qualifications about the reasons to avoid cynicism that we are considering here. First, these reasons are self-interested, but not in a narrow sense of self-interest. Cynicism will impede our living well, although it may not impede the maximization of our utility if utility is understood as the satisfaction of our unidealized preferences. Further, the reasons we have to avoid cynicism apply very broadly to any person who has normal human commitments, but they are not universal in the sense of applying to all rational beings. Reasons to develop realistic optimism are similarly derived from our interest in living well and widespread (though not necessarily universal) commitments.

Second, just as realistic optimism is an ideal that gives a person developing her character something at which to aim, so too cynicism is a negative ideal to be avoided. The cynic I will describe is one negative paradigm to be avoided in the context of a project of character development. The cultivation of good habits of thought is a complex, multifaceted process, and the ideal of realistic optimism and the negative ideal of cynicism are but two points of reference. One should not conclude from the argument below that each person ought to do everything she can to avoid a cynical character. Rather, the conclusion to be drawn is that each person has a reason to avoid cynicism, other things being equal. Each person must weigh these reasons within the overall project of her development as a reflective person. For some people, the risk of becoming cynical might be so small, and the risk of being foolishly naive so great, that it would not make sense for them to concentrate their attention on developing this aspect of their character.

6.2. THE VALUE OF BEING REALISTIC

A person who is realistic has a commitment to facing the facts and believing only what is consistent with them. There is much to be said from a prudential point of view for people who are realistic in this sense. Realistic people will be better prepared to achieve their ends despite setbacks, because they have faced the ways in which their projects or actions might fail. Further, realistic people can make better plans, because the successful implementation of plans depends on facts beyond one's own desires and intentions. If I am planning to see a particular film on Friday, I will make a better plan if I know where this film is playing. No matter how intently I plan, I will not succeed in seeing this film if I base my plan on an out-of-date newspaper listing. Good planning requires us to find out and confront the facts.

The ability to make effective plans is also essential for interpersonal coordination. People who have no commitment to discovering and making decisions on the basis of the facts, but who decide on the basis of private fictions, cannot be counted on to coordinate effectively with others. For example, plans to meet for lunch or dinner depend on both parties having the same beliefs about the location of the agreed-upon meeting place. The simplest way to ensure this convergence is for both parties to believe that the restaurant is where it in fact is.

Being realistic is also an important part of the virtue of self-awareness. The self-aware person knows her values, abilities, talents, interests, and emotional tendencies. In virtue of her self-knowledge, she is better off than the person who is not self-aware, because she is more likely to make decisions that stand up to her own standards and plans that allow her effectively to act on these choices. Being realistic is valuable in more than one way. If cynicism is a vice, then, it must be distinguished from the desirable quality of realism.[3]

6.3. CYNICISM

The vice of cynicism, as I intend it here, consists, first, in the disposition to judge that human beings are bad and therefore worthy of scorn or disdain, and, second, in the disposition to respond to others accordingly. Here I am restricting "cynicism" to cynicism about human nature.[4] One can, of course, be cynical about other things, but I will not argue that other kinds of cynicism

[3] Julia Driver (2001) has persuasively argued that being realistic is not always virtuous. We can agree with Driver's argument and still think that an account of cynicism as a vice must not ignore the many ways in which realism *is* beneficial.

[4] Thomas Hurka (2001) also emphasizes this form of cynicism. He says that "a cynic believes the world and people's lives are less good than they are commonly taken to be and, let us assume, actually are". He then goes on to specify that the usual subject of cynicism is virtue: "[the cynic]

are vicious in the same way.[5] The cynical person (in my sense) is disposed to judge that people are bad because she tends to ignore evidence of goodness in others, to look for the bad and dwell on it, and to interpret evidence so that it supports her negative conclusions. This negative outlook inclines the cynic to make global judgments about human nature and human potential. Her judgment that people are bad is not confined to individual cases. Rather, she tends to see human beings on the whole as bad in ways that matter morally: corrupt to the core, intrinsically selfish, greedy, base, and beyond hope. Of course, there are different uses of the term "cynic", and we do sometimes call people cynics when they do not exhibit all of the qualities I have mentioned here. But because my characterization is meant to describe cynicism as a vice, it may be the extreme version of a variety of types of cynicism that we recognize. Cynics in my sense doubt that human beings have truly good qualities; they attribute ugly ulterior motives to others without much evidence; and they react to other people with scorn and disdain, whether or not they have information about the particular person's character.

In dwelling on the bad and ignoring the good, the cynic is a pessimist. She differs from the pessimist in that the judgments constitutive of her cynicism are accompanied by a scornful or contemptuous affective orientation; the cynical person is disposed to feel scorn, disdain, or contempt toward others, and to ignore, avoid, or disengage from them.[6] Cynicism, then, has both cognitive and conative components: it includes dispositions to assess evidence and form judgments in certain ways, as well as dispositions to adopt certain attitudes. Because of her cognitive dispositions, the cynic judges that human beings, and human nature generally, are bad and worthy of scorn or disdain; here, the content of the cynic's judgments sustains her scornful attitudes toward others.

There are, then, two important differences between realism and the vice of cynicism. First, there is no particular affective orientation that accompanies being realistic; the realistic person's beliefs are not taken by her to be a basis for negative feelings about other people. In the cynical person, on the other

---

claims that people are less virtuous and more prone to vice than in fact they are" (Hurka 2001: 94). For Hurka, the viciousness of cynicism lies in the attitude behind these misperceptions: viz., the hatred of the good. This may well be the correct story about the moral viciousness of cynicism, but to understand cynicism as a reflective vice, we need a different kind of argument.

[5] Notably, one can be cynical about politics without being cynical about human nature generally.

[6] Pessimism may also include an affective orientation, perhaps one of gloom or dejection. My point is that pessimism does not include the same affective orientation as cynicism does.

hand, the pessimistic beliefs are accompanied by contempt toward other people and their perceived failings. She may take her views about human nature to warrant these negative emotions, but the cynic's contempt has a life of its own and can serve to further reinforce her pessimistic beliefs.

Second, the cynic's beliefs about human nature do not necessarily track the truth. The relevant judgments about human nature are judgments about the possibility of change and the grounds for hope given generalizations about all people, past, present, and future. Cynical judgments are negative, condemnatory judgments of this kind. For example, "people are selfish and mean; there's no hope for us", "people are narrow-minded and corrupt and they always will be", and "people are basically stupid". Given the sweeping nature of such judgments, our ignorance about the future, and the possibility of multiple interpretations and explanations of human behavior, the facts about particular people (past and present) are insufficient to determine specific judgments about the possibility of change or the warrant of scorn. When we make such sweeping judgments about human nature, then, our interpretation of the facts is shaped by our attitudes, and the gaps in information are filled by our interpretative analysis. The cynic's tendency to ignore the good and dwell on the bad, and her disposition to scorn others, will lead her to interpret the facts about human behavior in the most negative light and to infer that human nature itself is bad. The cynic's reaction here is different from the realist's, because the cynic's judgments reach beyond what is warranted by the facts.

Given this characterization, we can see that there are several objections to being cynical. We could argue that contempt for others is, prima facie, morally bad on the assumption that it violates a Kantian duty to respect them.[7] We could argue, as Thomas Hurka (2001) does, that cynicism is bad because it is the expression of hatred for good. For our purposes, however, the focus is on the ways in which cynicism may hamper a person's ability to value her ends in a way that will affect her ability to live well. To see how this might be, we need to think about examples of the kinds of ends that people tend to endorse. Let us consider two such ends from our discussion in Chapter 2.

First, in Chapter 2 I made a case for thinking that most people are committed to some moral ends, and would have them as part of their set of reflective values. There I defined moral ends as goals that benefit society

---

[7] Michelle Mason (2003) argues that contempt does not always violate moral imperatives, but her argument would not sanction the cynic's widespread contempt.

at large and that require coordinated human action for their achievement. Such goals are often represented as commitments to moral ideals, values, or principles such as the ideal that we ought to make the world a better place, the value of helpfulness, or the Golden Rule. Certainly, the moral commitments that people have are varied: some are committed to racial equality, some to gun control, some to the lives of fetuses, some to feeding the hungry, and some have less well-defined moral commitments such as the goal of "doing one's part".[8] Whatever the particular end endorsed, these moral commitments are often very important to people. They provide a larger cause with which a person can identify herself, and, as such, they provide a sense of purpose and meaning in life.

The pessimistic judgments about human nature and human motivations that are a component of cynicism affect our endorsement of moral ends, ideals, values, or principles by influencing our beliefs about the effectiveness of our actions in furthering these moral commitments and the ultimate point in maintaining them. Consider a person who is committed to the ideal of better treatment of animals who believes that human nature is hopelessly selfish, mean, and unsympathetic. Although she believes, for example, that there are excellent reasons for discontinuing the practice of factory farming, she has little hope that people will ever be persuaded by these reasons because she thinks that people's interests in profitable farming and in eating meat will determine their outlook on this practice. She is also doubtful that non-rational means of persuasion, which attempt to engage people's sympathies directly, will have any effect on their outlook. She believes that no matter what she does to discourage factory farming or to change people's minds, nothing is likely to change. While such an attitude may not change the judgment she makes about animal treatment, this attitude is likely to prevent her from achieving the motivational stance that is part of endorsing an end. It is hard to be motivated by a commitment to something that you believe is doomed from the outset. There are empirical findings that lend support to the claim that responses to moral commitments are inhibited by pessimism about human nature. According to Martin Seligman (1990: 57–9), pessimism is one of

---

[8] In calling these commitments "moral commitments", I do not mean to imply that they are good or correct. People's moral commitments in the descriptive sense intended here may be incorrect or unjustified. Further, some people's commitments to moral ends (in my sense) are not represented in moral terms. For example, someone might say that she values making a better world for her children and grandchildren.

the main ingredients in depression, and depression itself vitiates trying and inhibits response initiation generally.⁹

A related point is that pessimism may undermine a person's effectiveness in promoting her moral ends. As we learned in the previous chapter, positive illusions make us better able to pursue our ends in a variety of ways. Pessimists have no positive illusions—in fact, they have negative illusions—and, therefore, even if they are motivated, they may not be very good at doing what they are motivated to do. We can see how this too is a reinforcing mechanism. Unsuccessful efforts to pursue an end will reinforce the idea that the end is unattainable, which in turn lends support to beliefs about the cause of this lack of success: namely, for the pessimist and cynic, bad human nature.

Pessimism may even undermine our judgments about the *value* of our ends. A person who is committed to a moral ideal and who believes that human nature is such that this ideal will never become reality has some reason to question the role of this ideal as a goal or moral guide. How can an ideal provide guidance for us if we believe that human beings are constitutionally incapable of approaching it? For the pessimist, moral ends are more like pipe dreams or naive fantasies than like ethical models or long-term objectives. Insofar as judgments about the value or importance of a moral end depends on its having a practical role, coming to see one's end as a naive dream puts pressure on the person to devalue the end. Because morality is a fundamentally practical enterprise, judgments about the value of our ends very often depend on their practical role. We endorse moral ends as goals to be striven for. Therefore, when we believe that these ends cannot function in this way, our judgments about their value and importance may be undermined.

One might think that the negative effects of cynical beliefs are confined to problems with *bringing about* goals or ideal states of affairs. In other words, one might think that the above argument applies only to those with consequentialist moral commitments. But this is not the case. First, commitments to moral values and principles are often tied to commitments to ideals that one hopes will someday be achieved.¹⁰ Ideals give shape and direction to our principles and values. Second, even in the absence of ideals or ends to be brought about, there is reason to think that the emotional aspect of our commitments to moral values and principles will be undermined

---

⁹ On the correlation between pessimism and depression, see Sweeney *et al.* 1986.
¹⁰ Kant's Kingdom of Ends is an example of such an ideal, which cynicism about human nature would make a pipe dream rather than a guiding ideal.

by the belief that human nature is inherently corrupt. This is because the motivations to do good, or to follow a principle of beneficence, are often fragile and in need of support from our beliefs and other commitments. Moral motivations are fragile when they conflict with motivations that seem to be more certain means to more obvious and available sources of satisfaction. The belief that no one else is able to follow the principle that you are following, or that you are the only one promoting the value of helpfulness, could easily undermine a somewhat fragile motivation to act in accordance with your moral commitments. Moreover, the view that human nature is corrupt and hopeless is not easily confined to a view about the character of *other* people. Believing about ourselves that we are constitutionally incapable of having stable and reliable moral motivation undermines our moral commitments by making it seem that there isn't really any point in having these commitments anyway. We will do what our corrupt nature determines, regardless of our commitments to moral values and principles. The spread of cynicism to the self has other harmful effects, which I will discuss below.

So far we have talked about the problems with one component of cynicism: namely, pessimistic beliefs. But cynicism is worse for a person than pessimism by itself, because the scornful or contemptuous attitude that accompanies cynicism has additional deleterious effects on endorsement. Scornful and contemptuous attitudes reinforce pessimistic beliefs and render the pessimism of the cynical person more entrenched. This is because of the affective aspect of scorn and contempt. The visceral response toward others takes on a life of its own: it is taken to confirm the belief that human nature is hopelessly corrupt. Together with pessimistic beliefs about human nature, the visceral nature of scorn and contempt reinforce the cynic's disposition to accept negative interpretations of human behavior, as well as her unwillingness to consider evidence to the contrary. Pessimistic beliefs by themselves might give way to the facts, but the addition of scorn and contempt for others can cause us to turn a blind eye to these disconfirming facts.

We have now discussed the effects of cynicism on our moral ends. Let's turn to a second and equally pervasive example of an end we endorse: close relationships with friends and family. The true cynic seems to be less able to endorse such important relationships because of her cynical perspective on other human beings.[11] Valuable friendships require valuing the friend,

---

[11] Judith Shklar's (1984: 192–225) discussion of misanthropy emphasizes the opposition between friendship and the cynical contempt she takes to characterize the misanthrope.

at least in part, for her own sake. But a person who is suspicious of human motivation, and who thinks that human nature is hopelessly corrupt, is not disposed to value other people for their own sakes. The cynical person regards others as bad and therefore unworthy of being valued for their own sakes. According to a cynical view of human nature, then, other people are not deserving of the kind of commitment that friendship demands.

In addition to disposing the cynic emotionally to judge others harshly, it may be that cynicism also provides the cynic with more evidence for her pessimistic judgments. There is, in the cynical "theory" of human nature, a kind of confirmation bias. The main reason for this is that contempt for others is not easy to hide. Because contempt can be read or felt by others, and because others are likely to respond negatively to it, the cynic is more likely to incur responses from others that confirm her cynicism.[12]

Cynicism, then, influences what reasons the cynic thinks there are for valuing relationships with other people by providing a framework through which she interprets human behavior. Furthermore, the motivational component of endorsement is also hindered by cynicism. The judgment that others are not worthy of one's efforts undermines any motivation one might have had to act in ways consistent with friendship. And contempt for humanity conflicts with motivations (such as love) needed to engage in actions for the sake of others that are required by friendship.

This is not to say that no one who is at all cynical will have friends. Cynicism comes in degrees, and there are surely people who have a great deal of pessimism and contempt for most of humanity but have a few friends they have deemed worthy of their attention. The point is that people with the normal human need for friendship ought to avoid cynicism, other things being equal. For a person engaged in living a reflective life, the goal is to cultivate habits of thought that give her a reasonable expectation of living a life that will bear her own survey. If the argument in this chapter is correct, then avoiding cynicism about human nature and cultivating more optimistic habits of mind is a more sensible strategy than being cynical and hoping to avoid its costs.

Importantly, the disadvantages of cynicism are not confined to people who value the particular ends discussed above. First, as mentioned above, cynicism won't necessarily be confined to a view about others: because cynicism includes pessimistic beliefs about human nature and motivations in general, the cynical

---

[12] I would like to thank Martin Seligman for suggesting this point.

person will either have to engage in some creative self-deception or admit that she too is rotten.[13] Believing that we are unworthy of being valued for our own sake has profound effects on the ability to endorse any ends at all. First, contempt for our own nature and motivations can undermine confidence in our judgments about what ends have value for us. If I believe that my own nature is hopelessly corrupt, I am likely also to believe that I am not a good judge of what really has value. Second, believing that we are bad and unworthy of being valued for our own sakes hinders our ability to endorse our ends by diminishing our enthusiasm for, and our motivation to pursue, our own projects. If I believe that I am rotten (by my own standards), then I am not likely to be motivated to act in accordance with what I value because I will think that my valuing something only expresses my contemptible human nature. In short, cynicism may make it difficult for people to value themselves and, therefore, to endorse their own projects and commitments in general.

Second, we can see that cynicism impairs our rational agency in an even more general way if we think about the affective component of cynicism and the way it functions to reinforce cynicism's influence over judgment. If some of the capacities a rational agent has are the capacities to reflect, decide what to value, and make choices and plans that reflect these values, then contempt for humanity frustrates these capacities by severely limiting the range of options that we will consider and the responses we are likely to have toward the options we do consider. The contempt we find in cynicism is like depression in the way it influences our judgments about what has value: both contempt for humanity and depression severely limit what we find valuable by indiscriminately contaminating a large range of potential objects of choice. Depression does this by dampening all of our positive affective responses. Contempt for humanity accomplishes this feat by increasing our suspicion of any object of choice whose worth seems to us to depend on people, ourselves included, being worthy of our regard.

Further, the sense that people are worthy of our approval is indirectly implicated in the fulfilling pursuit of a great variety of possible ends. As Rawls noted, the enjoyment that human beings take in pursuing their ends increases with the realization of the capacities to achieve these ends and the complexity of the activity itself (1971: 426). For many ends, the process through which the pursuit becomes more complex and demands

---

[13] Thus, the relationship between cynicism and contempt for oneself is similar to the relationship between respect for others and self-respect in Kantian moral theory. On the latter, see Hill 1991.

new or more highly developed capacities of the agent is a process that involves other people. Of course, activities can become more internally complex without other people. Playing a musical instrument, for example, will become more complex and demanding for the musician as she plays more difficult pieces. But the other ways in which complexity is increased do involve others: taking lessons, engaging in competition, subjecting one's performance to criticism, involving oneself in discussion about the music or instrument, and listening to other musicians to obtain new input in the process of becoming better.[14] What's more, these modes of engagement have their counterparts in all sorts of ends we might pursue: sports, art, games, collecting, and so on.

The cynic's general contempt for human beings hinders her ability to take part in and benefit from the social means to developing and pursuing her own ends. Cynicism turns one away from or against the society needed to pursue many ends in a fulfilling way. It therefore competes with one's ability to maintain a positive motivational stance with respect to the ends one values. And this in turn handicaps the capacity for endorsement, which requires the maintenance of a positive motivational stance. Again, as discussed above in the case of friendship, I do not deny that it is possible to be cynical and to endorse important ends. Some cynical people manage to contain their contemptuous attitudes in such a way that certain people are exempt. The relevant question for the project of character development, however, is whether cynicism is a reasonable strategy for people concerned to live well. My point is that the way in which so many other people are implicated in the valuing of so many ends means that cynicism is not a reasonable strategy, in part, because its success depends on circumstances being quite different from what one can reasonably expect.

6.4. REALISTIC OPTIMISM

The above case for thinking of cynicism as a vice depends on the claim that cynicism interferes with an important component of living well: namely, our ability to endorse our ends. There are many ways to avoid being

---

[14] One might also think, following MacIntyre (1985), that successfully engaging in a practice such as music requires accepting the standards that are constitutive of this practice, which are formed and upheld by other people. A person who is contemptuous of people in general may be unable to give these human standards sufficient respect.

cynical: one can avoid just the affective component of cynicism by being merely pessimistic; one can avoid the cognitive and affective components by being realistic or optimistic. But some ways of avoiding cynicism are better than others, and hence more deserving of the status of a virtue. I will argue that the virtue corresponding to the vice of cynicism is a quality I will call *realistic optimism* (though I will not always add the qualifier). Before characterizing the virtue of realistic optimism, it will be helpful to consider some alternative ways of avoiding cynicism and why they do not constitute virtues.

First, consider the pessimist. The pessimist avoids cynicism because she does not have contemptuous attitudes toward others. But there are two problems with pessimism. Insofar as some of the disadvantages of cynicism can be traced to the cognitive content of the cynic's judgments, the pessimist is in the same boat as the cynic. Negative judgments about human beings and human nature generally, even without the cynical affect, can discourage our commitment to ideals, the success of which depends on people being capable of improvement. Moreover, if pessimistic beliefs about human nature are not warranted by the facts, then a reflective person committed to believing the truth ought to eschew pessimism. A further problem with pessimism is that it is reasonable to anticipate that pessimism will devolve into cynicism, thus making it a bad strategy for avoiding the problems with cynicism. Because the pessimist makes negative judgments about human nature and has cognitive dispositions that reinforce these judgments, it will seem to her that she has grounds for condemning human beings. The pessimist will have to make an effort to avoid feeling contemptuous of others, but it is difficult to see what strategy she could use to talk herself out of contempt, given her disposition always to see the bad in people.

Next consider a foolish optimism like that of the Pangloss. The naive or foolish optimist, perhaps less common than the cynic, judges that people are much better than they are and that they are, therefore, always worthy of association and attention. The foolish optimist lacks entirely the willingness to judge people ill, even when they deserve it, or to distinguish between those who are worthy of her attention and those who are not. Foolish optimists are susceptible to being taken advantage of and used by people who are not deserving of their trust. Moreover, they are unlikely to be able to act effectively on their commitments because they have a distorted picture of the obstacles that face them. The foolish optimist does not get the advantages to be gained from a realistic commitment to learning the truth and responding appropriately to it.

The virtue that corresponds to the vice of cynicism cannot abandon realism altogether. Realism requires a commitment to discovering the truth and responding appropriately to it, but this commitment can manifest itself in different ways. Let us first consider a kind of realism we might call conservative realism. The conservative realist aims to believe only what is well established by the facts and to have her attitudes and responses determined and justified by these beliefs. Given the inconclusive evidence about human potential and the insufficient grounds for generalized scorn, the conservative realist will not believe that human nature is hopelessly bad. She will either be agnostic about human nature, or she may have more cautious statistical beliefs about the likelihood that some person will be bad in certain ways, or about the percentage of people who are likely to demonstrate bad qualities in a given population. Further, the conservative realist will not adopt a negative emotional attitude toward human nature generally, since this would not be warranted by her beliefs.

Conservative realism surely has its advantages. The conservative realist will not be easy to take advantage of; nor will she tend toward the contempt of humanity that gets the cynic into trouble. Nevertheless, conservative realism is not ideal. If the conservative realist can keep herself from making judgments about human nature, she will have nothing to take as a basis for a positive affective attitude toward humanity. As the discussion in section 6.3 indicated, in order to endorse certain ends fully, we need to think that these ideals might be realized, and that at least some others are appropriate objects of our attention; it is not enough to refrain from believing that human nature is evil if the negative beliefs are replaced by indifference and detachment. In other words, we need to have hope, where hope is an attitude that goes beyond what is warranted by the facts. Hope, as I intend it here, is a positive attitude that includes an element of judgment—a positive appraisal of human nature, for example. It is not a belief, however, and it explicitly does not require evidence of merit in order to count as fitting its object (though it may be undermined by overwhelming evidence that contradicts its assessment). This is just what hope is: it is a positive attitude that goes beyond what the facts tell us; hope, by its nature, does not require justification in the way that beliefs do. The conservative realist who insists on believing only what is established by the facts and responding to people only in ways that are warranted by these beliefs, will not be hopeful about humanity.

Moreover, agnosticism about human nature is difficult to maintain, especially when we are deliberating about important projects. The very process of reflecting on what to endorse and what reasons we have to adopt some ends rather than others involves us in thinking about whether human nature is such that projects that depend on it are hopeless. It is not that we always have developed and reasoned views about human nature. Our judgments may be vague assumptions that are not well articulated or defended. The point is that it is difficult not to make such assumptions when what is at issue is the reasonableness of our commitment to an ideal. Statistical judgments about how likely it is that human nature is bad given the available evidence (the other option for the conservative realist) also seem difficult to maintain, though for different reasons. Human beings are notoriously bad at ascertaining probabilities and incorporating them into their practical lives in even simple cases (Kahneman *et al.* 1982). It therefore seems naive to think that we would be able to arrive at adequate judgments about how likely it is that human nature is hopeless given our evidence. (At least not without becoming obsessed with this evidence in a way not generally conducive to living wisely.) Further, such statistical judgments would also be susceptible to a kind of confirmation bias: a person who believes that there is a 70 percent chance that the next person she meets will be selfish and greedy is likely to find that people live up to her expectations.

From the Pangloss we learn that the virtue corresponding to cynicism cannot abandon realism. But from the pessimist and the conservative realist we learn that the virtue must include more than a commitment to discover and respond to the facts. The pessimist's negative judgments about human nature will lead to cynicism if unchecked, and, moreover, since the pessimist judges things to be worse than the facts warrant, pessimism is not the way to achieve the advantages of realism. We need to go beyond what the facts strictly warrant in our assumptions about, and our attitudes toward, human nature. The lesson of the cynic is that when we do so, it pays to be positive.

Given these constraints, it seems that the virtue corresponding to the vice of cynicism must be a kind of realistic optimism. We are now in a position to characterize this virtue. The virtuous optimist is committed to discovering and believing the truth. Like the realist, she is *open* to evidence for the goodness of human nature, but she goes beyond the realist in being disposed to look for such evidence and to make generalizations about human potential that are positive. When the optimist makes judgments under uncertainty, as we do when (on the basis of limited knowledge and experience) we generalize about human nature, she judges that human nature does not make people incapable of improvement or deserving of scorn. These judgments go beyond what the realist would believe if the realist believes only what is clearly warranted by the facts. Further, the realistic optimist's attitude toward humanity is neither scornful nor indifferent, but hopeful. She takes human beings to have at least the potential for good, and to be capable of change insofar as we are not good already.

According to the above characterization, the optimistic person has accurate, realistic beliefs about particular people, but has a positive or hopeful view about human nature and human potential. She is not a foolish optimist, because she does not ignore evidence that people are bad; nor does she tend to judge that particular people are good when they are not. She is realistic about particular people, and open to all kinds of evidence about human nature; but she has cognitive and affective dispositions that the conservative realist lacks. Notice that, as was the case with the cynic, the optimist's cognitive and affective dispositions are mutually reinforcing. The hopeful generalizations she makes about human nature encourage her positive attitudes toward human beings, and these positive attitudes in turn increase the likelihood that her generalizations will be hopeful.

The above suggestion that the realistic optimist has a disposition to seek evidence of the good in humanity requires some defense. First, it might seem that such a disposition is unnecessary, since the realist would be open to all kinds of evidence. While this is true, it is important to remember that virtues provide compensations for human limitations and weaknesses (Foot 1978). Because we simply do not have the time to seek out all the available evidence and process it thoroughly, the dispositions we have with respect to what we pay attention to and what we seek out will have a significant effect on our judgments about human nature. Further, our judgments are also shaped by what evidence we dwell on, which facts come to the fore and which ones impress us most as we are reflecting. Sometimes being optimistic is a matter of being able to shift our attention in reflection or change our habit of dwelling on the negative.

Second, one might object that the disposition to seek out support for positive judgments about human nature will bias the realistic optimist in an undesirable way. This disposition, the objection goes, is incompatible with the advantages of realism. But a disposition to seek out positive evidence does not imply a disposition to ignore negative evidence; the realistic optimist would not have the latter. Moreover, the disposition in question is to look for evidence, not to trump up pseudo-evidence in favor of positive judgments.

Therefore, while the optimist's judgments about human nature will be more positive than those of the conservative realist, they will not be wildly different. Finally, there is room for the optimist to be very realistic in circumstances in which accurate beliefs about particular other people are crucial to how things will go for her.

To some, optimism—even the *realistic* optimism defended here—will still seem naive or woefully out of touch with the harsh realities of life. In response to this concern, there are two points that should be emphasized. First, realistic optimism is not incompatible with believing that a number of particular people are very bad indeed, or with believing that improvements will be very slow and arduous. These may be very realistic judgments, and if they are, then the virtuous optimist will accept them. Second, the argument for realistic optimism as a virtue depends on the claim that the facts that we have underdetermine judgments about human potential. In the absence of conclusive evidence, what is the best strategy? The argument here is that if you choose the optimistic strategy, you will be more likely to be satisfied with your life upon reflection. That said, we cannot rule out in principle the possibility of conclusive evidence against the assumptions that optimism requires. Such evidence, if truly overwhelming, would even make hope impossible. If, ultimately, we find that we are in a world in which the belief in human potential for good is overwhelmingly contradicted by the facts, and hope is indeed impossible to maintain, then we would no longer have reasons to be optimistic. Of course, in such a world we would also lose many of our reasons for endorsing and pursuing the moral ideals to which we are currently committed, and life would be quite grim.

A different objection to realistic optimism is that it is a natural disposition, not a skill that can be cultivated and for which we can properly be praised. While it does seem to be true that some people are naturally more optimistic than others, this does not mean that the ideal of realistic optimism cannot help to guide people's deliberation and character formation. We can cultivate optimism by integrating the values that it recommends into our lives, by emulating those who have it, and by cultivating the habit of explaining events in more optimistic ways. Martin Seligman, in his self-help book *Learned Optimism*, suggests techniques from cognitive therapy to develop a more optimistic outlook (1990: 75–91). According to this approach, we should first recognize cynical patterns in ourselves, identify our pessimistic beliefs and cynical attitudes, and acknowledge the consequences that these patterns have in our lives. The next step is to respond to the cynical beliefs and attitudes that we observe in either of two ways: we can distract ourselves when they occur, or we can dispute them. Disputation is a successful technique of cognitive therapy that requires talking yourself out of your harmful beliefs, perhaps at first with the help of a therapist and then eventually on your own. Since cynicism is an attitude that is sustained by disputable beliefs (beliefs that are not warranted by the facts), these techniques ought to work to cultivate a more optimistic outlook in the domain that concerns us here.

Finally, given that the optimist seeks evidence of the good in human nature, another way to encourage optimism is to make an effort to find the good in humanity. We can do this by attending to the beauty in art, music, poetry, sport, or whatever human achievements one thinks express the best of human beings.[15] Or we can think about the lives of particular people who make us more hopeful. Judith Shklar (1984: 225) mentions the example of Montaigne, who warded off misanthropy "by remembering personal friendship and the occasional hero of the moral life".

6.5. THE VALUE OF OPTIMISM

We can now see that the optimist is well suited to endorse various commitments. First, when it comes to commitments to moral or political ideals, the optimist is not likely to see these values as doomed by human weakness from the outset. She is, therefore, more likely than the cynic to see her own contributions to these ideals as having purpose, to judge that these ideals are valuable in virtue of their practical role in her life, and to find it possible to sustain her motivation to pursue them. While her realism might incline her to believe that her moral ideals will not be realized in her lifetime, the optimist differs from the cynic in holding out hope that human beings will continue to make progress toward them.[16] Further, the optimist will not tend to think that human beings are simply incapable of following moral principles or being motivated by moral values in such a way that her own commitment to these principles and values looks either self-deceptive or foolish. The optimist's disposition to seek evidence for the goodness of

---

[15] I thank my colleague Joe Owens for reminding me of this point whenever he stops by my office to chat about politics.
[16] For example, Kant (1988 [1784]) discusses the need for hope in humanity if we are to make progress toward a perfect civic union. I thank Sarah Holtman for bringing this essay to my attention.

human nature and her positive attitude toward it leave her better off than the conservative realist, whose commitment to seeking the truth does not provide any particular support for the value or likely success of her ends.

Second, the optimist is, where the cynic is not, inclined to judge that others are deserving of association, attention, and interest. She is more likely to find deep and satisfying friendships and to endorse relationships with other people as valuable. If the endorsement of valuable ends is required for living well, then an optimistic disposition is valuable, because it facilitates our ability to value important ends such as moral ideals and friendships. We therefore have prima facie reasons to develop the virtue of optimism. Whether any of us has an all-things-considered reason will depend on our particular tendencies and the current state of our character.

Third, the optimist is better off than the cynic in a way that is independent of the particular goals and ideals mentioned above, because her capacity for endorsement has a greater range of use. Whatever ends a person values, she is better off being optimistic, because her capacity for pursuing these ends is not hindered by the cynical view that no human standards are worth striving to follow. Further, the realistic optimist will be more capable of finding ends she deems worthy of her endorsement and pursuit in the first place, because she is not encumbered by the cynical view that nothing that depends on the contributions of others is worth doing.

Finally, we should consider the empirical evidence for the benefits of optimism. Psychologists have shown that optimists have all sorts of advantages in terms of health, happiness, and success in their chosen pursuits (Buchanan and Seligman 1995; Seligman 1990; Snyder 2000). The question we need to ask is whether this research applies to the kind of optimism discussed here, and I think there are grounds for an affirmative answer, though the evidence is not yet conclusive. In a large part of the relevant psychological research, optimism and pessimism are defined in terms of explanatory style. Whereas optimists explain good events by citing permanent, personal, and pervasive features of the situation and bad events by citing temporary, impersonal, non-pervasive features, pessimists do the reverse (Seligman 1990). This definition of pessimism is related to the vice of cynicism as characterized here, because the cynic, on my account, scorns other people for what he takes to be permanent, personal, and pervasive features of human nature. It seems to follow that the cynic would take permanent, personal, and pervasive features of human nature to explain the bad things that human beings do, while the optimist would take such features of human nature to explain

the good things people do. Explanatory styles in this domain—explanations
that invoke positive or negative views about human nature to explain human
behavior generally—have not been studied, and we would certainly need
more evidence before allowing much of the argument to rest on this point.
Nevertheless, given the likely relationship between cynicism (in my sense)
and explanatory style, it seems reasonable to assume that the psychological
evidence about the benefits of optimism and the burdens of pessimism adds
to the case for the virtue of optimism made in this chapter.

The preceding argument that we have prima facie reasons to cultivate
realistic optimism rests on claims about the problems with cynicism and the
advantages of optimism that we can reasonably foresee. Such claims are made
by thinking about what effects it makes sense to expect a virtue or vice to
have when instantiated, given its profile and its relationship to other traits
and dispositions. The crucial claim for the argument that cynicism is a vice
is the claim that, given our imperfect information about the future, cynicism
is not a reasonable strategy for people interested in living well.

I hope to have demonstrated that realistic optimists are better suited than
cynics to engage in the endorsement of important ends and projects that
is vital to human flourishing. Optimism is a virtue, then, because we can
live better as optimists than as cynics. Or, more precisely, an optimist who
also has the other reflective virtues is more likely to live a life that she finds
satisfying on reflection. Cynicism is a vice because it frustrates our attempts to
live well. Optimism is valuable because it facilitates our abilities to find value
in things, to respond appropriately to the value we find, and to maintain the
enthusiasm and motivation needed to act for the sake of these values.

6.6. CONCLUSION

This chapter began with the observation that psychological research has shown
optimism to be beneficial for us in a variety of ways. There are two serious
concerns about deriving normative conclusions from this research. First, optimism can have negative as well as positive effects, and, second, optimism may
not be the kind of trait we can reflectively endorse. Addressing these concerns
requires a careful characterization of optimism that is sensitive to the reasons
we have for developing it and consistent with our other reflective concerns.

In trying to provide such a characterization, it is my hope that I have
also pointed the way to the kind of useful interchange that there might be

between philosophers and psychologists working on the virtues. Philosophers could benefit from discovering whether some of the empirical claims upon which we rely are supported by empirical evidence. For example, it would be interesting to investigate empirically whether cynical people are less likely to volunteer, give money to charity, or help people in other ways, or whether they are less likely to feel good about these activities if they do engage in them. On the other side, philosophers might have suggestions that could be useful to psychologists about the particular shape a virtue must take if it is to be part of a life worth living. From these suggestions, certain research programs might evolve. It would be interesting, for example, to include cynicism about human nature in the group of attitudes that are currently measured.

One of the conclusions we can draw from this chapter is that optimism not only helps us to live lives that are better from our own point of view, but that it also helps us live lives that are better from a moral point of view. This raises a question about the relationship between being a wise person (in the sense we have just explored in this part of the book) and being a moral person. This question is the subject of the next chapter, which begins Part III.

PART III

BEYOND THE FIRST-PERSON POINT OF VIEW

7

Morality and the Reflective Life

In Part II we saw that a person with reflective wisdom will have appropriately stable value commitments, perspective, attentional flexibility, self-awareness, and optimism. This is not necessarily an exhaustive account of reflective wisdom. Depending on a person's particular commitments, personality, and circumstances, there may be other habits of thought that it makes sense for her to develop, given the aim of living a life that will earn her reflective approval. But these are the qualities and habits of mind that it makes sense for most of us to cultivate, given various things that are true about us: that we have a plural set of values that includes life-satisfaction, self-direction, close personal relationships, and moral ends, and that we need to learn from experience how to instantiate these values in our lives in a way that will be satisfying in the long run.

In this third and final part of the book I turn to consider the bearing that this account of how to live wisely has on traditional philosophical questions about morality and normativity. As we have seen, for most of us, living well by our own lights will include commitments to friends and family, as well as to projects or goals that depend on other people in a variety of ways. Living well from our own point of view, then, is not the same as living egoistically or selfishly. Nevertheless, living well is not the same as living morally either, at least not insofar as one thinks that there are moral obligations that derive from something other than a person's personal commitments. Indeed, it seems obvious that morality and prudence (even prudence as broadly conceived as it is by the Reflective Wisdom Account) can pull us in opposite directions despite all the non-selfish commitments mentioned above.[1] Someone with

---

[1] I hesitate to use the word "prudence" to capture the kind of value that is at issue in the Reflective Wisdom Account, because it may connote self-interest in a narrower sense than I intend. Connie Rosati (2006) has suggested the term "personal value" for the broad category that I am concerned with. Since I think that this phrase is also somewhat misleading, I will stick with "prudence" and "prudential values", with the qualification that, on my view, prudential values include all of the commitments (including the moral ones) that the agent takes to be relevant to how successful her life is.

important friendships, for example, may have a moral obligation to forgo benefiting a friend for the sake of preventing harm to a stranger.

Questions about the relationship between prudence and morality are large and complex, but my aims in this chapter are modest. What I will do is articulate the implications of the Reflective Wisdom Account for two important topics. The first has to do with the nature of the gap between prudence and morality. Given my emphasis on not reflecting too much, one might worry that the person who lives wisely (in the sense recommended by the Reflective Wisdom Account) will not be living very well from a moral point of view. On this point, in section 7.1, I will argue that a person who lives well from her own point of view is also well suited for morality. In other words, there is a fair amount of overlap between prudentially good agency (broadly conceived) and morally good agency (conceived familiarly).[2] I do not take it to be a necessary condition for a successful account of how to live well from one's own point of view that it should end up establishing the complete coincidence of morality and prudence; as we will see, the Reflective Wisdom Account does not do this. However, the case for the Reflective Wisdom Account as a compelling normative theory is strengthened by showing that it is not at odds with other perspectives from which we evaluate our lives.

Despite the overlap between prudence and morality, there may be conflicts between moral and non-moral values even from the first-person point of view. The second topic addressed in this chapter is what to do about such conflicts. How to address conflicts between values in general is an important question for a pluralistic account such as this one, but the possibility of conflicts between moral and non-moral values makes the question a pressing one. I will argue that a person's reflective conception of a well-lived life provides an overarching standard that can help to adjudicate conflicts (taking the conflict between moral and non-moral commitments as my example), at least in principle. But the picture is complicated by the fact that, on my view, a reflective conception of a well-lived life does not have enough detail to provide a commensurating standard or super-value. The details of this picture will be explored in section 7.2, and in the third section I explore some possible problems and objections to the account.

---

[2] It is not my aim to define good moral agency here; rather, my point is to show that the reflectively wise person is a decent moral agent in an ordinary and intuitive sense. I take it that the familiar notion of a good moral agent emphasizes other-regarding actions, duties of beneficence, and the like.

7.1. REFLECTIVE VIRTUES AND MORAL AGENCY

Why do people behave badly, morally speaking? At least when such action is partly under a person's control (and not a matter of mental illness or coercion), there seem to be three likely (not mutually exclusive) explanations: (i) bad or insufficiently robust values, (ii) bad deliberation, or (iii) deliberation that has no effect on action. First, a person who has no moral values in the first place, or whose moral values are insufficiently strong, is likely to act badly whenever moral values conflict with something she does care about. Second, a person who has moral values but cannot figure out what actions they demand of her is not likely to act morally when the circumstances are the least bit complicated. Third, and finally, a person who can figure out what morality demands of her and recognize the importance of complying, but who is incapable of following these imperatives, would also be someone who tends to act wrongly whenever the going gets tough. These three explanations of immoral action are separated only artificially; they often go together. Some people reason poorly on the basis of lousy values, and some are led by their lousy values because their deliberation is ineffective (perhaps because absent entirely or perhaps because overwhelmed by selfish interests).

As far as the first problem goes, there are some reasons for thinking that a person with reflective wisdom would take some moral values to be important. First, a person with perspective has the ability and the incentive to appreciate moral values. Such a person cultivates her ability to find value in the world by appreciating the goods that are available rather than letting her emotional landscape be dominated by the negative emotional responses to assaults on some of the things she values. The reflective person I have described is also not loath to contribute to a communal or social good due to cynicism about human nature; nor is she unaware of her own needs for community and friendship.

Furthermore, the capacity for minimal sympathy that is part of perspective inclines its possessor to recognize the interests and concerns of others and acknowledge their similarity to her own. As was suggested in the discussion of Rachel in Chapter 4 (the sister who obsessed about the hole in her dress while children outside her door went hungry), the capacity for sympathy is not easily confined to taking away a reminder of one's own reflective values. Once one appreciates that another person is experiencing a threat to an important value, it is difficult not to have compassion for that person, to want this threat to stop, and to be willing to act for this reason. Sympathetic appreciation of other people's experiences is needed for perspective, because it forces us to see beyond our present concerns and, frequently, causes us to see that our problems are actually quite trivial in comparison to what is at stake in the concerns of others. But once we see that another person has bigger problems, and we are committed to the values at stake in her situation, it is difficult to stop the progression from minimal sympathy to a deeper compassion and appreciation of her plight. This is especially true for those of us—most of us—who care about other people and our relationships with them.

Finally, as Hume emphasized, because we are social creatures, our ability to survey our own lives with approval is very sensitive to the opinions of others. Since others have a keen interest in our having and abiding by a set of moral norms, their approval is more likely when we have certain moral commitments. The approval of others makes a difference to what values we can reflectively endorse, because conflicting opinions, especially from those we trust or want to please, can undermine our confidence in our reasons for valuing what we do.

People who have reflective wisdom are probably more likely to have moral commitments that are sufficiently strong to have a role in their decision making, but the Reflective Wisdom Account does not guarantee this coincidence. As we have seen, a naturalistic account that is responsive to individual differences does not sanction claims about values that we *must* have on pain of irrationality. It is, therefore, not well suited to answer skeptical worries about moral considerations that stem from concerns about people who do not have moral values at all or whose moral values are too weak to have any force in the face of conflict. But this kind of insufficiency of moral commitment does not seem to be the most likely cause of immorality in any case. More common are the other two kinds of cases, about which the Reflective Wisdom Account has more to say.

The two other sources of immoral behavior are problems for those who, like most of us, have moral values but who do not always act appropriately on them. The second problem I mentioned was the inability to figure out what our moral values require of us. Here, we can argue that the reflective agent has some skills and habits that are also necessary for moral deliberation: namely, the ability to reflect and make judgments without being overcome by current concerns. If we take the ideal point of view for moral deliberation to be an impartial point of view, then it is easy to see how a reflective person will be a better moral deliberator. She is capable of considering what is best without having her deliberation determined by her own short-term self-interest. This does not guarantee, of course, that she will be completely impartial, but it does ensure that at least one common source of partiality—namely, short-term self-interest—will be diminished. (Even if we reject the view that the moral point of view is impartial, we can still agree that reflective wisdom is useful for moral deliberation. If the ideal moral point of view is characterized by attachments to particular others, the ability to abstract from our current short-term self-interest is necessary for giving those particular attachments their due.)

The reflective person, then, avoids short-sighted thoughtlessness, which often causes us to improperly weight moral and narrowly self-interested considerations in deliberation. Many ordinary immoral actions result from rash decisions and facile judgments about what is appropriate in the circumstances. To see this, consider that often when people lie, cheat, or break promises, it is because they are narrowly focused on the troublesome spots they are in, and they give no thought to their commitment to treating others well, or even to the long-term consequences for their own interests.

In addition, a reflective person learns about herself and the effects of her actions on others from experience: she allows her own emotional responses and the reactions of others to sink in and inform her self-conception. This is important, because the brunt of our "everyday" bad behavior is borne by loved ones and acquaintances; fortunately, self-awareness can help us avoid the everyday immorality that results from our inattention. For example, attention to experience and the perspectives of others can bring a person to see that her contemptuous treatment of the waiters at a restaurant is embarrassing to her family, or that her condescending attitude toward her adult son humiliates him, or that her lack of help for a sick friend is seen as self-absorbed and uncaring by other friends. Gains in self-awareness, then, can help us see where our own responsibility lies in these failings, and this can spur efforts to change our patterns of behavior in the future.

Finally, the third problem mentioned above had to do with the connection between values and deliberation on the one hand, and action on the other. Here too we can see that a reflective person is better off because she tends to act in accordance with her own judgments about what matters, which likely include her moral judgments. This is so for various reasons. Given that the wise person has the virtue of perspective, her emotions conform to her judgments about what matters, and these appropriate emotions are motives for action. She is aware of her weaknesses and tendencies to fall short of her own standards, which allows her to compensate for them. Given her optimism, she is also prepared to act on her moral ideals, because she does not think that these ideals are doomed by corrupt human nature. Further, such a person is able to make discerning judgments about the relative merits of her values, and she knows when to shift her attention from a personal project to a moral ideal. Since the reflective person tends to act in accordance with her judgments about what really matters, she will be disposed not to sacrifice moral values for the sake of other things she judges to have less value. The reflective person has a vivid sense of the importance of her own moral commitments, and, insofar as these commitments figure prominently in her own set of values, they have more influence on her behavior than they do for the person who is committed to morality but who tends to get carried away by the concerns of the moment.

The argument above is that a reflective person avoids short-sighted thoughtlessness because of the habits of thought and action that she has cultivated, not because she eliminates her selfish interests or transforms into a different, more sensitive person. One of these habits is to reflect on the things that matter to her and to ask what she has learned from experience that is relevant to these values. Being a reflective person helps by drawing our attention to information about how we are treating what matters to us. Reflecting too much, of course, will preempt the very experiences from which we can learn, but good habits of reflection will take account of this fact. The relationship between reflective habits and moral behavior, then, is that reflection can change our beliefs about what is good for us in the long term by revealing the true costs of our bad behavior, thereby tapping into our motives for acting better. Importantly, this way of thinking about how reflective character can make us act better does not rely on cultivating robust dispositions that incline us to act differently in all circumstances. Rather, the idea is that we train ourselves to think in a way that engages motives we already have.

Having reflective wisdom does not guarantee that we will always act morally. However, those with reflective wisdom tend to be free from some common motives for giving insufficient weight to moral duties and good deeds, and they tend to be well suited to engage in the kind of reasoning that is required by morality. Moreover, because of her commitment to appreciating available value and her capacity for minimal sympathy, the person with perspective will be more likely to endorse certain moral values in the first place.

One might object that these prudential virtues do not give us moral reasons at all, but that rather they only give us a reason to develop traits that *happen* to produce moral behavior in people who have moral commitments.[3] To some extent, this is true: having perspective gives us prudential reasons to consider the plight of others, and these reasons are not themselves moral reasons. But as a general condemnation of the argument, it is unfair. Some of the particular reasons we will discover when we take on the project of developing reflective virtues will be reasons to act morally. For example, imagine that Rachel does have some typical moral concerns and that her sister persuades her to get some perspective. One thing she will find herself with reason to do is to reflect on what really matters to her and to pay more attention to it. This in turn might give her a reason to pay more attention to the needs of others. In this case it would be natural to say that Rachel has a reason to act better, morally speaking, by taking others' needs into account, that arises directly from the reason she has to develop the reflective virtues. In other words, prudential reasons lead her to engage in a reflective process, one outcome of which is that she comes to appreciate certain moral reasons. Further, what the reflective person learns about herself and her effect on others gives her moral reasons to behave better, given that she cares about those others. These *are* moral reasons insofar as they are other-directed; she behaves better for their sake, not for her own. While it is true that the reason to develop self-awareness is a prudential reason, this does not mean that every reason we come to have in virtue of developing our self-awareness is also a prudential reason.

Moreover, if it is correct that minimal sympathy is not easily constrained, and that the person who acknowledges the experiences of others will also tend to care about those others, then reflective character can do more than merely produce moral behavior. The reflective virtues, according to this line of argument, are conducive to having commitments to moral ends. These commitments, in turn, provide their own reasons for action. In the case of Rachel, her coming to care about the interests of others would give her reasons to promote their good, and these reasons would not be narrowly self-interested.

---

[3] This objection is due to Michelle Mason.

7.2. WISE DECISIONS AND VALUE CONFLICTS

Despite the happy connections between living morally and living well from one's own point of view, we cannot eliminate the possibility of conflicts between one's moral commitments and one's other value commitments. What does the Reflective Wisdom Account have to say about such conflicts? Before I proceed to answer this question, a few clarifications. First, as we saw in Chapter 2, conflicts between values sometimes indicate that one of the values should be abandoned. In our coherentist account of justification, the fact that the pursuit of one important project is undermined by another, less important one is evidence against the latter. The value commitments we are considering in this chapter are commitments to things that seem to have equal importance, or, at least, things that each have some legitimate claim to be part of one's conception of a good life. Second, such value conflicts are not confined to conflicts between moral and non-moral commitments. I focus on the case of moral versus non-moral values here because of its particular philosophical interest, but what I say in this section should apply to conflicts of all kinds. Third, I think it is interesting and important to discuss these conflicts, and doing so will help to fill out the details of the Reflective Wisdom Account, but this attention should not be taken to imply that this is a particular problem for my account. What to say about conflicts between values is a concern for any normative theory that recognizes plural values.

The problem with conflicts between moral and non-moral values, as many have noticed, is that there does not seem to be a single standard that can be used to assess the relative merits of both kinds of value.[4] Certainly, the Reflective Wisdom Account does not provide a single scale of value upon which we can plot moral and non-moral values; however, it does offer a deliberative perspective from which comparisons can be made. On my view, our reflective conception of how to live gives rough assignments of relative importance to the various values at stake in a particular choice. If we think of a conception of a good life as a kind of painting, then this conception tells us roughly how much "space" each value should occupy on the canvas. As we will see in more detail shortly, our conception of how to live does not give us

---

[4] This conflict is often expressed as a conflict between morality and prudence. Since, as explained above (n. 1), my broad conception of prudence includes moral commitments, it would be confusing for me to put it this way.

all the details we need to make a decision. Instead, reasons to choose one way rather than another in a particular decision context derive from the values at stake. To return to the painting metaphor, the reflective conception of how to live tells us roughly how much space each value will occupy, but *how* the space is occupied—scattered throughout the painting, all in one blob, colored blue or purple, and so on—will depend on the values in question.

This answer to the problem combines insights from two different approaches to value conflict in the literature, which Ruth Chang (1997) calls the *procedural approach* and the *covering value approach*. In the former, moral and prudential values are "put together", in Chang's terms, by a procedure such that the responses of an agent following the procedure perfectly determine the resolution of the conflict. In the latter, Chang's own approach, we choose rationally between moral and prudential values by referring to a more comprehensive value that includes both. According to Chang,

for any given conflict between particular moral and prudential values, there is some more comprehensive value—what I elsewhere call a "covering value"—that includes the conflicting values as "parts" and is that in virtue of which the conflict is rationally resolved if it is rationally resolvable. (2004: 119)[5]

The reflective conception of a good life that the Reflective Wisdom Account presupposes is a covering value, in Chang's sense, although it is one that is arrived at by a reflective process. Now a process (as I intend the term) is not a procedure; a process is not necessarily defined in value-neutral terms and does not necessarily lead to a single determinate outcome. Still, there is an insight from procedural accounts that informs my solution to the problem of conflicting values. To see the benefit of putting insights from these two accounts together, we need to see why they don't easily stand alone.

First, procedural accounts of normative concepts, in general, are notoriously subject to counterexamples.[6] For example, consider a procedural account according to which the good is the object of a fully informed desire. The advantage of such an account for our current purposes would be that a procedure that produces a single outcome answers the question of how to weight moral and non-moral values in decision making. The procedure is the method by which to weigh them, and, according to this account, their weights *just are* what is determined by the appropriate procedure. The problem is

---

[5] Note that Chang is not making the much stronger claim that there is *one* comprehensive value that can adjudicate every conflict.
[6] I discuss these in Ch. 2 n. 20.

that we have no guarantee that the addition of information will change our desires in ways that comply with the norms we accept.[7] This is, in fact, an instance of a general problem with attempts to reduce normative notions to non-normative ones: normativity gets lost in the translation. In Chang's words, such accounts fail because "neutral procedures for sanitizing desires will not yield the 'oughtness' of normativity" (2004: 122).

Chang's covering value approach does not attempt to reduce a normative notion to a non-normative one; however, it is unclear what kind of explanation it can offer for the respective weights of moral and non-moral values. As Elinor Mason (2006) puts it:

How does the covering value determine the relative weightings of the constituent values? One possibility is that it does it by pure stipulation—as a martini just is a certain proportion of gin and vermouth. However, stipulation does not have the right sort of explanatory power.

Chang claims that we know things about the structure of the covering value for morality and prudence. We know, for instance, that saving a child from drowning in a pond is more important than protecting our fancy new suede shoes from water damage. But what is the explanation of this fact? Why does saving children occupy more space than protecting shoes? Mason is right that stipulation won't do the job, because stipulation also undermines the normative force of the covering value (unless there were a "stipulator" whose decisions carry automatic normative weight). It seems, then, that the question about how rationally to assess the relative importance of two apparently different kinds of value simply reappears.

Procedural accounts resolve conflicts between morality and prudence by defining the relative importance of the values in terms of the importance they would have after applying an appropriate procedure. The complaint about this approach was that a procedure described without reference to norms does not guarantee a normative outcome. The covering value approach seems more promising because conflicts between moral and non-moral values are decided with reference to a *value* that has normative force already. However, this promise depends on its being able to provide a normatively compelling account of the content of the covering value, which includes an explanation of the relative importance of moral and non-moral values.

The answer to the question about conflicting values that is suggested by the Reflective Wisdom Account brings together aspects of these two

---

[7] For my diagnosis of the problem see Tiberius 1997.

approaches in the following way. It posits a covering value—namely, the value of a life lived well according to one's own standards—and it holds that the conception of a good life (in this sense) is arrived at through a reflective process. The process we use to construct our conception of a good life is the reflective process that was the topic of Part II; it is not a *procedure* that can be articulated without reference to norms. When we reflect on our values and their relative importance, our reflection is shaped by the reflective habits we have developed (the reflective virtues), by the stable commitments we have (not all of which we can scrutinize at once), and by what we have learned from our experience of living with these commitments. The wise person's reflective habits, together with her conception of a good life, determine what considerations are salient in particular circumstances. Then, when she is confronted with the need to make a decision between conflicting commitments, she decides by paying attention to the particular values that are salient within her current practical perspective.

To reiterate, the Reflective Wisdom Account holds that we can make rational choices between moral and non-moral values in virtue of a three-stage process. First, we develop a reflective conception of a good life, by thinking wisely and at an appropriate time. Second, our conception of how to live and our reflective habits set the constraints for our choice; these constraints delimit which considerations count as reasons for us to choose one way rather than another. This step does not involve explicit deliberation; nevertheless, it is not arbitrary, because it is the consequence of having appropriate reflective habits. Third, within these constraints, we appeal to the values themselves as a source of reasons for choice. In what follows I will illustrate some of the details of this picture with an example.[8]

The initial process of reflection on a conception of a good life is not a "neutral procedure" for improving our desires, because we cannot engage in the process appropriately, or assess whether someone has done so, without employing norms. Whether a person's reflective conception of how to live is appropriate will depend on whether that person's emotions and actions are *proportional* to her value commitments and whether she has allowed herself to be *suitably* absorbed by experiences that are relevant to her values. Appropriate reflection requires thinking about what kind of information might undermine our value commitments and judging whether this outcome

[8] My view is structurally similar to Ruth Chang's (2004) view that there are two conceptions of choice. Chang distinguishes between the decision about what choice situation we are in from the decision within that choice situation.

would be legitimate or not, given our other commitments. For example, imagine that you are considering what role the value of donating a portion of your income to charity should play in your conception of a good life. You know about yourself that vivid reflection on a new set of speakers, or an expensive new jacket, would cause you to have an overwhelmingly strong desire to keep your money to spend on yourself. You also know that getting these things wouldn't be all that you imagine in terms of your long-term happiness, and that you really do care about helping those less fortunate than you. The process recommended by the Reflective Wisdom Account would have you not think much about the new speakers or jacket. Whether you have reflected well on the matter can be ascertained only by employing evaluative standards about the appropriateness of vivid reflection on various facts. Contrast this with a "full information" procedure, which requires vivid reflection on all the facts. One might hope that vivid reflection on the joys of new speakers and on the children who will eat only if you donate your money to charity would result in a desire to give the money to the children and forgo the speakers. But I see no reason to think that this is necessarily how things will go. Absent my own judgments about how it is *best* to react, I might just be more moved by dwelling on speakers than I am by dwelling on the problems of strangers.

For most of us, our conception of a good life tells us to make room for moral obligations of charity *and* for the projects that give us satisfaction and enjoyment. But the conception of a good life does not tell us exactly how much room to give to each. A conception of a good life that answered this question would be far too detailed. The problem with such a detailed plan for how to live, as we saw in Chapter 3, is that in order to follow it, we would have to consult it so frequently that we would be engaged in reflection all the time. There would be no room for experience to influence and shape our conception of how to live. Further, a conception of a good life that determined exactly how each of our values ought to be manifested in our choices and how to respond to each conflict between value commitments would be extremely difficult to devise. Again, this kind of vast undertaking would have us reflecting far too much and would interfere with our actually *living* good lives as opposed to just thinking about them.

If our conception of a good life does not tell us how much weight to give to our various commitments, how do we make rational or non-arbitrary decisions about particular matters such as how much of our income to give to charity, or whether to give to this organization or that one? The reasons we have for giving this or that amount, or to this or that group, come from the value commitments that are relevant to the decision we are trying to make and the constraints that have been established by our conception of a good life. The value of charity makes the needs of others salient, but given the constraints imposed by a conception of the good life that also includes other commitments, the reasons we have to give almost everything we have to charity are, for most of us, off the table.[9] For most of us, our pluralistic conception of how to live makes salient reasons of compromise and accommodation. One set of considerations of this kind are reasons of fairness: what amount of money is such that, if everyone were to give their share, poverty and hunger would be eliminated? Fairness is a reason here, because it has some independent moral weight, and because it moves us toward a solution that is compatible with the conception of a good life that most of us have.[10]

One advantage of the Reflective Wisdom Account's three-stage process is that it avoids problems with extremes. A rigid, deterministic covering value that allows us to commensurate values on a single scale, or one that appeals to a single principle or plan, seems not to do justice to the nature of the values at stake. On the other hand, a covering value that does not give us any guidance undermines the possibility of rational choice. The Reflective Wisdom Account offers a solution that is between these extremes. Further, it contains an explanation of the normative authority of the covering value (the reflective conception of a good life): this conception is normative insofar as it is arrived at via the reflective process of a wise person.

Another advantage of the three-stage view is that it seems to be true to the phenomenology of what we often do when confronted with such questions. Consider an example from a *New York Times* reporter contemplating what he ought to do in the face of the extreme poverty he confronted as a journalist covering Africa:

My own code is simple: I never give people money in advance of an interview, even when the person is clearly in need. I argue that the value of educating the world about their problems is reason enough to talk. When I am personally moved by an

---

[9] This statement may strike some readers as reprehensible. Remember, though, that the Reflective Wisdom Account is not a moral theory. The question I am trying to answer here is not "What is the right thing to do?" but "How can we choose rationally between the various value commitments we have?" I take up further concerns about this position in the next section.

[10] For an approach to the problem of the demandingness of morality that takes fairness as the crucial moral reason, see Murphy 2000.

individual's situation, I sometimes offer help after completing an interview, and tell myself that I cannot also help all his neighbors and friends without impoverishing myself. Those rules are no panacea. They don't even answer many of the questions raised here. But better to light one candle, so to speak. That said, it can be haunting to realize that it is in fact usually just one candle, and usually in places where bonfires are needed. (Wines 2006)

This reporter's views about the morality of helping the impoverished people he interviews are complicated. He thinks one ought to do something, but he's not sure how much. He recognizes that more needs to be done, and also that he cannot be the one to do everything that needs to be done. It is also important to him to uphold the norms of his profession and not to jeopardize his credentials as a journalist. When he is in the field, forced to decide whether to give someone money, buy a child some candy, or pay for a sick person's medications, he follows a code which does some justice both to his moral values and to the value he places on his journalistic career; he compromises. We might say that his code determines what considerations count as reasons in a particular situation for him. And the content of the code is shaped by his conception of how to live, which tells him to make room for both values, in some way.

7.3. SOME PROBLEMS: DISCRETION, COMPLACENCY, AND INTRACTABLE CONFLICTS

Despite its advantages, the Reflective Wisdom Account's solution seems to have its own problems that arise because of the apparent indeterminacy in the account of wise choice. The fact that the conception of a good life constrains, but does not determine, which considerations count as reasons might be thought to leave too much discretion in our choices. One might think that we are left with a degree of discretion in fulfilling our moral commitments that is foreign to our moral practice and our intuitions about living well.

To answer this worry, we need to see that absolute commitments are compatible with the Reflective Wisdom Account. A reflective conception of a good life is not deterministic, but this does not mean that all of our commitments allow for discretion. Given the role of commitments, standards, and ideals in a person's conception of a good life, there is a natural way to understand the ones that always guide our action, no matter what particular perspective we occupy. Our ideals give us direction and a basis for a sense of achievement and satisfaction. But not every ideal provides a goal that can be worked towards intermittently; not every standard is one that admits of degrees of fulfillment. There are some ideals we have, in other words, that we just cannot see ourselves as upholding unless we meet certain minimal standards in all of our actions. For example, many moral commitments function in such a way that to violate them is to jeopardize our identity as a morally decent person and our self-conception as someone who has moral ideals at all.[11]

This reply depends on people having some absolute moral commitments that shape the conception of a good life in the first place. A related worry arises when we think about people whose moral commitments are weak. Since the conception of a good life determines what considerations count as reasons, it might seem that a person without stringent moral commitments from the outset could have no reason to improve. In fact, this objection could take a more general form: If which considerations count as reasons is determined at the first stage of the three-stage process described in the previous section, then there won't be grounds for criticizing, improving, or acquiring new reasons at the final stage. And this in turn implies that when we are deciding what particular choice to make, we will have no grounds for considering that morality (or some other particular project or value) ought to occupy more (or less) space in our conception of a good life. This might be thought problematic, because it is often when we are making specific choices that we have the motivation to reconsider our commitments in this way.

This objection has things partly right. The fact that our conception of a good life constrains which reasons we consider in making specific choices will prevent a certain amount of reflection on our commitments. But this is as it must be if we are going to make decisions and take action without being paralyzed by reflective rumination. It is precisely because active reflection can compete with living that the Reflective Wisdom Account highlights the importance of stable commitments that we are not always poised to reconsider and the ability to shift between reflection and other engaged perspectives. Indeed, we can think of the three-stage process I have described in terms of

---

[11] David Velleman's philosophy of action provides support for the view I develop here. He argues that people are motivated to act in ways that make sense to them given their conceptions of themselves and their other beliefs. Moral motivation is often a matter of being motivated to act in accordance with an idealistic self-conception. According to this theory, "a person refrains from stealing because he cannot assimilate stealing into his self-conception" (Velleman 2000: 226). See also Velleman 2002*b* and Tiberius 2005*a*.

perspective shifts. The perspective from which we decide on our conception of a good life and the place for moral and self-interested values is the reflective perspective discussed in Chapter 3. The perspective from which we make a particular choice, such as a choice about how much of our income to give to charity, or, even more specifically, whether to give more to a particular charity, is a perspective from which certain values are salient and taken for granted, while other considerations are not on the table.

Thinking of the process of negotiating choices between moral and prudential values in terms of perspective shifts reminds us that we do not yet have the whole story. Though it is true that making a specific choice does not invite reconsideration of all our commitments, it is also true, as we noted earlier, that perspectives are not entirely isolated from each other. This means that as we think about the reasons involved in making a particular choice, we may become aware of reasons for modifying the value commitments that we are taking as starting points.[12] We need to be able to forestall a complete reflective overhaul of our values in order to decide and act. But, compatibly with this goal, we can plan to reflect on the matter later when we have the time to give it attention. Reasons for moral improvement, or for shifting the balance of our value commitments, are certainly relevant considerations from the reflective point of view.

These replies to the appearance of too much discretion raise another problem: If particular value commitments can themselves be rigidly demanding, and if reasons for moral improvement can be found within one's conception of a good life, how can we be sure that it will always be possible to fit our various commitments into a single conception of how to live? For example, if a person begins to develop very demanding moral standards, then it would seem that morality will begin to take up more space in her conception of a good life. If this happens without other commitments diminishing in importance, then the resulting conception of a good life will contain competing goals that cannot be mutually secured. Moral commitments that are both extremely demanding and overriding would seem to crowd out other pursuits from one's conception of a good life in such a way that all choice situations

---

[12] Again, Velleman's philosophy of action is in agreement. According to Velleman (2002*b*: 322), motives that are not part of the agent's current story (in my terms, the motives that are not most salient in the current perspective) "are nevertheless present", and "they have two chances to prevent him from getting carried away". These motives can constrain the agent's actions from the outside without being explicitly acknowledged. Or, if this kind of unreflective restraint fails, these motives can obtrude on the agent's attention so that he "comes to think of himself, under the circumstances, as having more than one end at stake" (Velleman 2002*b*: 322).

would be ones where moral considerations are the overwhelmingly relevant reasons. How can we put very demanding moral commitments together with other values in a single conception of how to live? The answer is that we might not be able to; there is a real possibility of some *intractable* conflicts between values. What does this mean for the Reflective Wisdom Account? Is the possibility of intractable conflicts an objection to a view such as this, which requires a conception of a good life that includes all our values? If not, what should we say about these conflicts? Can we live good lives while acknowledging permanent conflict among our ideals, or must conflicts always be eliminated?

To give some detail to the sketch of this supposed conflict, consider Utilitarian arguments for our duties to alleviate global poverty and hunger. Utilitarians are famous for arguing that our ordinary commitments to helping others and preventing tragedy, as seen in cases of children drowning in ponds, lead to extreme demands upon those of us who live in relative affluence (Singer 1972; Unger 1996). Just as we are morally obligated to save the drowning child despite some cost to ourselves, so too we are obligated to save children who are suffering or dying from poverty, hunger, and preventable disease. While there are variations on this theme, and while some versions of the argument allow more attention to one's own personal projects than others, on any Utilitarian view the demands of morality are much higher than the demands that most of us actually meet.[13] Moreover, philosophers have recently begun to argue that it is not just Utilitarianism that forces this uncomfortable conclusion on us: contractualism, virtue ethics, and other theories may have similar implications.[14] Moral ideals such as these come into conflict with even modest personal commitments to careers, friends, and hobbies. A dinner party for friends, a new garden tool, or a family vacation do not seem like justified uses of resources when those resources could be used to cure deadly illnesses, or provide uncontaminated drinking water for people who need it.

Can a Utilitarian (or anyone who is impressed by the arguments that we ought to do much more than we do) have an integrated conception of a good life for her that does justice to her moral commitments as well as to the value of her personal projects and relationships? Again, it is not clear that

---

[13] Singer (1972) distinguishes a weak and a strong version of his principle, but either principle demands much more of us than most of us actually do.

[14] Elizabeth Ashford (2003) persuasively argues that Scanlon's (1998) contractualism is as demanding as Utilitarianism. Garrett Cullity (1994) makes a similar case about virtue ethics.

she can. The right thing to say here might be, as Elizabeth Ashford does, that integrity (a harmonious conception of a good life for us) is not possible in our current circumstances.[15] Certainly, this possibility is unfortunate, because a conception of a good life that contains incompatible goals cannot support a complete endorsement of one's life. If my conception of how to live requires doing everything I can to prevent extreme suffering *and* paying special attention to my friends and family, then I will never be in a position to reflect on my life and assess that I am meeting all of my own standards, or even coming close to it. But it is not clear that the possibility of intractable conflict is an objection to the Reflective Wisdom Account. After all, it may be that it is just not possible in our current circumstances to live a life we can endorse wholeheartedly and in every respect. This is not so hard to accept. The Reflective Wisdom Account is committed to the claim that it would be better for us if we could wholeheartedly endorse our lives in this way, not that it is possible for us to do so now.

It would be different if the conflicts were in principle intractable. If it were the case that moral commitments are necessarily so all consuming that we cannot pursue other projects compatibly with fulfilling them, no matter what the world is like, then we would have a case of in principle intractability. If this were the case, the good life for a person according to the Reflective Wisdom Account would be necessarily unachievable, which seems wrong, or at least highly counterintuitive. But there is little reason to suppose that this is the case, even for Utilitarian moral commitments, as Ashford (1997) convincingly argues. If we lived in a world in which poverty, hunger, and disease were problems of the past, Mill's (1979 [1861]: 17–19) view that we would all do best at promoting utility by focusing on ourselves and the people nearest us would probably be correct.

Granting that the possibility of intractable conflicts is not an objection to thinking that a good life would be one we can endorse on reflection, we might still ask whether we ought to eliminate conflicts where we can. Does the Reflective Wisdom Account imply that it is always better for us to eliminate conflicts? Certainly, there are reasons to eliminate conflicts. For instance, we cannot wholeheartedly endorse how our lives are going if we have mutually unachievable goals. Further, as we saw in Chapter 2, conflicting value commitments would constitute some evidence against each other in our

---

[15] Ashford (1997) argues that the current circumstances of those of us who enjoy relative affluence with respect to the global poor undermine our capacity to achieve integrity.

reflection on our values. Given these reasons, in cases in which conflicts can be eliminated by changing the commitments we have in ways that do justice to the values at stake, this can be a sensible thing to do. For example, if you want to be a gourmet chef and you are an ethical vegetarian, you may modify your personal goal so that it is compatible with your value commitments by aiming to bring gourmet skills to vegetarian food.[16]

Getting rid of conflicting value commitments in order to secure a better life for oneself, where the changes do not do justice to the values at stake, is a different matter. Sometimes, of course, this is exactly what we should do. We can't pursue every project that holds some interest for us; we can't have unlimited commitments, and so we have to "prune". But in cases such as the one we have been discussing, pruning may mean too much of a sacrifice. In order for the Utilitarian sympathizer to rid herself of the conflict between morality and prudence, she would either have to radically alter her understanding of what morality requires or abandon all of her non-utility-maximizing personal projects. The former tack would likely seem arbitrary even from her own point of view, and therefore not a strategy that would itself survive reflection. The latter tack is unlikely to increase her chances of living a life that is good for her: eliminating conflict only eliminates one source of misery, after all. The other option, I have suggested, is to live with the conflict, recognizing that one's conception of a good life cannot be fully realized in the world as it unfortunately happens to be.

The Reflective Wisdom Account, then, does not require that we eliminate all conflicts among our value commitments. Although value conflicts do generally impede our ability to live well, removing every such impediment may not be the best overall strategy for living as best we can. When such conflicts arise—as they will for a person whose moral commitments are strongly Utilitarian but who will not abandon her personal projects—making a rational decision between moral and prudential values will be difficult. Because this person's conception of a good life does not constrain how much

---

[16] It may also be possible to modify your ethical commitment, though this seems the more complicated route. For example, you could decide that the commitment to vegetarianism is to bringing about certain consequences in the long term, and you might think that there are many things one can do to promote this goal while cooking meat for a living. Part of the story here might be that before you can really influence the culinary scene in positive ways, you must establish yourself as a chef, and this may require cooking some meat. The food critic for the *Star Tribune*, Jeremy Iggers, reported having such an attitude toward his career and ethical commitments, as I discovered during our mutual participation on a panel on Consumer Choices and Food at the University of Minnesota, 1 Mar. 2005.

space moral projects will take up, it will not constrain what considerations are relevant in a choice situation in which morality and prudence seem to conflict. This seems to be an implication of the claim that such a person cannot fully realize her conception of a good life: decisions between moral and prudential values will have to be made somewhat arbitrarily. One strategy that a person with an intractable conflict of value commitments might adopt is to limit arbitrarily the space that moral commitments occupy and to proceed as if her conception of a good life were one that placed limits on when to consider moral considerations as reasons. We could see this as a strategy for coping with an imperfect world.

The Reflective Wisdom Account implies that, for most of us, in cases of conflict between moral and prudential values, our conception of a good life constrains which considerations we ought to take into account. We then decide what to do on the basis of the values that are at stake in the conflict, against the background of the overarching goal of finding a place for all of our value commitments. Importantly, this is not to say that the value of a good life for a person overrides moral values; there is no single scale of value on which to rank them.[17] Rather, the Reflective Wisdom Account gives us a way of conceiving of a wise, non-arbitrary choice between values where there is no single scale of value. For people whose commitments create intractable conflicts, my account concedes that there may not be a resolution that makes things better for that person.

7.4. CONCLUSION

Living well, on my account, will coincide to a significant extent with living a morally decent life. This is so because most of us have moral commitments, some of which are absolute, and because the habits of reflection that the wise person has will prepare her to act on these moral commitments. Even with substantial overlap between a reflective and a moral life, conflicts among our plural values are inevitable. Where there are conflicts, the best we can do is to weigh the values at stake with the habits of wise reflection in the background.

---

[17] For this reason I do not think that the possibility of intractable conflicts constitutes an argument against Utilitarian moral commitments, as some seem to think. The covering value, on my account, is used to make wise decisions, but this does not mean that it subsumes other values such that they have value only in virtue of their contribution to the good life for a person. See Stocker 1976 and Williams 1973 for a critique of Utilitarianism along these lines.

Sometimes, it won't be possible to adjudicate conflicts in a way that puts everything together neatly, and in such cases we must choose to hone our conception of the good life or to live with some conflict.

It seems to me that these implications are attractive. The view that the world is such that certain packages of commitments cannot be achieved together is realistic; in fact, the alternative seems naive. The idea that a life in which one must find coping mechanisms for conflicts might be better than a life in which one eliminates conflict altogether also shows an appropriate respect for the complexity that people's patterns of commitments tend to have.

8

Normativity and Ethical Theory

Living well requires developing helpful habits of thought, sometimes reflecting on our conception of a good life, and developing a set of values that are appropriate for us. Having reflective values is not sufficient, however; we need also to *act* in accordance with these commitments, and to get positive emotional feedback from doing so. I have suggested that in the context of a life of reflection *and* action, reflection on our values and choices does not undermine those values. Stable commitments, supported by experience and their respective roles in a conception of a good life, will not be undermined by appropriate reflection on the reasons for having them.

There is another kind of reflection, however, which does seem more threatening. This is a kind of philosophical reflection that seeks an ultimate foundation for our value commitments and the reasons we take ourselves to have for them, where we do not take for granted the value of anything. The Reflective Wisdom Account might seem vulnerable to this kind of reflection, because it does not supply an inherently normative foundation for the authority or legitimate force of the reasons we have to change our habits of thought or act on our values.

Psychologists who write self-help books chock full of reason-giving prescriptions avoid this problem by assuming that they are simply informing people of the means to the ends they have already. "If you want to be happier, count your blessings"; "If you want to be more satisfied with your life, spend time with your friends"; and so on. The self-help prescriptions assume that there is a worthwhile goal, which their advice helps you realize. This is one option for the Reflective Wisdom Account: assume that the end of living a life that survives your own reflective survey is a worthwhile one, and point out that the prescriptive claims are instrumental to this end. This is not an unattractive option. As I said in the Introduction, the only reasonable strategy for living a good life is to try to lead a life that lives up to the standards that you think are the right ones. You might take your judgments about the right standards to track something with an objective foundation, but your own commitments are where you must start. On this way of seeing it, the Reflective Wisdom Account is meta-ethically neutral. The recommendations to develop appropriate habits of reflection and pursue your reflective values are practical strategies for living that are compatible with a variety of meta-ethical views about the foundations of our values, and it is these views that answer to the kind of deep philosophical reflection mentioned above.

While it is true that the Reflective Wisdom Account can be neutral about the ultimate source of normativity, it is also true that it fits particularly well with a naturalistic, Humean meta-ethical theory according to which the ultimate foundation for norms is our commitments and passions.[1] So, the other option for the Reflective Wisdom Account is to embrace the meta-ethics that it most naturally suggests and answer the charge of arbitrariness directly. This is what I will do in this chapter, in part because this exploration will help to display the Humean account of normativity (which I think has independent plausibility) to its greatest advantage. The meta-ethics suggested by the Reflective Wisdom Account locates the source of normativity for its prescriptive claims in the stable network of commitments of a reflective agent who has a concern to live a life she can endorse. When we engage in reflection on our commitments, some of them must be taken for granted in order to reflect critically on others (though, of course, not necessarily the same ones all the time). In particular, the underlying commitment to living a life that meets our reflective standards is always taken for granted and cannot itself be justified. On this picture, then, our reasons for pursuing the things we value and for living up to our standards ultimately derive from our concern to live well and from other particular commitments we have. I have not assumed any imperatives of nature or rationality that provide an ultimate foundation for the reasons and values that make up the reflective life.

Taking a step back now, we may have some concerns about the tenability of this picture in the face of deep philosophical reflection, because we might think that an awareness of the source of normativity that the picture implies would undercut our normative commitments. In other words, we might think that my account of how to live well is, ultimately, self-effacing: a person who believes it to be true would not be able to take herself to have reasons for upholding the various standards she endorses. This sort of criticism is similar to criticisms of expressivist meta-ethical theories, according to which

---

[1] See Introduction for more discussion of naturalism.

the ultimate authority of norms derives from our commitments, attitudes, or desires.[2] The fundamental worry about such meta-ethical theories is that motivational states (desires, passions, commitments, and the like) are not well suited to play an essential role in an account of normativity because they are always, in the end, arbitrary. Russ Shafer-Landau (2003: 29) puts the problem this way: arbitrariness "is problematic because it infects all justificatory efforts. If our evaluative attitudes rely for their justification on attitudes which themselves lack justification, then the whole network is corrupt." Along these lines, one might worry that the commitments that are essential to living wisely will not be sustained if the reflective agent realizes that these commitments are ultimately arbitrary.

The defense of my account against this challenge has two stages, presented in section 8.1.[3] First, I isolate the place where arbitrariness might be thought to enter. On my view, the most natural thing to say about the source of normativity is that it is ultimately our desire to live well that gives us a reason to develop the reflective virtues, which in turn make us into the kind of people who take some of our commitments to be genuinely justified and normative. The real concern about this account is that the particular desire to live a good human life on which I am relying is itself arbitrary. The second stage of the argument aims to show that this desire to live well is not arbitrary in a sense that gives rise to serious objections.

Though the values and reasons in the Reflective Wisdom Account are not arbitrary, it is true that they are contingent in various ways. It might be argued that this contingency undermines their normative authority, even once we have eliminated the worry about arbitrariness. In section 8.2 I argue that the fact that the reasons we have to develop reflective virtues and act for the sake of our values are contingent does not provide any independent cause for concern about their normative status.

The contingency of normative reasons also gives rise to a concern about the legitimacy of normative theory in a naturalistic framework. In this framework, where there are no ethical facts woven through the fabric of the universe, or rational principles with independent authority, one begins to worry that there is no legitimate role for the philosopher in telling us what reasons we have. The philosopher, on this view, can tell us what kinds of things reasons *are*, psychologically or conceptually. But what we actually have reason to do is not

---

[2] The best examples of such theories are found in Gibbard 1990, 2003, and Blackburn 1998.
[3] James Lenman (1999) makes an analogous argument against the view that moral imperatives must be categorical.

a legitimate philosophical topic: either it follows simply from what we want, or there's no fact of the matter, or it is far too relative to the individual for there to be anything interesting to say. I think that this picture oversimplifies matters. In contrast to this circumscribed vision of philosophy's domain, I argue in section 8.3 that there is an important role for philosophers in the business of telling us what reasons we have, even within a naturalistic framework.

8.1. ARBITRARINESS AND THE DESIRE TO LIVE WELL

According to the Reflective Wisdom Account, the desire to live a life that can bear our own reflective survey is, ultimately, the source of normativity. I will explain this claim in more detail below, but for now I want to consider what it means for the individual deliberator. Consider the psychology of the reflective person. First, the reflective person is disposed not to reconsider her commitments indiscriminately, and when she does engage in critical consideration of their merits, she has a rich set of commitments, attitudes, and experiences upon which to draw. Because of her willingness to learn from experience and her ability to modify her actions in response to what she has learned, her set of commitments, attitudes, and experiences will be (to some degree) tried and tested. Moreover, because the reflective person does engage in deep reflection on the justification of her values when appropriate, she will know that the background she has to draw on in deliberation is (more or less) reliable.

Second, because of these features of her psychology, the person who has developed the reflective virtues does not see her commitments as arbitrary. For a person with the reflective virtues, the justification of a particular commitment takes place within her larger network of values and proceeds by locating that commitment within this network. The justificatory end point for particular commitments is the set of reasons we have for endorsing them. The reflective person has reasons for valuing friendship, for example, and her reasons will likely be multiple: some will have to do with her own happiness; some may have to do with the social nature of human beings; some may have to do with the role of friendship in pursuing other goals; and some may have to do with features of friendship that appear good for their own sakes (conversation, sharing, or love itself). Moreover, if these reasons are arrived at through a process of reflection of which she approves, then she will have no reason to doubt their credibility. She will trust her experience and past deliberation enough to have confidence in the results of her reflection on the justification of her current commitments.

The above account describes an agent who has fully developed the reflective virtues. Notice that even those of us whose reflective capacities are not well developed (that is, most of us) will have the relevant features to some degree. While the reflection of those of us with only some reflective wisdom may not be ideal, and our patterns of commitments, experiences, and attitudes therefore not quite as trustworthy, we will have some sense of the reasons for our important projects. Moreover, insofar as we are trying to live reflective lives, we will be concerned to deepen our stable value commitments, improve our reasons, and learn more from experience. This project of developing wisdom is at odds with taking our value commitments to be arbitrary. And certainly, we wouldn't have this project without a desire or concern to live a life that can bear our own reflective survey.

The concern to live a life that goes well according to its own standards, then, is in one sense the source of normativity. But it is important here to distinguish between the source of normativity and the justification of particular values and commitments. To say that the ultimate source of normativity is the concern to live well is not to say that our particular values are valuable only as means to this end, or that the concern to live well constitutes our ultimate reason for having these values. For the reasons to be a reflective valuing agent are different from the reasons for having particular values or commitments.

One way to make this distinction clear is by analogy to epistemic rationality. Like reflective agents, truth-seeking agents have certain kinds of commitments and accept certain kinds of norms. Questions about the justification of particular beliefs are answered by the reasons peculiar to those beliefs. For example, one reason to believe that it is raining in London is that the Weather Channel reports that it is. When a truth-seeking agent stands back from her beliefs, norms, and epistemic practices and asks why she ought to be such an agent in the first place, she is asking a very different kind of question. In answer, we may offer some prudential reasons for being a truth-seeker: people who form beliefs with the constitutive goal of truth are more likely to get what they want and avoid harm. The practical payoff of being a truth-seeker is no part of the reason for believing that it is raining in London, but it may partly explain the normative authority of a particular epistemic practice.[4]

Similarly, the idea that being a reflective agent is necessary for living well from our own point of view is the source of normative authority for the practice of practical deliberation. It is so in the sense that if we were creatures without the concern to live well from our own point of view, we would have no use for this kind of reflection with its constitutive norms and virtues. Nevertheless, creatures who are reflective in the relevant sense do not take this fact to be the reason that they have for valuing what they value. Just as it would not be in keeping with norms of truth seeking to believe that it is raining in London because it is in my interest to do so, so too an agent who took her interest in living a good life to be the reason for her valuing friendship would not be reflective in the right way.

The analogy between the practical and the epistemic case goes some way to alleviating concerns about the Reflective Wisdom Account being self-effacing or undermining, because it deflates the objection that our values are *directly* based on an arbitrary desire. Still, the objection has not disappeared entirely. If the desire to live well from our own point of view is itself arbitrary, then doubts about the normative moorings of the account reappear.

In contrast to the Humean view according to which normativity derives ultimately from human desires, passions, and commitments, the Kantian view is that normativity derives from our rational nature. The Categorical Imperative is the law of a rational will, and it is its constitutive connection with reason that gives the law normative authority.[5] As Korsgaard (1996: 103–4) puts it, "The reflective structure of consciousness requires that you identify yourself with some law or principle which will govern your choices. It requires you to be a law to yourself. And that is the source of normativity." For Korsgaard, the "reflective structure of consciousness" is that which explains and makes sense of the normative enterprise of justifying to ourselves and looking for reasons.

I will argue that, in a similar way, the reflective concern to live well from one's own point of view can be the source of normativity without raising the worry about arbitrariness. To defend this claim, it will be helpful first to see why Korsgaard's explanation of the source of normativity is not arbitrary in any troublesome way. I take the answer to be that we can have no reason to

---

[4] Or it may not. My point here is just to use the analogy to make the distinction in the case of values easier to see.

[5] See, e.g., Korsgaard 1996: 98.

reject the law that governs our reflective consciousness. Since the Categorical Imperative just *is* the law that constitutes rationality—in fact, it has no other content at this stage in Korsgaard's argument—there can be no reason to question the law. To question the law of a rational will would be akin to asking what truth-conducive reason there might be to aim at true beliefs. The law of a rational will is constitutive of practical reasoning in such a way that it makes no sense to ask for practical reasons to follow it.

The desire to live well from our own point of view does not enjoy quite this status, but there is an important sense in which it too is not arbitrary. While it may be true that we are not rationally required to have the desire to live well from our own point of view, it is still a desire we have in virtue of our rational or reflective nature.[6] For reflective creatures like us, the concern for reflective success—the concern to approve of how our lives are going on the basis of standards we take to be justified—shapes the desire to live well from our own point of view. In this way, the desire to live well is an essential part of being a reflective person. Furthermore, it is essentially through our reflective capacities that we become capable of finding normativity in the world. As I argued in Chapter 2, part of what it is to take a commitment to be normative is to have a sense that the commitment is justified, and this requires some ability to reflect on what is good about it and how it is supported by other commitments we have. We distinguish values from mere desires because we are able to reflect on the reasons we have for our various positive affective responses, to think about how our future experiences are likely to affect them, and to conceive of our identity in terms of certain ends, but not others. We would not see the world in normative terms if we did not have these reflective habits and skills.

But, one might ask, why be like this? Why see the world in these terms at all? When we begin asking such questions, we are no longer looking for reasons for valuing friendship or pleasure or anything else in particular; rather, we are questioning the whole normative enterprise at once. Questioning the whole normative enterprise at once amounts to looking for a justification for being the kind of person who takes things to be reasons, has stable commitments, and sees things in normative terms. But what kind of answer could there be to this question other than "This is how we are"? Any other answer—say, "Being reflective will make you happy"—must presuppose the

---

[6] I use the term "rational" here because Korsgaard does. But this term does have strong Kantian connotations. I therefore prefer the term "reflective" to indicate the aspect of a person that engages in deliberation, reasoning, and conscious evaluation.

reason-giving force of the considerations it invokes. We ought to be reflective because we are creatures who want to find our lives to be worth living. Ultimately, the desire to live well from our own point of view is the reason to be the kind of person who takes certain considerations to be reasons, maintains stable commitments to valuable ends, and reflects on how these commitments contribute to our conception of a good life. There is no deeper answer, but there is also no need for one.[7]

The view I am defending is in agreement with Korsgaard's claim that our rational or reflective nature is the source of normativity. But, according to what we might call *Humean* constructivism, instead of rational nature being guided by a law, it is guided by our value commitments and the reflective virtues. I submit that this difference does not make a crucial difference to the problem of arbitrariness. From the outside, the desire to live well from a person's own point of view is not arbitrary, because it is part of what it is to be a reflective creature.[8] This desire to live well, in turn, justifies developing reflective wisdom in a way that will make reflective success more likely.

Of course, one can also wonder about the desire to live a reflective life from the inside—that is, from the perspective of a particular person thinking about how to live her life. From this perspective there are resources for responding directly to doubt. The development of reflective wisdom makes sense because we have a concern to live well from our own point of view; living well, in other words, is the ultimate ground of being a virtuously reflective agent. But once we are on the path of becoming a reflective agent, we already have some stable value commitments, habits of reflection, and patterns of action and emotional response. We are, in other words, already committed in the way that a reflective agent is. Given this, when we ask what reasons there are to be a reflective agent, we cannot abandon all our views about what considerations count as reasons. These views are an integral part of the point of view from which we ask for reasons.

If we cannot abandon our normative commitments when we ask what reason we have to be reflective agents, then these commitments can be part

---

[7] As Jimmy Lenman (unpublished MS 2007: 11) puts it in his defense of Humean constructivism in moral theory, "What gives the whole [normative] landscape its shape is indeed just us, just humanity in all our stark contingency. But that surely need not be thought of as a bleak or a despairing view. From the standpoint of humanity, so inescapably our own, humanity is not so bad."

[8] I do not want to go so far as to say that a person who lacks the desire to live well from her own point of view is irrational. She is lacking a kind of rationality that the Reflective Wisdom Account takes for granted, but she would certainly not be entirely lacking in rational capacities.

of the answer. The fact that we have stable commitments to life-satisfaction, friendship, enjoyment, achievement, and so on, and that we take these commitments to give us good reasons for acting, means that a good life for us already has a certain shape. By the time we get to asking whether there is any good reason to be reflective in the first place, we are already committed to living a reflective life, and the particular commitments that constitute this good life count as reasons for continuing to pursue it.

To summarize, the desire to live well from our own point of view gives us reasons to develop the reflective virtues. Developing the reflective virtues consists (in part) in developing our normative capacities, and once we have these capacities, we do not find all of our own commitments and desires to be arbitrary. In particular, from the inside, the fact that our desire to live well is the ultimate source of normativity does not give us any reason to give up the normative enterprise. Further, the desire to live well is not arbitrary in an interesting sense even from the outside, because this desire is the *sine qua non* of rational deliberation about how to live. The fact that a person has developed as a reflective agent in a way that allows her to live well from her own point of view is what makes her capable of engaging normative questions about what it makes sense to want or to do in the first place. From the outside, this makes the desire to live well, if not compulsory, at least rationally unimpeachable.

8.2. CONTINGENCY

I have defended a naturalistic account of the source of normativity that highlights the importance of our reflective capacities. On this view, there are reasons and values (rather than merely desires) because we are reflective creatures who commit ourselves to the development of our capacities to reflect, justify, and value. The development of these capacities is not compulsory; nor is our reflective practice guided by anything that might be called a law. Given this, one might be concerned that despite the additional attention to our rational capacities, the account seems to include too much contingency to be satisfying. The Reflective Wisdom Account of living well is contingent in several respects. The normativity or reason-giving force of any of our value commitments ultimately derives from a contingent concern to live a certain kind of life. The justification of particular reflective values is based on contingent facts about the kinds of commitments and concerns we tend to have. And the reasons we have to develop reflective virtues are likewise dependent on these contingent claims about our values and other features of our psychology.

These contingencies weaken any claims to universal or necessary reasons that the Reflective Wisdom Account might have had. This would be a serious problem if it is indeed a normative theory's job to provide such reasons. I do not think that this is the role of normative theory, but I do see why some might find this disappointing. To dispel the aura of disappointment, we must first be clear about what the implications of contingency really are; only then can we see clearly the advantages and disadvantages of the account. In my view, the advantages of Humean ethical theory—a normative theory that embraces naturalism by admitting contingency and taking our psychology seriously—have not been sufficiently well explored. One reason for this is that Humeans have tended to be more interested in meta-ethical theories than in first-order normative theories, and this has meant that there are few good examples of Humean normative theories to demonstrate their attractions.[9] With an example in hand, we can better appreciate that a normative theory that is compatible with Humean naturalism is not merely a consolation prize.

According to the Reflective Wisdom Account, the reasons we have for developing virtues are contingent, and this is one area where the worries about contingency arise. For example, as we saw in Chapter 6, the reasons we have to develop optimism and shun cynicism are prima facie and conditional. The reasons are prima facie because they can be overridden by other demands on the development of our character. They are contingent on our being a certain kind of person: namely, the kind of person whose commitments include friendships and moral ideals and who has a concern to live well by upholding and pursuing her values and goals. People who are concerned with nothing more than getting what they want from day to day, who do not care at all about anyone else or for anything larger than themselves, may not have reasons to develop this virtue.[10] Our reasons for developing self-awareness are similarly contingent on our having long-term projects and a concern to find our lives satisfying.

---

[9] Notable exceptions are Jimmy Lenman's recent defense of Humean constructivism (unpublished MS 2007 and 2007) and Annette Baier's work (1991 and 1994).

[10] I say "may not" because if it is true that an optimistic disposition makes people happier (and there does seem to be some evidence for this), then even a short-sighted egoist will have some reason to develop a certain kind of optimism.

When it comes to the reasons for acting morally that derive from the Reflective Wisdom Account of living well, contingency might seem all the more problematic. On this account, our moral projects and commitments are a typical but contingent part of our human nature. People who have no such commitments have no reasons to act morally from their own point of view. As we saw in Chapter 7, morality and a good life from one's own point of view may overlap significantly for most people, but this congruence does nothing to show that everyone necessarily has a reason to be moral, or even that all rational or reflective beings have such a reason. Considering this conclusion, one might think that if a Humean normative theory can provide reasons only of this sort, then so much the worse for the Humean approach. This reaction is unfortunate, however, for it may be that conditional reasons of this sort are the only kind of reasons there are in ethical theory. If this is so, then Humeanism provides a viable alternative to the Kantian paradigm of universal, unconditional moral reasons.

One of the main reasons for thinking that Humeanism is not a viable alternative is that contingent reasons of the kind available to the Humean are thought to be merely motivating reasons, without any normative force. Here we must be careful to distinguish contingency from arbitrariness. If the problem is really that reasons on the Humean view are too arbitrary to be authoritative, then this is the problem we tackled in the previous section. I have argued that the reasons we have according to the Reflective Wisdom Account, although contingent, are not arbitrary. Insofar as arbitrariness is what is thought to undermine their authority, the claim to authority that Humean reasons have remains unharmed.

What we need to consider is whether contingency itself undermines normative authority. To isolate a case in which we have contingent reasons that are non-arbitrary, imagine the simple case of an instrumental reason. Consider a person who has a reason to take an umbrella on a trip to England. This reason is certainly contingent on many features of the agent and her situation: for example, her desire to stay dry, her lack of other means of keeping dry, and the likelihood of rain in England. Does the contingency of the reason to take the umbrella undermine its authority? It seems natural to say that it does not, as long as the person does indeed want to stay dry, and so on. We might go on to consider the fact that her desire to stay dry is arbitrary (why not be cool and wet?), which again turns the objection into an objection about the arbitrariness of desire. As I have argued, though, the desire to live well from one's own point of view is not arbitrary in a relevant sense, and this means that reasons that can trace their authority back to this desire are not subject to the objection.

Contingency by itself, then, does not undermine authority. The objection to reasons that are contingent seems to have to do with our convictions that there are overriding and universally binding reasons, such as the reasons we have to be moral. Here it is important to point out that the Reflective Wisdom Account does not preclude us from criticizing others on moral grounds that they do not endorse, or from claiming that others have moral reasons that they fail to see. The moral commitments that are part of the conception of a good life from one's own point of view can provide the grounds for moral criticism of others who do not share them. Moreover, as we saw in Chapter 7, we can make sense of overriding reasons on the Reflective Wisdom Account. Such reasons will be sustained by commitments or ideals that cannot be upheld in a partial way if we are going to continue to identify with them.

Furthermore, the Humean alternative has attractive features of its own. The nature of the reasons we are discussing is clear and comprehensible: reasons to develop virtue and shun vice derive from our interest in living well. (This is not to say that these reasons are all instrumental; insofar as a virtue is *constitutive* of living well, the reasons to develop it would not be instrumental.) The fact that we are, for the most part, motivated to act on reasons is also naturally explained. Moral reasons motivate us, when they do, because of our own commitments to others and to bettering the world. Paying attention to the kind of life that is good from the point of view of most reflective people allows us to see reasons for acting morally that we may not have seen before. Finally, the account of the authority of the reasons we have in virtue of our concern to live good lives renders normativity comprehensible within a naturalistic picture of the world.

8.3. THE PAINTER AND THE ANATOMIST

If the argument above is successful, there is no reason to think that normativity and Humean naturalism are incompatible. This fact, however, does not entirely clear the way for normative theory. The Reflective Wisdom Account relies on generalizations about human nature that may or may not be true of particular individuals; it does not defend universal principles or find reasons that are reasons for anyone. Aside from the worries about the normative authority of such contingent reasons, values, and principles, some might be concerned that there is no legitimate role for philosophical argument or theory in the context of a substantive engagement with these normative claims.

We can put the problem this way: if there are no universal principles to articulate and defend, then all we are doing in normative theory is exhorting people to virtue—and exhortation is not philosophy. When Hume, at the end of the *Treatise*, sings the praises of virtue by pointing out its many advantages, he stops and adds:

> But I forbear insisting on this subject. Such reflexions require a work a-part, very different from the genius of the present. The anatomist ought never to emulate the painter: nor in his accurate dissections and portraitures of the smaller parts of the human body, pretend to give his figures any graceful and engaging attitude or expression. (1978 [1739–40]: 620–1)

Philosophers can describe human nature, analyze language and concepts, and point out the implications of commitments that people already have. But exhortation and persuasion, one might think, are best left to preachers and advice columnists.

Two questions arise from reflecting on Hume's metaphor. First, to what extent is normative theory really analogous to painting? In other words, to what extent does a normative theory that is in keeping with Humean naturalism count as exhortation or persuasion? Second, insofar as normative theory does count as exhortation, is there really no role for philosophers in this task?

On the first question, we would do well to notice that there is much more to normative theorizing than exhortation. Taking the Reflective Wisdom Account as our example, we can see that much of the work of a normative theory is in describing what we are like and in drawing out the implications of our commitments. If the empirical claims discussed in Chapter 2 are correct, then most people will recognize the values of satisfaction, friendship, and the like as their own. A normative theory that reflects our real concerns in its description of us is really like a set of directions for reaching a goal that people already have rather than a piece of persuasive rhetoric that aims to exhort people to a goal they find alien.

Moreover, the set of directions produced by a philosophical theory is of a particular kind; normative theories are not self-help manuals. A normative theory of this kind tells us what reasons we have to do certain things, given our various commitments; its directions are designed to warrant our reflective approval. In this way, philosophical advice is different from the advice given by many psychologists. It is the business of philosophy to articulate a goal that we have good reason to think is worth pursuing. Psychologists, on the other hand, make assumptions about the goals we want to achieve, but they usually aim to be neutral about the ultimate value of these goals.[11]

Granted, not everyone will immediately recognize themselves in the description that the Reflective Wisdom Account offers. Yet, by portraying the reflective person and the reflective life in an attractive light, some who do not immediately recognize themselves may come to appreciate the ideal and see how it relates to their own aspirations. There may be some persuasion involved in a normative theory like this one, which leads us to our second question: Is there no legitimate role for philosophy in exhortation or persuasion?

To see that there is, it will be helpful to shift to a different analogy. Instead of an anatomist, consider the bird illustrator Roger Tory Peterson. Peterson's illustrations of birds for bird-identification books revolutionized the genre of nature guides, because they combined a specialized knowledge of bird anatomy and habitat with artistic skill and vision. Although Peterson's illustrations are not as precise as photographs, many bird-watchers find it easier to use his guides because he emphasizes features that are key to a correct identification. In this example the anatomist and the painter are combined, and what results is something better than either alone for a particular purpose. If we think of the philosopher as analogous to the nature illustrator, then we can allow that the persuasive aspect of normative theory is not illegitimate. What counts as a good description is relative to the purposes of the description. A normative theory is meant to guide people's thinking about how to live their lives, and this purpose may best be served by a description that makes certain ways of living seem appealing.

Of course, if exhortation implies coercion by non-rational means, then philosophical theories are not compatible with exhortation. What is compatible with philosophical theory is appealing to people's commitments and the reasons they take themselves to have in order to make a certain kind of life attractive to them. The persuasive dimension of description in this sense is not in tension with the standards that govern philosophical analysis and argument, because a description of an ideal that makes it appealing need

---

[11] Of course, their advice is often useful because the goals they assume—life-satisfaction and health, for example—are ones that *are* worth pursuing. But this does not undermine the point that there are important questions that philosophy can answer that psychology cannot.

not be an inaccurate description. The persuasive description may emphasize certain features rather than others, but one does not necessarily misrepresent something by drawing people's attention to one aspect of it. For example, my discussion of the virtue of perspective emphasized the way in which we tend to make ourselves unhappy by dwelling on trivial problems. This is not the only way in which one can fail to have perspective, but it is one which, in our current social context, may be the most useful in helping us to identify perspective as an ideal we ourselves endorse.

8.4. CONCLUSION

In Korsgaard's version of the objection to Humeanism, the problem with desire-based accounts of normativity is that there is nothing to stop the reflective regress. When we begin to ask what reason we have to perform some action, we need to find an answer that does not give rise to another "Why do that?" On the Kantian view, desires do not provide the right kind of stopping point for this regress of why-questions; we need laws or rational principles for that. The answer to the challenge put forward in this chapter is complex. First, it is misleading to call the kind of Humean account I have defended a desire-based account. The desire to live well from our own point of view is crucial, this is true; but this desire cannot really be understood without invoking our concern to live in accordance with reasonable standards, a concern that seems to be equally a part of our reflective nature.

Second, I have argued that the reflective regress can go only so far, given what it means to be a reflective agent. A reflective agent is the kind of person who is concerned to act for reasons and who takes some considerations but not others to be good reasons for acting. Moreover, a reflective agent takes up perspectives that are defined by particular values, perspectives that are not compatible with a totalizing normative skepticism. Could you, as a reflective agent now, abandon this way of being? Yes. Do you have reason to? Well, you might: If a madman offers you the choice between abandoning your rational faculties and his destroying the world, it may make sense to take the former option, given your commitments. But in ordinary cases, you have no such reason, and the commitments you do have give you ample reason to continue to try to live a reflective life. From within the reflective point of view, then, there are many reasons for many different things, but no reason to abandon reflection and the hope of living well by your own lights.

I have also argued that normative theory is compatible with Humean naturalism. Even with all the contingency that a Humean naturalist must accept, a normative theory of how to live wisely has a real contribution to make. The philosopher can point out rational connections between the various components of our lives in such a way that we can recognize the goal of living wisely as a good one for us and appreciate what we must do to attain it. For the Humean, I have suggested, the role of the philosopher in constructing normative theory is analogous to that of the nature illustrator: the anatomist and painter combined. I have argued that this way of seeing philosophy's role opens the door for philosophical advice and counsel. This role for philosophy certainly has a long history, but it is a role that has been under something of a cloud in recent times.[12] It is my hope that understanding how this role is compatible with a thoroughgoing naturalism will help to lift this cloud.

Another important implication of the metaphor is that moral philosophers may benefit from paying more attention to anatomy—or perhaps to anatomy of a different kind—than we are accustomed to doing. As empirical research in the psychology of happiness, well-being, virtue, and strengths of character develops, it is likely to inform naturalistic philosophy in interesting ways.[13] I hope that this book has illuminated some of these possibilities and paved the way for even better and more inspiring illustrations of the good life.

---

[12] For the ancient idea of philosophy as therapy, see Nussbaum 1994 and Annas 1993. My evidence that this role has been the object of some suspicion recently is mostly anecdotal. For example, many philosophers I know reacted with scorn and raised eyebrows to the news that some philosophers are now offering "philosophical therapy".

[13] An excellent example of the way in which positive psychology is beginning to influence philosophical work on happiness and well-being is Dan Haybron's book, *The Pursuit of Unhappiness* (forthcoming).

9

Conclusion

The question "How should I live?" demands an answer that is satisfying from the first-person point of view. According to the Reflective Wisdom Account, we live well when we have a point of view that will ground positive assessments of our choices and actions. Whether we will be able to make a positive assessment depends partly on luck and external circumstances, but partly on us. The primary aim of this book has been to explore the contribution to living well made by us, by articulating the nature of reflective wisdom.

One of the things that wisdom requires is having stable value commitments and a conception of a good life that situates these commitments with respect to each other. I have made certain assumptions about the value commitments we tend to have that are described in very general terms (for example, a commitment to "friendship"). An individual person trying to live a reflective life will have to give particular content to these generally described commitments. People typically do not value "social relationships"; they value particular relationships with particular other people. We do not value "moral ends"; we value particular causes, goals, or ideals. To live well, one has to have some stable value commitments, and these values will, in all likelihood, be specific values that no theory can anticipate. The theory can give direction about how to reflect on our values, but it cannot do the work of figuring out what in particular we ought to value and commit ourselves to.

Wisdom also includes cultivating habits of thought that allow us to live a good life by our own lights. People who have no perspective are likely to focus on the wrong things when they ask how well their lives are going. People who have no commitment to seeing themselves and the world accurately, or who pay no attention to the results of their experiences, are likely to make choices that don't work. Those with an exaggerated sense of the importance of believing only the truth about themselves and other people are likely to find many reasons to be dissatisfied with their relationships and the progress on their personal projects. Those who do not develop an appropriate habit of reflection on their lives may reflect so much that they undermine the very activities that make life worthwhile, or they may reflect so little that when they do wonder how their lives are going, they have no resources for coming to a convincing conclusion. The project of character development as I have described it, then, is one of changing our habits of thought to overcome the disruptive, distracting, and unhealthy patterns that we tend to have.[1]

The second, meta-ethical aim of the book has been to show by example how Humean naturalists, who are committed to the empirical contingency of any normative theory, can nevertheless construct a genuinely normative theory. One of my strategies here has been to insist on taking the first-person point of view as the starting point for inquiry. From the first-person point of view, I have argued, empirical contingency does not undermine the action-guiding authority of the norms and values we reflectively endorse.

A theory of how to live that takes seriously the person's own point of view must be a theory that recommends "from the inside" rather than imposing external imperatives. The Reflective Wisdom Account does this in four ways. First, it begins with an assumption about goals that belong to anyone who is interested in the normative question of how to live. The shared target of living a life that can bear one's reflective survey provides a ground for the normative claims of the theory that would be part of the practical reasoning of any person who has an interest in living well. Second, it makes generalizations about values that are open-textured enough for a wide variety of people to identify with them. Third, its recommendations about character and the cultivation of habits of thought are based, in part, on empirical evidence about what most people are like and what are their shared goals and value commitments. Finally, the Reflective Wisdom Account does not prescribe a particular balance of commitments or a particular program of character development. It leaves many of the details of what will count as a good life open to individual creation and discovery.

Another strategy for meeting the meta-ethical aim of the book has been to show how empirical research might be relevant to the construction of a naturalistic normative theory without making a direct inference from how

---

[1] Of course, the particular shape of the project will also depend on the person. Since people have these bad patterns to varying degrees, there will be individual variation in what kind of changes make sense. For example, a person who is severely critical of herself and others may need to attend much more to developing habits that promote perspective and optimism than she does to cultivating habits of self-awareness.

things are to how they ought to be. Such direct inferences fail to capture normativity in any interesting sense; so Humeans who want to develop normative theories must articulate a more subtle relationship between *is* and *ought*. According to the Reflective Wisdom Account, this relationship is mediated by an agent who has reflective interests, capacities, and virtues.

I have given two examples of the ways in which empirical research is relevant to normative theorizing about how to live. First, facts about what we value, how we are emotionally disposed, and what projects we take to be important measures of how well our lives are going, are an important basis for generalizations that ground specific recommendations about how to live. Second, facts about our capacity to acquire self-knowledge, and the consequences of pursuing knowledge about ourselves and the world, are relevant to what counts as good character. In neither example is it the case that the empirical facts are the foundation for normative claims. The fact that people claim to value something on a survey does not by itself establish what counts as a reflective value; rather, such facts must be considered in the light of reflective norms. Similarly, the fact that positive illusions have good consequences does not by itself establish a norm against an uncompromising commitment to the truth. We must think about the implications of positive illusions for our other commitments as we reflect on the reason for our commitment to truth.

Deciding what to make of empirical findings, then, is a normative matter. When we (individual people to whom the account applies) are making decisions about how to live our own lives, the facts that we might learn from reading some psychology will be helpful, but they will not eliminate the need for reflection. Similarly, when we (philosophers) are making decisions about what normative claims to include in our theories, we need to consider the empirical facts reflectively.

The Reflective Wisdom Account is a theory that aims to give guidance to people who are concerned about how to live their own lives. We might now wonder whether this theory gives us any guidance when we are concerned about the lives of others. This is the question I raised in the Introduction, but which I have not yet addressed: What light does an answer to the first-personal question of how to live shed on third-personal questions about what it is for a human life to be a good one? This is a big question, and not one that can be answered in the short space that remains; but I think it will be helpful to say a few things that will indicate directions for further inquiry.

The crucial shift here is from thinking about one's own life to thinking about the lives of others, lives that one cannot control from the inside. Since one of our primary interests in thinking about how other people's lives are going concerns how to help them, let us focus on the question of how to *improve* the lives of others. As a first pass, there is an obvious way in which the Reflective Wisdom Account bears on our concerns about other people's lives. It assumes that living a life we can endorse on reflection is a good thing. This assumption could have been shown to be unwarranted, had it turned out that reflective lives bear little resemblance to what we ordinarily think of as good lives. But this has not been the case: reflective lives, in the relevant sense, are (for most people) lives that do resemble good lives from other evaluative points of view. We might say, then, that being able reflectively to approve of how your life is going is a necessary condition of its going well. In further support of this claim, think about its intuitive appeal. A person who achieves all sorts of things that we on the outside think are valuable, but who does not care about achieving any of them, and does not see anything he does as making his life worthwhile, would seem to be missing something important. In fact, this phenomenon is one of the marks of serious depression.

The claim that reflective endorsement is one necessary feature of a good life for a person gives us one way in which the Reflective Wisdom Account is relevant to improving lives. Of course, we can't make other people live their lives well; we can't make them be reflective, become wise, self-aware, and so on. But we can help ensure that people have the preconditions that are necessary for living their own lives well. Much of what is required here will line up with the recommendations of many other accounts of well-being, prudential value, or flourishing. To be able to be reflective about our own lives and values, to make good choices and to act on them, we need to be free of urgent material needs that crowd out all other concerns. In short, according to the Reflective Wisdom Account, providing people with the means to live reflective lives on their own is a good thing to do.

Given that the Reflective Wisdom Account includes a target, a reflective ideal that we can achieve more or less well, we can say more. The target is a life lived in accordance with our reflective values; it is not a life that *seems* good to us. The latter could perhaps be achieved by brainwashing or drugs, whereas the former can be achieved only by developing good habits of reflection, learning from experience, and making good choices. Moreover, living in accordance with our reflective values (as opposed to just thinking that we are) requires that some things in the world go our way. There are conditions of life that are beyond our control, so that whether we live our lives in accordance with our reflective values is not entirely a matter of how we've chosen to live. The Reflective Wisdom Account presumes, therefore, that some success is necessary for reaching the target. This reveals another way in which the Reflective Wisdom Account is relevant to improving others' lives. There may be things we can do (as part of a political agenda) to help people achieve their values that go beyond providing the basic preconditions for their own reflection. Such actions would include increasing opportunities for the development of certain widely shared and important values such as community and social interaction, giving people information that would improve their reflection, and organizing society so that predictable value conflicts are minimized.

We are reflective creatures who want to live well and to be able to judge that our lives are going well. These concerns are normative concerns that carry with them the assumption that there are ways of being better or worse, ways of getting things right or wrong. To try to get things right or better, we need to have a point of view from which to assess how they are. And to have such a point of view is to have a set of reflective values and a conception of a good life for us. We are not merely reflective creatures, of course, and our reflective capacities are not always in tune with our emotions and experiences. This means that we cannot develop an appropriate point of view by the pure power of thought. Nor can we live our lives well without allowing our emotions and experiences to influence our reflection, choices, and actions.

I have argued that living a reflective life means developing certain habits of thought and pursuing things we care about. Living reflectively, in this sense, will not give us the kind of complete rational control over our lives that we may once have envisioned. But living a reflective life along the lines suggested in this book does engage the part of us that seeks control. The Reflective Wisdom Account proposes balancing thinking and feeling, reflection and passion, leading one's life and living one's life. There are no step-by-step instructions for getting this balance right, and, in fact, no picture of exactly what such a life would look like. To live life wisely is to engage in the process of figuring it out.

Bibliography

Adler, M. D., and Posner, E. A. (unpublished MS), "Does Happiness Research Undermine Cost–Benefit Analysis?"

Annas, J. (1993), *The Morality of Happiness* (New York: Oxford University Press).

——— (2005), "Comments on John Doris' *Lack of Character*", *Philosophy and Phenomenological Research*, 71/3 (November): 636–42.

Argyle, M. (1996), *The Social Psychology of Leisure* (London: Penguin).

——— (1999), "Causes and Correlates of Happiness", in D. Kahneman, E. Diener, and N. Schwarz (eds.), *Well-Being: The Foundations of Hedonic Psychology* (New York: Russell Sage Foundation), 353–73.

Aristotle (1984), *Nicomachean Ethics*, trans. W. D. Ross, rev. J. O. Urmson, in *The Complete Works of Aristotle*, ii, ed. Jonathan Barnes (Princeton: Princeton University Press).

Arpaly, N. (2003), *Unprincipled Virtue* (Oxford: Oxford University Press).

Ashford, E. (1997), "Utilitarianism, Integrity, and Partiality", *The Journal of Philosophy*, 97/8: 421–39.

——— (2003), "The Demandingness of Scanlon's Contractualism", *Ethics*, 113/2 (January): 273–302.

Audi, R. (1993), "Self-Deception and Practical Reasoning", in *Action, Intention, and Reason* (Ithaca, NY: Cornell University Press), 209–30.

Augst, T. (2003), *The Clerk's Tale: Young Men and Moral Life in 19th Century America* (Chicago: University of Chicago Press).

Austen, J. (1991 [1813]), *Pride and Prejudice*, Repr. edn. (New York and Toronto: Alfred A. Knopf, Inc., 1991).

——— (1995 [1818]), *Persuasion*, ed. Patricia Meyer Spacks (New York and London: W. W. Norton & Company).

——— (2000 [1816]), *Emma*, ed. Stephen M. Parrish (New York and London: W. W. Norton & Company (2000).

Baier, A. (1991), *A Progress of Sentiments: Reflections on Hume's Treatise* (Cambridge, Mass.: Harvard University Press).

——— (1994), *Moral Prejudices: Essays on Ethics* (Cambridge, Mass.: Harvard University Press).

Baltes, P. B., Gluck, J., and Kunzmann, U. (2002), "Wisdom: Its Structure and Function in Regulating Successful Life Span Development", in C. R. Snyder and S. J. Lopez (eds.), *Handbook of Positive Psychology* (Oxford and New York: Oxford University Press), 327–47.

Baron, M. (1998), "What is Wrong with Self-Deception?", in B. P. McLaughlin and A. O. Rorty (eds.), *Perspectives on Self-Deception* (Los Angeles, Berkeley, and London: University of California Press), 431–49.

Bittner, R. (1989), *What Reason Demands*, trans. T. Talbot (Cambridge: Cambridge University Press).

Blackburn, S. (1984), *Spreading the Word: Groundings in the Philosophy of Language* (New York: Oxford University Press).

_____ (1998), *Ruling Passions* (Oxford and New York: Oxford University Press).

Boehm, J. K., and Lyubomirsky, S. (in Press), "Enduring Happiness", <http://www.faculty.ucr.edu/~sonja/papers/BLinpressa.pdf.>, accessed 1 Oct. 2007.

Braithwaite, V. A., and Law, H. G. (1985), "Structure of Human Values: Testing the Adequacy of the Rokeach Value Survey", *Journal of Personality and Social Psychology*, 49/1 (July): 250–63.

_____ and Scott, W. A. (1991), "Values", in J. P. Robinson, P. R. Shaver, and L. S. Wrightsman (eds.), *Measures of Personality and Social Psychological Attitudes* (San Diego, Calif.: Academic Press, Inc.), 661–753.

Brandt, R. (1979), *A Theory of the Good and the Right* (Oxford: Clarendon Press).

Bratman, M. (1987), *Intention, Plans and Practical Reason* (Cambridge, Mass.: Harvard University Press).

Broadie, S. (1991), *Ethics with Aristotle* (New York and Oxford: Oxford University Press).

Buchanan, G. M., and Seligman, M. E. P. (1995), *Explanatory Style* (Hillsdale, NJ: Erlbaum).

Butler, J. (2006 [1726]), "Upon Self-Deceit", in *The Works of Bishop Butler*, ed. David E. White (Rochester, NY: University of Rochester Press), 103–9.

_____ (1983 [1726]), "Sermon 1 Upon Human Nature". in S. Darwall (ed.), *Five Sermons* (Indianapolis: Hackett Publishing Company), 25–33.

Cantril, H. (1965), *The Pattern of Human Concerns* (New Brunswick, NJ: Rutgers University Press).

Carroll, L. (1895), "What the Tortoise said to Achilles", *Mind*, 4/14 (April): 278–80.

Chabon, M. (2000), *The Amazing Adventures of Kavalier and Clay* (New York: Random House, Inc.).

Chang, R. (1997), "Introduction", in R. Chang (ed.), *Incommensurability, Incomparability and Practical Reason* (Cambridge, Mass.: Harvard University Press), 1–34.

_____ (2004), "Putting Together Morality and Well-Being", in M. Betzler and P. Baumann (eds.), *Practical Conflicts* (Cambridge: Cambridge University Press), 118–58.

Clark, A., Diener, E., Georgellis, Y., and Lucas, R. E. (2004), "Lags and Leads in Life Satisfaction: A Test of the Baseline Hypothesis", Delta Working Paper 2003–14, <http://www.delta.ens.fr/abstracts/wp200314.pdf.>

Csikszentmihalyi, M., and Csikszentmihalyi, I. S. (1992) (eds.), *Optimal Experience: Psychological Studies of Flow in Consciousness* (Cambridge: Cambridge University Press).

Cullity, G. (1994), "International Aid and the Scope of Kindness", *Ethics*, 105/1 (October): 99–127.

D'Arms, J., and Jacobson, D. (2003), "The Significance of Recalcitrant Emotions (Or Anti-QuasiJudgmentalism)", *Philosophy*, supp. 52: 127–45.

Darwall, S. (1983), *Impartial Reason* (Ithaca, NY, and London: Cornell University Press).

Diener, E. (2000), "Subjective Well-Being: The Science of Happiness and a Proposal for a National Index", *American Psychologist*, 55/1 (January): 34–43.

_____ and Biswas-Diener, R. (2002), "Will Money Increase Subjective Well-Being? A Literature Review and Guide to Needed Research", *Social Indicators Research*, 57: 119–69.

_____ and Seligman, M. E. P. (2002), "Very Happy People", *Psychological Science*, 13: 80–3.

_____ _____ (2004), "Beyond Money: Toward an Economy of Well-Being", *Psychological Science in the Public Interest*, 5/1: 1–31.

_____ Sapyta, J., and Suh, E. (1998), "Subjective Well-Being is Essential to Well-Being", *Psychological Inquiry*, 9: 33–7.

Doris, J. (2002), *Lack of Character: Personality and Moral Behavior* (Cambridge: Cambridge University Press).

Driver, J. (2001), *Uneasy Virtue* (Cambridge: Cambridge University Press).

Elga, A. (2005), "On Overrating Oneself … and Knowing It", *Philosophical Studies*, 123: 115–24.

Elliott, C. (2003), *Better than Well: American Medicine Meets the American Dream* (New York and London: W. W. Norton & Co.).

Emmons, R. A. (2003), "Personal Goals, Life Meaning, and Virtue: Wellsprings of a Positive Life", in J. Haidt and C. L. M. Keyes (eds.), *Flourishing: Positive Psychology and the Life Well-Lived* (Washington: American Psychology Association), 105–28.

_____ and McCullough, M. E. (2003), "Counting Blessings versus Burdens: Experimental Studies of Gratitude and Subjective Well-Being in Daily Life", *Journal of Personality and Social Psychology*, 84: 377–89.

Erwin, E. (1998), "Psychoanalysis and Self-Deception", in B. McLaughlin and A. O. Rorty (eds.), *Perspectives on Self-Deception* (Los Angeles, Berkeley, and London: University of California Press), 228–45.

Falk, D. (1986), "Hume on Practical Reason", in *Ought, Reasons and Morality: The Collected Papers of W. D. Falk* (Ithaca, NY, and London: Cornell University Press), 153–4.

Foot, P. (1978), "Virtues and Vices", in *Virtues and Vices and Other Essays in Moral Philosophy* (Oxford: Blackwell), 1–18.

——— (2001), *Natural Goodness* (Oxford: Clarendon Press).

Frank, T. (1997), *The Conquest of Cool: Business Culture, Counterculture, and the Rise of Hip Consumerism* (Chicago and London: University of Chicago Press).

Frankfurt, H. (1988), "Identification and Wholeheartedness", in *The Importance of What We Care About* (Cambridge: Cambridge University Press), 159–76.

——— (1993), "On the Necessity of Ideals", in G. C. Noam and T. Wren (eds.), *The Moral Self* (Cambridge, Mass.: MIT Press), 16–27; repr. in *Necessity, Volition, and Love* (Cambridge: Cambridge University Press, 1999), 108–16.

——— (1994), "Autonomy, Necessity, and Love", in H. F. Fulda and R. P. Horstmann (eds.), *Vernunftbegriffe in der Moderne: Stuttgarter Hegel-Kongress 1993* (Stuttgart: Klett-Cotta); repr. in *Necessity, Volition, and Love* (Cambridge: Cambridge University Press, 1999), 129–41.

——— (2002*a*), "Reply to J. David Velleman", in S. Buss and L. Overton (eds.), *Contours of Agency* (Cambridge, Mass., and London: MIT Press), 124–8.

——— (2002*b*), "Reply to Richard Moran", in S. Buss and L. Overton (eds.), *Contours of Agency* (Cambridge, Mass., and London: MIT Press), 218–26.

——— (2004), *The Reasons of Love* (Princeton: Princeton University Press).

Gage, N. L. (1991), "The Obviousness of Social and Educational Research Results", *Educational Researcher*, 20/1 (Jan.–Feb.): 10–16.

Gibbard, A. (1983), "A Noncognitivistic Analysis of Rationality in Action", *Social Theory and Practice*, 9: 199–221.

——— (1990), *Wise Choices, Apt Feelings* (Cambridge, Mass.: Harvard University Press).

——— (2003), *Thinking How to Live* (Cambridge, Mass.: Harvard University Press).

Gilbert, D. T. (2006), *Stumbling on Happiness* (New York: Knopf).

——— and Ebert, J. E. J. (2002), "Decisions and Revisions: The Affective Forecasting of Changeable Outcomes", *Journal of Personality and Social Psychology*, 82: 503–14.

——— Lieberman, M. D., Morewedge, C. K., and Wilson, T. D. (2004), "The Peculiar Longevity of Things Not So Bad", *Psychological Science*, 15: 14–19.

——— Pinel, E. C., Wilson, T. D., Blumberg, S. J., and Wheatley, T. P. (1998), "Immune Neglect: A Source of Durability Bias in Affective Forecasting", *Journal of Personality and Social Psychology*, 75: 617–38.

Gollwitzer, P. M., and Kinney, R. F. (1989), "Effects of Deliberative and Implemental Mind-Sets on Illusion of Control", *Journal of Personality and Social Psychology*, 56/4 (April): 531–42.

Griffin, J. (1986), *Well-Being: Its Meaning, Measurement and Moral Importance* (Oxford: Clarendon Press).

Gruen, L. (2004), "Empathy and Vegetarian Commitments", in S. Sapontzis (ed.), *Food for Thought: The Debate over Eating Meat* (New York: Prometheus Press), 284–94.

Haidt, J. (2005), *The Happiness Hypothesis: Finding Modern Truth in Ancient Wisdom* (Cambridge, Mass.: Basic Books).

Halberstadt, J. B., and Levine, G. M. (1999), "Effects of Reasons Analysis on the Accuracy of Predicting Basketball Games", *Journal of Applied Social Psychology*, 29: 517–30.

Hamlyn, D. W. (1971), "Self-Deception", *Proceeding of the Aristotelian Society*, 45: 45–60.

——(1983), "Perception", in P. Kegan (ed.) *Learning and the Self* (London: Routledge), 162–77.

Harman, G. (1998–9), "Moral Philosophy Meets Social Psychology: Virtue Ethics and the Fundamental Attribution Error", *Proceedings of the Aristotelian Society*, 99: 315–31.

——(2000), *Explaining Value and Other Essays in Moral Philosophy* (Oxford: Clarendon Press).

Haybron, D. (forthcoming), *The Pursuit of Unhappiness: Well-Being and the Limits of Personal Authority* (Oxford: Oxford University Press).

Hill, T. E. Jr. (1973), "Servility and Self-Respect", *The Monist*, 57/1 (January): 87–104; repr. in *Autonomy and Self-Respect* (Cambridge: Cambridge University Press, 1991), 4–18.

——(1991), "Pains and Projects", in *Autonomy and Self-Respect* (Cambridge: Cambridge University Press), 173–88.

——(1986), "Darwall on Practical Reason", *Ethics*, 96: 604–19.

Hume, D. (1978 [1739–40]), *A Treatise of Human Nature*, ed. L. A. Selby-Bigge, 2nd edn. (Oxford: Clarendon Press).

Hurka, T. (2001), *Virtue, Vice, and Value* (New York: Oxford University Press).

Hursthouse, R. (1999), *On Virtue Ethics* (New York: Oxford University Press).

Inglehart, R. (2006), "Inglehart–Welzel Cultural Map of the World", <http://www.worldvaluessurvey.org/>, accessed 15 May 2007.

——Basánez, M., Díez-Medrano, J., Halman, L., and Luijkx, R. (2004) (eds.), *Human Beliefs and Values: A Cross-Cultural Sourcebook Based on the 1999–2002 Values Survey* (Mexico: Siglo XXI Editores).

Ishiguru, K. (1989), *Remains of the Day* (New York: Knopf).

Kahneman, D. (1999), "Objective Happiness", in D. Kahneman, E. Diener, and N. Schwarz (eds.), *Well-Being: The Foundations of Hedonic Psychology* (New York: Russell Sage Foundation), 3–25.

——— Slovic, P., and Tversky, A. (1982), *Judgment under Uncertainty: Heuristic and Biases* (Cambridge: Cambridge University Press).

Kamtekar, R. (2004), "Situationism and Virtue Ethics on the Content of Our Character", *Ethics*, 114/3 (April): 458–91.

Kant, I. (1988 [1784]), "Idea for a Universal History with a Cosmopolitan Intent", in T. Humphrey (ed.), *Perpetual Peace and Other Essays* (Indianapolis: Hackett Publishing Company), 29–39.

Kasser, T. (2002), *The High Price of Materialism* (Cambridge, Mass.: MIT Press).

Kekes, J. (1995), *Moral Wisdom and Good Lives* (Ithaca, NY: Cornell University Press).

King-Farlow, J. (1973), "Review of Herbert Fingarette's *Self-Deception*", *Metaphilosophy*, 4: 76–84.

Kingsolver, B. (1998), *The Poisonwood Bible* (New York: Harper Collins Books).

Kleinman, A. (2006), *What Really Matters: Living a Moral Life amidst Uncertainty and Danger* (New York: Oxford University Press).

Knobe, J. (2006), "Experimental Philosophy", *Philosophy Compass*, 2/1: 81–92.

Korsgaard, C. (1996), *The Sources of Normativity* (Cambridge: Cambridge University Press).

——— (1997), "The Normativity of Instrumental Reason" in G. Cullity and B. Gaut (eds.), *Ethics and Practical Reason* (New York: Oxford University Press), 215–54.

Kraut, R. (1997), "Desire and the Human Good" in T. L. Carson and P. K. Moser (eds.), *Morality and the Good Life* (Oxford: Oxford University Press), 164–76.

Kross, E., Ayduk, O., and Mischel, W. (2005), "When Asking 'Why' Does Not Hurt: Distinguishing Rumination from Reflective Processing of Negative Emotions", *Psychological Science*, 16/9: 709–15.

Layard, R. (2005), *Happiness: Lessons from a New Science* (London: Penguin).

Lenman, J. (1999), "Michael Smith and the Daleks: Reason, Morality and Contingency", *Utilitas*, 11: 164–77.

——— (2007), "What is Moral Inquiry?", *Proceedings of the Aristotelian Society*, supp. vol. 81/1: 63–81.

——— (unpublished MS, 2007), "Humean Constructivism in Moral Theory".

Lovibond, S. (2002), *Ethical Formation* (Cambridge, Mass.: Harvard University Press).

Lucas, R. E., Clark, A. E., Georgellis, Y., and Diener, E. (2003), "Re-Examining Adaptation and the Setpoint Model of Happiness: Reactions to Changes in Marital Status", *Journal of Personality and Social Psychology*, 84: 527–39.

Lyubomirsky, S., Sheldon, K. M., and Schkadeet, D. (2005), "Pursuing Happiness: The Architecture of Sustainable Change", *Review of General Psychology*, 9/2: 111–31.

MacIntyre, A. (1985), *After Virtue* (London: Duckworth).

Martin, M. (1986), *Self-Deception and Morality* (Lawrence, Kan.: University Press of Kansas).

Mason, E. (2006), "Pluralism", in *Stanford Encyclopedia of Philosophy*, <http://plato.stanford.edu/entries/value-pluralism/>, accessed 4 Jan. 2008.

Mason, M. (2003), "Contempt as a Moral Attitude", *Ethics*, 113/2 (January): 234–72.

—— (unpublished MS), "Living Well and Faring Well".

McDowell, J. (1979), "Virtue and Reason", *The Monist*, 62: 331–50.

—— (1996), "Deliberation and Moral Development", in S. Engstrom and J. Whiting (eds.), *Aristotle, Kant, and the Stoics: Rethinking Happiness and Duty* (Cambridge: Cambridge University Press), 19–35.

Mele, A. (1983), "Self-Deception", *Philosophical Quarterly*, 33: 365–77.

Merritt, M. (2000), "Virtue Ethics and Situationist Personality Psychology", *Ethical Theory and Moral Practice*, 3: 365–83.

—— (forthcoming), "Aristotelian Virtue and the Interpersonal Aspect of Ethical Character", *Journal of Moral Philosophy*.

Mill, J. S. (1979 [1861]), *Utilitarianism* (Indianapolis: Hackett Publishing Company).

Moran, R. (2001), *Authority and Estrangement: An Essay on Self-Knowledge* (Princeton: Princeton University Press).

Murdoch, I. (1970), *The Sovereignty of the Good* (London: Routledge).

Murphy, L. (2000), *Moral Demands in Nonideal Theory* (New York: Oxford University Press).

Murray, S. L., Holmes, J. G., and Griffin, D. W. (1996), "The Benefits of Positive Illusions: Idealization and the Construction of Satisfaction in Close Relationships", *Journal of Personality and Social Psychology*, 70/1 (January): 79–98.

—— —— Bellavia, G., and Griffin, D. W. (2002), "Kindred Spirits? The Benefits of Egocentrism in Close Relationships", *Journal of Personality and Social Psychology*, 82/4 (April): 563–81.

Myers, D. G. (1999), "Close Relationships and Quality of Life", in D. Kahneman, E. Diener, and N. Schwarz (eds.), *Well-Being: The Foundations of Hedonic Psychology* (New York: Russell Sage Foundation), 374–91.

Nichols, S. (2004), *Sentimental Rules: On the Natural Foundations of Moral Judgment* (New York: Oxford University Press).

Nussbaum, M. (1986), *The Fragility of Goodness: Luck and Ethics in Greek Tragedy and Philosophy* (Cambridge: Cambridge University Press).

Nussbaum, M. (1994), *Therapy of Desire: Theory and Practice in Hellenistic Ethics* (Princeton: Princeton University Press).

_____ (1995), "Aristotle on Human Nature and the Foundations of Ethics", in J. E. J. Altham and R. Harrison (eds.), *World, Mind, and Ethics: Essays on the Ethical Philosophy of Bernard Williams* (Cambridge and New York: Cambridge University Press), 86–131.

_____ (2001), *Women and Human Development: The Capabilities Approach* (Cambridge: Cambridge University Press).

Parfit, D. (1984), *Reasons and Persons* (Oxford: Oxford University Press).

Patchett, A. (2001), *Bel Canto* (New York: Harper Collins).

Pavot, W., and Diener, E. (1993), "Review of the Satisfaction With Life Scale", *Psychological Assessment*, 5/2: 164–72.

Peterson, C., and Chang, E. C. (2003), "Optimism and Flourishing", in C. L. M. Keyes and J. Haidt (eds.), *Flourishing: Positive Psychology and the Life Well-Lived* (Washington: American Psychological Association), 55–79.

_____ and Seligman, M. E. P. (2004*a*), "Hope", in C. Peterson and M. E. P. Seligman (eds.), *Character, Strengths, and Virtues: A Handbook and Classification* (Oxford and New York: Oxford University Press), 569–82.

_____ _____ (2004*b*), "Perspective [Wisdom]", in C. Peterson and M. E. P. Seligman (eds.), *Character Strength and Virtues: A Handbook and Classification* (Oxford and New York: Oxford University Press), 181–96.

Piliavin, J. A. (2003), "Doing Well by Doing Good: Benefits for the Benefactor", in C. L. M. Keyes and J. Haidt (eds.), *Flourishing: Positive Psychology and the Life Well-Lived* (Washington: American Psychological Association), 227–48.

Prinz, J. J. (2007), *The Emotional Construction of Morals* (Oxford: Oxford University Press).

_____ (1986), "Moral Realism", *The Philosophical Review*, 95/2 (April): 163–207.

Railton, P. (1984), "Alienation, Consequentialism and the Demands of Morality", *Philosophy and Public Affairs*, 13: 134–71.

Rawls, J. (1971), *A Theory of Justice* (Cambridge, Mass.: Harvard University Press).

Reis, H., Sheldon, T. K. M., Gable, S. L., Roscoe, J., and Ryan, R. M. (2000), "Daily Well-Being: The Role of Autonomy, Competence, and Relatedness", *Personality and Social Psychology Bulletin*, 26/4: 419–35.

Rokeach, M. (1973), *The Nature of Human Values* (New York: Free Press).

_____ and Ball-Rokeach, S. J. (1989), "Stability and Change in American Value Priorities, 1968–1981", *American Psychologist*, 44 (May): 775–84.

Rorty, A. O. (1975), "Adaptivity and Self-Knowledge", *Inquiry*, 18: 1–22.

Rosati, C. S. (1995), "Persons, Perspectives, and Full Information Accounts of the Good", *Ethics*, 105: 296–325.

_____ (2006), "Preference-Formation and Personal Good", *Royal Institute of Philosophy Supplements*, 81: 33–64.

Ryan, R., and Deci, E. (2000), "Self-Determination Theory and the Facilitation of Intrinsic Motivation, Social Development, and Well-Being", *American Psychologist*, 55/1 (January): 68–78.

—— —— (2001), "On Happiness and Human Potentials: A Review on Hedonic and Eudaimonic Well-Being", *Annual Review of Psychology*, 52: 141–66.

Sandvik, E., Diener, E., and Seidlltzet, L. (1993), "Subjective Well-Being: The Convergence and Stability of Self-Report and Non-Self-Report Measures", *Journal of Personality*, 61/3 (September): 317–42.

Scanlon, T. M. (1998), *What We Owe to Others* (Cambridge, Mass.: The Belknap Press of Harvard University Press).

Schimmack, U., Diener, E., and Oishi, S. (2002), "Life-Satisfaction Is a Momentary Judgment and a Stable Personality Characteristic: The Use of Chronically Accessible and Stable Sources", *Journal of Personality*, 70/3 (June): 345–84.

Schwartz, B. (2000), "The Tyranny of Freedom", *American Psychologist*, 55/1 (January): 79–88.

—— (2004), *The Paradox of Choice: Why More Is Less* (New York: HarperCollins Publishers, Inc.).

Schwartz, S. (1992), "Universals in the Content and Structure of Values: Theory and Empirical Tests in 20 Countries", in M. Zanna (ed.), *Advances in Experimental Social Psychology*, 25 (New York: Academic Press), 1–65.

—— (2006), "Basic Human Values: Theory, Measurement, and Applications", *Revue française de sociologie*, 47/4. (Pages from author's preprint)

—— and Bilsky, W. (1987), "Toward a Universal Psychological Structure of Human Values", *Journal of Personality and Social Psychology*, 53/3 (September): 550–62.

Schwarz, N., and Strack, F. (1999), "Reports of Subjective Well-Being: Judgmental Processes and Their Methodological Implications", in D. Kahneman, E. Deiner, and N. Schwarz (eds.), *Well-Being: The Foundations of Hedonic Psychology* (New York: Russell Sage Foundation), 61–84.

Seligman, M. E. P. (1990), *Learned Optimism: How to Change Your Mind and Your Life* (New York: Free Press).

—— (2002), *Authentic Happiness* (New York: Free Press).

—— (unpublished MS), "Introduction to Positive Psychology", Paper presented at the Conference on the Philosophical History of Strength and Virtue, University of Pennsylvania, 10–12 April 2003.

Shafer-Landau, R. (2003), *Moral Realism: A Defense* (New York: Oxford University Press).

Shklar, J. (1984), *Ordinary Vices* (Cambridge, Mass.: The Belknap Press of Harvard University Press).

Singer, P. (1972), "Famine, Affluence, and Morality", *Philosophy and Public Affairs*, 1/3: 229–43.

Smith, M. (1994), *The Moral Problem* (Oxford: Blackwell Publishers Ltd.).

Snyder, C. R. (2000), *Handbook of Hope: Theory, Measures, and Applications* (San Diego, Calif.: Academic Press).

Sreenivasan, G. (2002), "Errors about Errors: Virtue Theory and Trait Attribution", *Mind*, 111: 47–68.

Stanovich, K. (2004), *The Robot's Rebellion: Finding Meaning in the Age of Darwin* (Chicago: University of Chicago Press).

Stocker, M. (1976), "The Schizophrenia of Modern Ethical Theories", *Journal of Philosophy*, 73: 453–66.

Stohr, K. (2006), "Contemporary Virtue Ethics", *Philosophy Compass*, 1/1: 22–7.

Sumner, L. W. (1996), *Welfare, Happiness, and Ethics* (New York: Oxford University Press).

Svenson, O. (1981), "Are We All Less Risky and More Skillful than our Fellow Drivers?", *Acta Psychologica*, 47: 143–8.

Sweeney, P. D., Anderson, K., and Bailey, S. (1986), "Attributional Style in Depression: A Meta-analytic Review", *Journal of Personality and Social Psychology*, 50: 974–91.

Taylor, C. (1976), "Responsibility for Self", in A. O. Rorty (ed.), *The Identities of Persons* (Berkeley: University of California Press), 281–99.

Taylor, S. E. (1991), *Positive Illusions: Creative Self-Deception and the Healthy Mind* (New York: Basic Books).

_____ and Brown, J. D. (1994), "Positive Illusions and Well-Being Revisited Separating Fact From Fiction", *Psychological Bulletin*, 116/1 (July): 21–7.

_____ _____ (1988), "Illusion and Well-Being: A Social Psychological Perspective on Mental Health", *Psychological Bulletin*, 103: 193–210.

Tiberius, V. (1997), "Full Information and Ideal Deliberation", *Journal of Value Inquiry*, 31/3 (September): 329–38.

_____ (2000*a*), *Deliberation about the Good: Justifying what We Value* (New York: Garland Publishing, Inc.).

_____ (2000*b*), "Humean Heroism", *Pacific Philosophical Quarterly*, 81/4: 426–46.

_____ (2005), "Value Commitments and the Balanced Life", *Utilitas*, 17/1 (March): 24–45.

_____ (2006), "Well-Being: Psychological Research for Philosophers", *Philosophy Compass*, 1/5: 493–505.

_____ and Plakias, A. (forthcoming), "How's it Going?: Positive Psychology, Ethics, and Conceptions of Well-Being", in J. Doris and S. Stich (eds.), *Rethinking Moral Psychology: Interdisciplinary Conversations on Ethics and the Human Sciences* (Oxford: Oxford University Press).

Townsend, M. A. R. (1995), "Effects of Accuracy and Plausibility in Predicting Results of Research Findings on Teaching", *British Journal of Educational Psychology*, 65/3: 359–65.

Unger, P. (1996), *Living High and Letting Die* (Oxford: Oxford University Press).

Velleman, J. D. (1988), "Brandt's Definition of Good", *The Philosophical Review*, 97/3 (July): 353–71.

—— (2000), "From Psychology to Moral Philosophy", *Philosophical Perspectives*, 14 (October): 349–77; repr. in *Self to Self* (New York: Cambridge University Press, 2006), 224–52.

—— (2002*a*), "Identification and Identity", in S. Buss and L. Overton (eds.), *The Contours of Agency: Essay on Themes from Harry Frankfurt* (Cambridge, Mass., and London: MIT Press), 91–123; repr. in *Self to Self* (New York: Cambridge University Press, 2006), 330–60.

—— (2002*b*), "Motivation by Ideal", *Philosophical Explorations*, 5 (May): 89–104; repr. in *Self to Self* (New York: Cambridge University Press, 2006), 312–29.

—— (2005), "The Self as Narrator", in J. Anderson and J. Christman (eds.), *Autonomy and the Challenges to Liberalism: New Essays* (Cambridge: Cambridge University Press); repr. in *Self to Self* (New York: Cambridge University Press, 2006), 203–23.

Walzer, M. (1994), *Thick and Thin: Moral Argument at Home and Abroad* (Notre Dame, Ind.: Notre Dame University Press).

Watson, G. (1975), "Free Agency", *Journal of Philosophy*, 72/8: 205–20.

Weinstein, N. D. (1989), "Optimistic Biases about Personal Risks", *Science*, 246: 1232–3.

Williams, B. (1973), "A Critique of Utilitarianism", in B. Williams and J. J. C. Smart (eds.), *Utilitarianism: For and Against* (New York: Cambridge University Press), 77–150.

Wilson, T. D. (2002), *Strangers to Ourselves: Discovering the Adaptive Unconscious* (Cambridge, Mass., and London: The Belknap Press of Harvard University Press).

—— and Dunn, D. S. (1986), "Effects of Introspection on Attitude-Behavior Consistency: Analyzing Reasons versus Focusing on Feelings", *Journal Experimental Social Psychology*, 22: 249–63.

—— —— (2004), "Self-Knowledge: Its Limits, Value, and Potential for Improvement", *Annual Review of Psychology*, 55 (February): 493–518.

—— and LaFleur, S. J. (1995), "Knowing What You'll Do: Effects of Analyzing Reasons on Self-Prediction", *Journal of Personality and Social Psychology*, 68: 21–35.

—— and Schooler, J. W. (1991), "Thinking Too Much: Introspection Can Reduce the Quality of Preferences and Decisions", *Journal of Personality and Social Psychology*, 60: 181–92.

—— Dunn, D. S., Bybee, J. A., Hyman, D. B., and Rotondo, J. A. (1984), "Effects of Analyzing Reasons on Attitude-Behavior Consistency", *Journal of Personality and Social Psychology*, 47: 5–16.

Wilson, T. D., Hodges, S. D., and LaFleur, S. J. (1995), "Effects of Introspecting about Reasons: Inferring Attitudes from Accessible Thoughts", *Journal of Personality and Social Psychology*, 69: 16–28.

—— Lindsey, S., and Schooler, T. Y. (2000), "A Model of Dual Attitudes", *Psychological Review*, 107/1 (January): 101–26.

—— Lisle, D., Schooler, J., Hodges, S. D., Klaaren, K. J., and LaFleur, S. J. (1993), "Introspecting about Reasons Can Reduce Post-Choice Satisfaction", *Personality and Social Psychology Bulletin*, 19: 331–9.

Wines, M. (2006), "To Fill Notebooks, and Then a Few Bellies", *The New York Times* (27 August).

Index